Routledge Author Guides

Macaulay

Routledge Author Guides

GENERAL EDITOR: B. C. SOUTHAM, M.A., B.LITT. (OXON)
Formerly Department of English, Westfield College, University of London

Titles in the series

Browning by Roy E. Gridley

Byron by J. D. Jump

William Cobbett by James Sambrook

Macaulay by Jane Millgate

Nietzsche by R. J. Hollingdale

Tolstoy by Ernest J. Simmons

Routledge Author Guides

Macaulay

by

Jane Millgate

*Department of English, Victoria College,
University of Toronto*

Routledge & Kegan Paul
London and Boston

First published in 1973
by Routledge & Kegan Paul Ltd
Broadway House, 68–74 Carter Lane,
London EC4V 5EL and
9 Park Street
Boston, Mass. 02108, U.S.A.
Printed in Great Britain by
Cox & Wyman Ltd, London, Fakenham and Reading

ISBN 0 7100 7663 0 (c)
ISBN 0 7100 7685 1 (p)

Library of Congress Catalog Card No. 73–80373

To Michael

General Editor's Preface

Nowadays there is a growing awareness that the specialist areas have much to offer and much to learn from one another. The student of history, for example, is becoming increasingly aware of the value that literature can have in the understanding of the past; equally, the student of literature is turning more and more to the historians for illumination of his area of special interest, and of course philosophy, political science, sociology, and other disciplines have much to give him.

What we are trying to do in the Routledge *Author Guides* is to offer this illumination and communication by providing for non-specialist readers, whether students or the interested general public, a clear and systematic account of the life and times and works of the major writers and thinkers across a wide range of disciplines. Where the *Author Guides* may be seen to differ from other, apparently similar, series, is in its historical emphasis, which will be particularly evident in the treatment of the great literary writers, where we are trying to establish, in so far as this can be done, the social and historical context of the writer's life and times, and the cultural and intellectual tradition in which he stands, always remembering that critical and interpretative principles are implicit to any sound historical approach.

BCS

Contents

Preface and Acknowledgments

To approach Macaulay in the latter half of the twentieth century is to be confronted by two basic questions: how to account for his immense popularity with the Victorian public, and how to assess the continuing value of his literary achievement – his significance for readers who share few of his political and historical assumptions and fewer still of his tastes. In pursuing both these questions a good deal of emphasis must be placed on two elements, discrete yet complementary, which characterize the literary productions of Macaulay's maturity. He had, first of all, an acute sense of audience. Almost everything he wrote demonstrates his capacity to identify his readers and to speak directly and clearly to them, to arouse their interest and carry them with him through the difficult issues of contemporary politics or into the lives of individuals long dead, the complexities of situations long past. He had also an extraordinary gift for narrative. In the brief anecdotes incorporated in his speeches, legislative minutes, and notes to the Indian penal code, in the balladry of the *Lays of Ancient Rome*, in the larger terms of the later essays and the *History of England*, the same essentially narrative art shapes, supports, and makes attractive what may often have originated in a polemical or educational impulse.

I have tried in this study to identify and define the characteristics of that art through the analysis of particular texts. The specific texts discussed have been chosen largely for their representativeness – the light they throw upon the sheer variety of Macaulay's interests and techniques and upon different stages of his development – but the advantage of the selective method of itself seemed to lie in the opportunity it offered for detailed examination of works which have rarely been subjected to close critical scrutiny. Attention is paid throughout to the non-literary aspects of Macaulay's career – for in some ways it is the combination of a distinguished public life with sustained literary success which constitutes the most striking feature of his whole achievement – and the attempt is made to place his literary works in their political, historical, and biographical contexts. But I have in no sense sought to write a 'life and times'. The emphases of this study are critical, its essential aims the exploration of the range and quality of Macaulay's writing and the demonstration of the validity of continuing to approach him – above all in the mature essays and the *History of England* – as a major narrative artist.

Part of one of my chapters appeared in an earlier form in the *University of Toronto Quarterly* and I am grateful to the Editor for permitting me to re-use it here. I wish also to thank the Canada Council for generous support during the research for this study. I gladly acknowledge the permission of the Master and Fellows of Trinity College, Cambridge, to quote from their collection of Macaulay manuscripts, and the assistance I have consistently received from the Librarian of Trinity College and his staff. My thanks are further due to the National Trust, the British Museum, the Cambridge University Library, the Fitzwilliam Museum, the Bodleian Library, and the Pierpont Morgan Library for access to other Macaulay materials. I am especially grateful to Mrs Humphry Trevelyan for allowing me to use the Macaulay items in her possession and for enduring my repeated visits with such unfailing cheerfulness, and to Mrs Pauline Dower for all her kindness and thoughtful hospitality.

It gives me great pleasure to record my appreciation of the assistance and advice I have received from many people. Among those who have patiently answered my inquiries or helped me with specific problems relating to Macaulay or his family I should like particularly to mention Mr Alistair Elliot of the University of Newcastle upon Tyne; Professor P. L. Heyworth of the University of Toronto; Viscount Knutsford; Mrs Mary Moorman; Mr D. S. Neill of the Bodleian; Dr R. Robson of Trinity College, Cambridge; and Professor Peter Shillingsburg of Mississippi State University. I am especially indebted to those who read earlier versions of parts of this study or shared with me their own expert knowledge of Macaulay and the Victorians: Dr Louis James and Professor Leland Lyons of the University of Kent; Professors Daniel Aaron and John Clive of Harvard; Professor George Levine of Rutgers; Professor J. M. Robson of the University of Toronto; and Professor Bert James Loewenberg, formerly of Sarah Lawrence College, who first encouraged my interest in Macaulay. The greatest of my debts are to Professor Thomas Pinney of Pomona

College, who so unselfishly made available to me the rich resources of his own research, to Dr A. N. L. Munby of King's College, Cambridge, whose help, enthusiasm, and imaginative generosity have sustained me throughout this enterprise, and to my husband, Michael Millgate, from whose critical and scholarly insights this study has benefited at every point and without whose patience, encouragement, and good humour it would never have been completed.

Victoria College
University of Toronto

Preface and Acknowledgements

Chronology

1800   Macaulay born at Rothley Temple, Leicestershire (25 October).

1802   Family moves from the City to Clapham.

1813–18   Attends Mr Preston's boarding school.

1818   Family moves from Clapham to Cadogan Place. Macaulay goes up to Trinity College, Cambridge.

1819   Wins Chancellor's Medal for 'Pompeii'.

1821   Wins Chancellor's Medal for 'Evening'.

1822   Wins prize for an essay on William III.

1823–4   Contributes articles and poems to *Knight's Quarterly*.

1824   Elected to a Trinity Fellowship. Speech to the Anti-Slavery Society.

1825   First contribution to the *Edinburgh Review*, 'The West Indies', published in January issue; Milton essay published in August issue.

1826   Called to the bar and joins Northern Circuit.

1830   Southey essay published in January issue of *Edinburgh Review*. Elected M.P. for Calne. Visits France immediately after the July Revolution.

1831   Death of his mother. Croker essay published in September issue of *Edinburgh Review*.

1831–2   Famous speeches in Reform Bill debates.

1832   Appointed Commissioner on the Board of Control for India. Elected M.P. for Leeds.

1834   Leaves for India (February) to become Law Member of Governor General's Supreme Council. Death of his sister, Margaret, and marriage of his sister, Hannah, to Charles Trevelyan (December).

1837   Indian Penal Code completed. Bacon essay published in July issue of *Edinburgh Review*.

1838   Death of his father shortly before Macaulay's arrival back in London from India (June). Leaves for a visit to Italy (October). Temple essay published in October issue of *Edinburgh Review*.

1839   Elected M.P. for Edinburgh (June). Enters Cabinet as Secretary-at-War (August).

1840   Clive essay published in January issue of *Edinburgh Review*.

1841   Government resigns (August); Macaulay resumes intensive work on his *History of England*, begun in 1839. Warren Hastings essay published in October issue of *Edinburgh Review*.

1842   *Lays of Ancient Rome* published.

1843   First authorized collected edition of his *Critical and Historical Essays*. Addison essay published in July issue of *Edinburgh Review*.

1844   Last *Edinburgh Review* essay, on Lord Chatham, published in October issue.

1846   Accepts Cabinet office as Paymaster-General. Re-elected for Edinburgh.

1847   Defeated in General Election (July).

1848   First two volumes of *History of England* published (December).

1852   Re-elected for Edinburgh. Suffers heart attack.

1854   Authorized edition of *Speeches* published.

1854-9 Contributes biographies of Atterbury, Bunyan, Goldsmith, Johnson, and Pitt to *Encyclopaedia Britannica*.

1855   Volumes III and IV of *History of England* published. Report on the Indian Civil Service by Macaulay and others.

1856   Resigns his Edinburgh seat because of continuing ill health. Moves from his rooms in Albany to Holly Lodge on Campden Hill.

1859   Raised to the peerage as Baron Macaulay of Rothley.

1859   Dies (28 December).

Textual Note

Quotations from Macaulay's letters and manuscript journals have been made wherever possible from the originals, and reference to the source is given in the notes. Where passages cited also appear in the two major published collections of such material – G. O. Trevelyan's *Life and Letters of Lord Macaulay* or Macvey Napier Jr's edition of *Selections from the Correspondence of the Late Macvey Napier, Esq* – the relevant reference is also included in the notes, using the abbreviations *LL* and Napier respectively.

Macaulay's published works are quoted throughout from the texts of their first authorized publication. For the essays this means *Knight's Quarterly Magazine*, the *Edinburgh Review*, or the eighth edition of the *Encyclopaedia Britannica*. For the *Lays of Ancient Rome*, the *History of England*, and the *Miscellaneous Writings* the first English editions are used. The speeches are quoted from the edition of 1854 prepared by Macaulay himself, not from the Vizetelly piracy of a year earlier, but comparison has been made with earlier printings such as those in Hansard and significant variations are noted.

Page references to Macaulay's contributions to the *Edinburgh Review* and the *History of England* are incorporated within parentheses in the text. For the *Edinburgh* volume and page numbers are given in arabic numerals, thus: (68:117). For the *History* the volume is indicated by a roman numeral, thus: (I,125).

I

Beginnings

The Early Literary Essays

Thomas Babington Macaulay was born at Rothley Temple, Leicester-shire, the home of his uncle Thomas Babington, on 25 October 1800; following his death on 28 December 1859, as Baron Macaulay of Rothley, he was buried with great ceremony in Westminster Abbey. His father, Zachary Macaulay, had also been buried in the Abbey, and there were those ready to say at the son's death that the father, though less famous, had been in some respects the greater man. The Rev. Frederick Arnold, in *The Public Life of Lord Macaulay* (1862), observes: 'It was not the son's great lot to be a sufferer for mercy's and righteous-ness' sake, to be so active an agent in a beneficent movement which has changed the current of our history, to be one of those who will here-after be found to have sensibly lessened the sum of the world's misery and degradation.'[1]

The 'beneficent movement' was, of course, the Anti-Slavery cause, with which Zachary Macaulay became identified in the early 1790s after an experience of religious and moral conversion under the guid-ance of Thomas Babington, the husband of Zachary's favourite sister, Jean. Babington was a committed member of the circle already forming around the charismatic figure of William Wilberforce, and it was through Babington's influence that Zachary Macaulay was appointed first as Member of the Council and then, at the age of twenty-six, as Governor of Sierra Leone, the settlement founded by leading members of the Anti-Slavery movement as a home for former slaves who had fought on the British side in the American War of Independence. Upon his return to England in 1799 he became Secretary of the Sierra Leone Company; in 1802 he took over the editorship of the newly established Evangelical journal, the *Christian Observer*; and in 1803 the final seal was set upon his membership of the leading group of Evangel-ical reformers when he moved with his family to a house on the fringe of Clapham Common – in the vicinity of the Clapham 'saints', of what was later to be known as the Clapham Sect.

The chief members of the Clapham Sect were two distant cousins, William Wilberforce and Henry Thornton, and the focus of the group was Thornton's house at Clapham, Battersea Rise. The two men lived there together for a few years until Thornton's marriage in 1796; when Wilberforce married a year later he moved into Broomfield, the house next door. At different periods during the 1790s and early 1800s Clapham was home to James Stephen, John Venn, Lord Teignmouth, Charles Grant, and many others who shared Wilberforce's beliefs. David Newsome has described Clapham as 'the power-house of the Evangelical revival' from which Wilberforce 'launched the projects and created the organisation which were to convert Evangelicalism into a national force',[2] and Noel Annan has charted the Clapham origins of so many members of the late-nineteenth-century 'intellectual aristocracy'.[3] By its single-minded devotion to specific objectives, this small group of friends was able to extend its influence into every sphere of the moral and religious life of the country and of its overseas possessions. James Stephen, the son of the James Stephen who had been one of the key figures of the original group, described the Sect's activities in an *Edinburgh Review* article of 1844:[4]

> Bibles, schools, missionaries, the circulation of evangelical books, and the training of evangelical clergymen, the possession of well-attended pulpits, war through the press, and war in Parliament, against every form of injustice which either law or custom sanctioned – such were the forces by which they hoped to extend the kingdom of light, and to resist the tyranny with which the earth was threatened.

At home they sought to place as many Evangelical clergymen as possible into livings whose gift they controlled or could influence, with such success that the Rev. Sydney Smith had his Peter Plymley warn in 1807 against 'that patent Christianity which has been for some time manufacturing at Clapham, to the prejudice of the old and admirable article prepared by the Church'.[5] Abroad, the admission of missionaries to India was a major Clapham objective, eventually realized under the terms of the new East India Company Charter of 1813. By far the greatest of their aims, however, was the abolition of the slave trade and of slavery itself in all British colonies. The first legislative blow was struck in 1788 when a bill limiting the number of slaves which could be carried in one ship was passed by parliament, but it took another twenty years for the trade itself to be stopped in 1807, and it was not until 1833 that the Emancipation Bill was passed.

From his first introduction to Wilberforce in the early 1790s Zachary Macaulay worked ceaselessly but inconspicuously for the abolitionist cause. James Stephen described him as 'a man possessed by one idea, and animated by one master passion',[6] while Sir Henry Taylor evoked the relationship between him and Wilberforce in terms which reflect a little unkindly on the latter: 'A winning amenity of manner, peculiar grace and fervour in conversation, and an easy eloquence in public speaking, planted [Wilberforce] the foremost of his party in the eyes of mankind, and placed his name in the title-page (as it were) of a great cause. But Mr. Zachary Macaulay was the man who rose and took pen in hand at four o'clock in the morning.'[7] The role, however, was one which Zachary Macaulay had chosen for himself. He recognized all the qualities that made Wilberforce such a great leader; he also knew that he himself had been denied such qualities and believed that it was his duty to use to their utmost the talents he did possess. Stephen's portrait brings out something of the strength which his silence paradoxically expressed:[8]

> That much was passing within, which that ineloquent tongue and those taciturn features could not utter; that nature had compensated her other bounties by refusing him the means of a ready interchange of thought; and that he had won, without knowing how to court, the attachment of all who approached him closely – these were discoveries which the most casual acquaintance might make, but which they whom he honoured with his intimacy, and they alone, could explain.

One attachment so won, and the most important of all, was that of Selina Mills, daughter of a Bristol Quaker family, whom he met during a visit to Miss Hannah More and her sisters in 1795. Though she lived in the Somerset countryside – first at Cowslip Green, later at Barley Wood – devoting herself to the education of the local poor and to writing in support of Evangelical causes, Hannah More maintained close ties with the Clapham group. Selina Mills had been a pupil of the Miss Mores when they ran a school for young ladies and Miss Patty More made some protest at the loss of her special favourite; but once this minor obstacle had been overcome, and Zachary had served out the remaining years of his Sierra Leone commitment, the couple were married in 1799, settling first in Lambeth and then over the offices of the Sierra Leone Company in Birchin Lane in the City of London. This was their home at the time when their eldest son was born, and for the first two years of his life.

The genial household of the Miss Mores was to be scarcely less important for that son than for his parents. The young Tom Macaulay was often sent to Barley Wood for his holidays, and following a nostalgic visit to the house at the age of fifty-one he refers to it affectionately in his *Journal* as 'the place where I passed so many happy days in my childhood'.[9] The period of Hannah More's youthful celebrity as a member of Dr Johnson's circle was long past, but the intelligence, wit, and charm which had won her such great literary friends were as much in evidence as ever. Marianne Thornton, Henry Thornton's daughter, later recalled:[10]

> Surely there never was such a house, so full of intellect and piety and active benevolence. They lived in such uninterrupted harmony with each other, were so full of their separate pursuits, enjoyed with such interest and vivacity all the pleasures of their beautiful home, or wholly laid aside all the forms of society that were irksome, that young or old one felt oneself in a brighter and happier world, alloyed indeed by the most fearful attacks of illness occasionally, but even when these occurred the patience and cheerfulness of both patient and nurses never failed.

Marianne Thornton adds that Hannah More, 'in many ways a charming companion for children', had 'very little power of resisting either persuasion or fun',[11] and one of the especial treats of that indulgent household for her, as it must have been for Macaulay, was to get the old lady to reminisce about the days of her London triumphs: 'Hannah More was always ready to talk about the literary set with whom she passed her youth. Many an evening has she amused me by describing Johnson and Burke, Horace Walpole, Mrs Montagu and the many personages I had read of in Boswell, and for this reason I suppose no period in history interests me so much.'[12] Many of the most charming anecdotes of Macaulay's precocity in G. O. Trevelyan's biography relate to Hannah More. It was to that high-principled old lady that the four-year-old boy offered, on their meeting quite early one morning, 'a glass of old spirits' – on the precedent that 'Robinson Crusoe often had some'.[13] It was she who encouraged him with his great project of an epic on Olaus Magnus, King of Norway, and bought him books with which to lay the foundation of his library, while the books at Barley Wood itself were also important to him: 'I could point out the very place where the Don Quixote in four vols stood,' he recorded on his 1852 visit, '& the very place from which I took down at ten years old the Lyrical Ballads. With what delight & horror I read the Ancient Mariner.'[14] It is not surprising that Macaulay should have recalled a stay with the Miss Mores at the age of six as 'a great event in [his] life', and there can be no doubt that they delighted in his precocity and encouraged his showier side: 'In parlour and kitchen they could not make enough of me. They taught me to cook; and I was to preach, and they got in people from the fields, and I stood on a chair, and preached sermons. I might have been indicted for holding a conventicle.'[15]

But Hannah More was for the holidays. The great influences at Clapham were his father and his mother, and their contrasted yet complementary personalities were to have a profound effect upon their son's later development. On the eve of Zachary Macaulay's marriage his brother-in-law, Thomas Babington, wrote to him with all the frankness that the Evangelicals so valued in each other. He saw Zachary's strengths and weaknesses as closely allied, the product of 'natural ardour of mind and firmness of character' – qualities capable of encroaching on 'that smiling serenity of soul which is so amiable in itself, and so nearly connected with Christian love and meekness', and of diminishing the capacity for 'true Christian sensibility',[16] by which Babington seems to have meant sensitivity to the feelings of others. 'Part of your duty,' Babington gently admonished the intending husband, 'will consist in improving yourself in an art you never yet studied, the art of relaxing in a way which may suit a pious, affectionate, and amiable wife.'[17] In the event, Zachary Macaulay never entirely mastered this art, but his wife seems not to have blamed him for its absence. Their letters show a complete confidence in each other and a sympathy of interests which ensured that although Selina Macaulay's role was always to be the subordinate one of loyal supporter, confidante, and comforter, Zachary's statement on her death that 'for thirty-two years we have been the sharers of each other's joys and sorrows and cares'[18] was a tribute both sincere and amply deserved.

Only his wife and a few intimate friends seem to have had the clue to what lay behind the harsh exterior Zachary Macaulay turned to the outside world. James Stephen asked in his 1844 article on the Clapham Sect:[19]

But what might be suggesting that expression of countenance, at once so earnest and so monotonous – by what manner of feelings those gestures, so uniformly firm and deliberate, were prompted – whence the constant traces of fatigue on those overhanging brows, and on that athletic though ungraceful figure – what might be the charm which excited amongst his chosen circle a faith approaching to superstition, and a love rising to enthusiasm, towards a man whose demeanour was so inanimate, if not austere?

All too often in childhood and early manhood what Zachary Macaulay's eldest son saw turned towards him was 'that expression of countenance, at once so earnest and so monotonous', while the concern for his children's welfare which lay behind it was not always easy to discern or appreciate. It is clear, in fact, that Zachary Macaulay wished to cure his brilliant son of the faults he recognized as inherited from himself, in the hope that the talents in which the boy far surpassed his father – 'If I had only Tom's power of speech', he once exclaimed[20] – might be more effectively employed in God's service. In that 1799 letter already quoted, Thomas Babington mentioned the faults of which he felt his brother-in-law had already cured himself – 'impatience, self-confidence, and a love of praise'[21] – and by way of guarding against any backsliding he characterized their symptoms:[22]

In the style of your letters and your tones in reading being too oratorical; in something of this in your conversation also at times; in a boldness in your looks, and a hardness and spirit of opposition in arguing, and in joining in conversation sometimes as master, sometimes as an equal in knowledge, on subjects on which your degree of information would have made it more decorous and useful for you to have taken a lower station.

Zachary Macaulay was well aware of these failings, and in an auto-biographical fragment composed two years earlier he had attributed to his having been assigned as a child to teach his younger brothers and sisters 'the rise of several tempers which have caused me no small trouble in after life, particularly my impatience and self-confidence, my imposing tone, and dogmatical, magisterial style as well in writing as speaking'.[23]

Since these were precisely the characteristics he saw developing in his son from an early stage, it is understandable that he should have repeatedly sent him letters urging restraint and self-discipline. On 28

February 1814 he wrote to Tom, who was away at school at Little Shelford, near Cambridge, to recommend the language of 'diffidence and humility' as especially suited to youth:[24]

> When you came to us last Christmas I found you had acquired at School a loud and intrepid and confident tone which was not a little opposed to the modesty becoming youth. I think you had improved in this respect during your stay with us; but the tendency to this evil was far from having been thoroughly corrected. I trust my Dear Tom that things have not been retrograding since your return to school, but that by the aid of Divine grace earnestly sought in prayer you have been getting the better more and more of this propensity.

Even when Macaulay was up at Trinity College, Cambridge, and already winning considerable academic distinction, his father continued to urge on him the necessity for tidiness and order, for curbing his tongue and repressing the violent display of his opinions and emotions. Some years after Macaulay's death, his sister, Hannah, recorded that he 'used to say he could not recall an instance in which his Father had ever praised him or shewn any sense of his abilities'. Hannah herself dissents from this judgment, pointing out that Zachary did show his estimation of his son by 'writing to him from a very early age as to a man', but she admits that 'in the desire to keep down any conceit, there was certainly in my Father a great outward show of repression and depreciation.'[25]

Marianne Thornton thought Zachary Macaulay had been a very judicious parent. Writing to Hannah More on 21 January 1822, she commented on Tom's having been denied the chance to sit for the Chancellor's medal at Cambridge because of his inadequate mastery of mathematics: 'Tho' his is not a mathematical head, they say this little may be gained by almost any body who will read with attention, and I am therefore doubly sorry, not on his own account only, but on that of his sire, who has been so wise and so wary in his management of his "son of genius". Perhaps it may be of use to Tom in showing that there is no royal way to Honours.'[26] There may, however, be a touch of sisterly satisfaction in this account of Tom Macaulay's come-uppance. Marianne's own brother, Henry, who had gone up to Trinity at the same time as Macaulay, had just been named Fourth Wrangler, and this achievement was something to set in the scale against Tom's triumphs in the Union debates and his successes in winning a Craven scholarship and the prize for Latin Declamation as well as the Chancellor's prize for an English poem on two out of the three occasions for which he was eligible.

Zachary Macaulay had largely entrusted his wife with the upbringing of their nine children. At the time of her death he wrote to Hannah More:[27]

> With what unwearied resolution and self-denial her time and thoughts were devoted to the formation of the infant mind, to the development of the infant faculties, to the implantation from the earliest dawn of reason of those principles of piety, truth, reverence, love, devotion, and all kindly affections no one can know so well as I do – for unfortunately I could bear but a small part in the work – I could only admire and encourage and cheer her in the task.

Selina Macaulay seems never to have enjoyed society beyond the limits of her family circle and of holiday visits to the Miss Mores or to her sister-in-law, Jean Babington, at Rothley Temple. Even during the years she and Zachary lived at Clapham she rarely figures in accounts of the doings of that active and gregarious extended family centred upon Wilberforce and Henry Thornton. Within her own family she was loved and trusted with complete devotion, and by no one more than her eldest son; it was to her, naturally enough, that he turned for companionship, encouragement, affection openly expressed, delight in literature publicly displayed. Viscountess Knutsford notes of Selina that 'Her love of reading was inherited by her eldest son',[28] for although Zachary Macaulay, by his own confession, had originally had 'a strong passion'[29] for literature and always kept up with current trends in English and French writing, his religious conversion and his dedication to the Anti-Slavery cause had taught him to subordinate his literary interests to his more serious work. He saw indulgence in the wrong kind of literature as one of the vices of his misspent Edinburgh youth: 'When I was not draining the midnight bowl, I was employed in wasting the midnight oil by poring over such abominable, but fascinating works as are to be found under the head of novels in the catalogue of every circulating library.'[30] While the children associated their mother with the enjoyment of reading Shakespeare aloud, it is surely her father that Hannah is quoting when she says that in the Macaulay household reading poetry and novels in the daytime was equated with 'drinking drams in the morning'.[31]

The entire family was stricken with grief at the sudden death of Selina Macaulay in 1831. Her husband took the loss austerely, attempting to shoulder his cross and carry on his Anti-Slavery activities with as little interruption as possible. Tom's 'first burst of grief' was, as his sister, Selina, noted in her journal, 'overwhelming',[32] but he quickly turned his attention to comforting the others. There is little doubt that the energy he put into enlivening the home for his two youngest sisters, Margaret and Hannah, in 1831 and 1832 – when they and their brother, Charles, were the only ones living with Zachary – was an instinctive attempt to compensate for the warmth and happiness of which they had been deprived by their mother's death. It was at this period that Macaulay came so close to these two girls ten years his junior and learned to depend on them for that open expression of pleasure in his achievements which he had formerly received from his mother.

Macaulay's relationship with his father seems to have remained to the end both uneasy and remote, despite his anxious attempts to gain parental approval by demonstrations of support for the causes closest to Zachary's heart. He accepted the task of compiling an index for the thirteenth volume of the *Christian Observer* in 1814, and wrote from Cambridge on 23 October 1818: 'I am far less desirous to return loaded with medals or distinguished on the tripos-paper, than to acquire here those accomplishments and that information which may qualify me to inherit your public objects, and to succeed to your benevolent enterprises.'[33] It is instructive to compare this solemnly formal letter with one written to his mother at the same period in which he discourses with great gaiety and energy, and with complete naturalness, on his horror of mathematics.[34] Perhaps the saddest story in Trevelyan's biography concerns the brilliant speech the young Macaulay made to the Anti-Slavery Society in 1824. Though deeply moved by his son's success in such a cause, Zachary's only comment was that 'it was ungraceful in so young a man to speak with folded arms in the presence of royalty.'[35]

Macaulay never abandoned the Anti-Slavery cause. His first article for the *Edinburgh Review*, that on 'The West Indies' in January 1825,[36] dealt with the slavery question, as did the article on 'The Social and Industrial Capacities of Negroes', published in the *Edinburgh* two years later. Like the occasion in the early 1830s when he showed himself ready to resign from government office over the same question when scarcely launched on his public career, these were not empty gestures of filial piety but the product both of a deep emotional need to prove himself to his father and of a strong personal commitment to liberal principles. But before he had begun to contribute to the great Whig journal Macaulay had already attempted a declaration of literary independence from his father. In 1823 Macaulay supplied a variety of items in prose and verse to *Knight's Quarterly Magazine*, a short-lived periodical for which he and some of his Cambridge friends provided the literary content and the publisher, Charles Knight, the commercial impulse. On 7 June 1823 Zachary Macaulay wrote to his wife:[37]

> The more I look into this magazine in which Tom cuts so conspicuous a figure the more am I dissatisfied with it, and the more pained am I at the associations which Tom has formed. It is a loose, low, coarse, and almost blackguard work in *some* of its parts. In others, where there is less of coarseness there is still a strain of voluptuousness and even licentiousness which is quite intolerable and which almost rivals Little's poems. There is one poem of Tom's own which would find its place very well as far as the sentiments go in that vile repository. I am quite shocked & pained that a son of mine should have linked himself with such associates and should countenance and even compose such mischievous effusions. This matter presses heavily on my mind at present; but I wish to consider it more calmly. Something however must be done and that speedily. I did not want this at present to add to my cares – but I desire to receive it as a part of my merited chastisement at the hand of God.

This letter was duly forwarded to Macaulay, and in a prompt response to his father he defends himself and his fellow-contributors with considerable spirit, showing no willingness to consider the abandonment either of his friends or his literary career: though he feels 'deep pain', it is 'pain without remorse. I am conscious of no misconduct, and whatever uneasiness I may feel arises solely from sympathy for your distress.'[38] According to Hannah, both sides eventually gave ground: Macaulay agreed to break his connection with the magazine in deference to his father's feelings, only for Zachary in his turn to withdraw his objections.[39] At all events, the contributions of 'Tristram Merton', as Macaulay called himself (whether for chivalric or Shandean reasons is not entirely clear), continued until *Knight's Quarterly* itself foundered on the disregard of some of the young gentlemen for the realities of publishing and to the accompaniment of a certain amount of proprietorial recrimination on the part of Knight himself.[40]

To read the contributions which Macaulay made to *Knight's Quarterly* and to the *Edinburgh Review* in the 1820s is to have the sense of watching a young man trying to discover both his subject and the methods which will enable him to control it. Year by year his techniques become more skilful, the assurance of tone and the narrative verve increase, and there is a drawing-back from subjects and approaches which he finds himself unable to handle effectively. Essentially the process is one of progressive refinement rather than of major change, and this exploratory phase continues in certain respects into the essays of the early 1830s. The solidity of his subsequent achievement as essayist and historian amply confirmed the rightness of Macaulay's judgment as to what he could and could not do; from the mid-1830s his grasp was always to determine the extent of his reach. To say this is not to diminish the stature of the later works – above all the *History of England* – or detract from their distinctiveness and range. It is simply to recognize the nature of the artistic achievement involved. Yearnings for a perpetually growing sensibility and technical range can only prevent the reader from appreciating the kind of success which Macaulay's mature writings so triumphantly represent. If at times the sureness, the accomplishment, the consistency produced what Matthew Arnold was to characterize as that appearance of always hitting the nail on the head, they also produced the confident sweep of the famous third chapter of the *History of England* and the controlled brilliance of the whole series of scenes and portraits which occur throughout the *History*'s five large volumes.

Macaulay's greatest successes were to be achieved in the writing of history and of narrative essays on historical subjects, but he did not arrive immediately at this kind of material or form. Indeed, access to the pages of *Knight's Quarterly* gave him an early opportunity to try his hand at a variety of literary modes in prose and verse.[41] Hindsight – the kind of Whig perspective of which Macaulay himself was often to be accused – prompts anyone now turning the pages of *Knight's* to notice first of all the contributions which seem clearly to foreshadow the later *Edinburgh* career: the article on Dante which has so many features in common with its more famous successor on Milton; the essay on slavery which was actually to be reworked for Macaulay's first *Edinburgh* appearance. But some of the more frivolous items deserve attention as well, not only as assertions of independence from his father but because they represent the false starts through which the young writer was to discover his literary identity.

It was not difficult for Macaulay to supply poems to the new magazine, but his father's objections to the two conventional love lyrics he published in the first issue led him, when he resumed his contributions in the third, to confine himself to historical subjects.[42] In prose he ranged from book reviews to imaginary conversation and satirical allegory. Beneath this apparent variety there existed, however, a connecting link. The more ambitious poems were those which took for their occasion historical events; the most finished review was of Mitford's *History of Greece;* the imaginary conversation was between two seventeenth-century figures; the comic allegory dealt with late eighteenth- and early nineteenth-century events. A fascination with men and actions from the past thus emerges as a characteristic feature of Macaulay's contributions to *Knight's Quarterly*, but what gives this material particular interest is the way in which – under pressure of the conventions of light literature then current – much of it takes a fictional turn.

The heavy-handed comic satire of the allegory of St Dennis and St George, or the prophecy of a Wellingtoniad to be published in the year 2824 – these make rather tiresome reading today, but the attempt to use historical situations for literary purposes connects these sketches not only with more substantial *Knight's* pieces but even with the *Lays of Ancient Rome* which Macaulay was to publish in mid-career. It is perhaps significant that the two most interesting attempts at historical fiction in *Knight's Quarterly* deal with classical subjects, resembling the *Lays* in this and in their overall concern with questions of historical perspective. All the irony available from knowledge of later Roman history hangs over Macaulay's very first contribution, 'Fragments of a Roman Tale', an anecdote about the saving of Julius Caesar from the plots of the Catiline conspirators who would implicate him or destroy him outright. Zoë, the dark-eyed Greek slave-girl to whom Caesar owes his life, has no historical future, and her flimsy and sentimentalized figure is doomed as certainly by the patterns of romance as by the ironies of history: three years after the publication of *Ivanhoe* readers hardly needed to be reminded of the likely fate of dark maidens of alien descent who were so unfortunate as to fall in love with heroes. In the dramatic fragment, 'Scenes from "Athenian Revels"', the hero is Alcibiades on the eve of the Sicilian expedition, and Macaulay clearly expects his readers to bring to bear a knowledge both of the traditional patterns of tragedy and of the specific events of history. That sacrilege and blasphemy are dangerously hubristic enterprises, that the would-be conqueror who goes forth in confident glory may be disappointed, that wives of heroes often live to weep – all these are frequent elements in tragic design, and they are confirmed by what the Classical historians tell of the recall from Sicily and consequent flight to Sparta which lie, at the moment of the drama, in Alcibiades' future.

One of Macaulay's childhood delights was to hear his mother read aloud the plays of Shakespeare; as a young man, like the rest of his generation, he waited in eager anticipation for each successive Waverley novel, and in 1823 the succession looked as though it might go on for ever; both Shakespeare and Scott were to be invoked in Macaulay's attempt in the 1828 *Edinburgh* essay on history to discriminate between the role of the creative artist and that of the historian. There is therefore nothing surprising in his trying at the age of twenty-two or -three to produce something effective in the forms of historical fiction and drama. He failed. There is no life in either Roman tale or Athenian revel, and the insistent historical detail, extending even to footnotes, suggests that the basis in fact commanded far more of his imaginative allegiance than the fanciful construct he sought to erect on that foundation. It is none the less interesting to ponder whether it was the example of Shakespeare – in *Coriolanus*, say – which led him to focus on a famous individual, or, on the other hand, how far the example of Scott might have suggested that first scene in the 'Athenian Revels' where an unimportant and fictional young man is shown in comic rebellion against his father's ideas and attitudes. The Shakespearian influence seems, if anything, the stronger; in both Roman and Athenian pieces it is finally the great man himself – Caesar or Alcibiades – who holds centre-stage, and this is, of course, quite different from Scott's use of most of his *Welthistorische* figures.

The recognition of this instinctive tendency to centre attention on the chief actors in any particular moment of historical drama may well have been one of the most valuable lessons the young writer learned from his *Knight's* experience, but it also presented him with certain problems. The central position of individual great men in Macaulay's early historical fictions suggests at first glance an heroic conception of history. But his attitude to major figures and their influence on the course of events is not as clear-cut as this impression suggests. In the 'Fragments of a Roman Tale', Caesar is presented in the archetypal situation of a hero about to be called from a life of retirement at a crucial moment in his nation's history; he is allowed an oblique prophecy of his own destiny:[43]

'Time will show. I would hope that there may arise a man, whose genius to conquer, to conciliate, and to govern, may unite in one cause an oppressed and divided people; – may do all that Sylla should have done, and exhibit the magnificent spectacle of a great nation directed by a great mind.'

'And where is such a man to be found?'

'Perhaps where you would least expect to find him. Perhaps he may be one whose powers have hitherto been concealed in domestic or literary retirement. Perhaps he may be one, who, while waiting for some adequate excitement, for some worthy opportunity, squanders on trifles a genius, before which may yet be humbled the sword of Pompey and the gown of Cicero.'

Whether 'Time will show' implies some kind of active process of historical generation, or whether what is envisaged is simply revelation, is not entirely apparent from the passage, but elsewhere in *Knight's Quarterly* Macaulay provides a very clear formulation of the notion that the times produce the man, or at any rate that achievements are attributable as much to external factors as to innate genius. The essay, 'On the Athenian Orators', incorporates a pronouncement about the relationship of great literary productions to the times in which they occur, and while the formulation is crude, its very baldness helps to make inescapably plain a theory which Macaulay continued to entertain, though varying the range of its applicability, throughout his life:[44]

It may be doubted whether any compositions which have ever been produced in the world, are equally perfect in their kind with the great Athenian orations. Genius is subject to the same laws which regulate the production of cotton and molasses. The supply adjusts itself to the demand. The quantity may be diminished by restrictions, and multiplied by bounties. The singular excellence to which eloquence attained at Athens is to be mainly attributed to the influence which it exerted there.

A fascination with great men and crucial moments does not sit well with the kind of theory just outlined, and this undoubtedly caused Macaulay difficulties in both his critical and historical writings in the 1820s. An additional complication arose from the increasing emphasis he placed on the importance of social history in coming to any full understanding of the men and events of the past. The review of Mitford's *History of Greece* in *Knight's Quarterly* contains the first full statement of a view Macaulay was to express in similar terms on a number of subsequent occasions:[45]

> I would hope that there may yet appear a writer who may despise the present narrow limits, and assert the rights of history over every part of her natural domain. Should such a writer engage in that enterprise, in which I cannot but consider Mr. Mitford as having failed, he will record, indeed, all that is interesting and important in military and political transactions; but he will not think any thing too trivial for the gravity of history, which is not too trivial to promote or diminish the happiness of man. He will portray in vivid colours the domestic society, the manners, the amusements, the conversation of the Greeks. He will not disdain to discuss the state of agriculture, of the mechanical arts, and of the conveniences of life. The progress of painting, of sculpture, and of architecture, will form an important part of his plan. But above all, his attention will be given to the history of that splendid literature from which has sprung all the strength, the wisdom, the freedom, and the glory, of the western world.

Earlier in the Mitford essay Macaulay had remarked that the best sources for such history might well be found in 'works not professedly historical',[46] the literary documents of the period. Paradoxically, however, it is in the handling of the creators of such documents that the problem of the great man recurs for Macaulay in its most acute form.

What we encounter in the early critical essays in both *Knight's Quarterly* and the *Edinburgh Review* are a series of attempts to expound and exemplify theories – theories of art having to do with such fundamental concepts as realism and the imitative nature of all art, theories of cultural development charting the decline of imaginative power and the accompanying growth of technical accomplishment, and theories of general history concerned to relate individuals to their times. Macaulay excels when invoking a whole string of concrete instances in support of an isolated abstract generalization, and he is skilful enough at logical gymnastics to allow himself the valuable room for manoeuvre supplied by the occasional exceptions which manage somehow to prove the very rules they seem at first sight so markedly to contradict. But he cannot make all his theories work in concert together to solve the cluster of problems about the characters and achievements of individual great artists at given historical moments. Indeed, Macaulay's eventual turning away from literary criticism may be attributable in part to his own recognition that, no matter how dazzling the detail of individual essays, he had failed to account for the existence of a Dante, a Milton, or a Byron in their particular historical moment, or to make a viable connection between purely critical evaluation of their works and assessment of their status as historical figures.

The theory of literature which Macaulay expounds in the *Knight's* essays on Dante and Petrarch and in the *Edinburgh* articles on Milton and Dryden is basically historical, concerning itself with change as it occurs in time. It embodies the standard Romantic commonplace that imagination is a predominant faculty in primitive societies, and supports it by the usual analogies with childhood. The Milton essay of 1825 states quite bluntly, 'We think that, as civilization advances, poetry almost necessarily declines.'[47] The absoluteness of this view is slightly modified in the Dryden essay of 1828, for although Macaulay still insists that 'Our judgment ripens, our imagination decays' (47:8), he is at pains to point out that 'the instruments which the imagination employs' are refined in the course of time; therefore 'In poetry, as in painting and sculpture, it is necessary that the imitator should be well acquainted with that which he undertakes to imitate, and expert in the mechanical part of his art' (47:10). This leads Macaulay to posit 'a short period of splendid and consummate excellence' (47:11) when the arcs of imaginative power and technical skill intersect. Such a theory will account for a Shakespeare; when allowance is made for the force of exceptional imaginative power in combination with an extraordinary range of technical ability, and for something as unpredictable as blindness, it will also account for a Milton. Since the theory allows for a revival period of imitative greatness when the accomplishments of an earlier golden age are echoed – 'a Saint Martin's Summer, which, after a period of dreariness and decay, agreeably reminds us of the spleandour of its June' (47:13) – certain resurgences of poetic power can further be accommodated. The theory, in short, works quite well for a view of English literary history which sees the eighteenth century as a decline from the heights of the early seventeenth century, and it in no way interferes with a belief in the intimate connection between artists and their period.

This latter theory of the link between man and moment is taken up in the opening pages of the Dryden essay: 'it is the age that forms the man, not the man that forms the age. Great minds do indeed re-act on the society which has made them what they are; but they only pay with

changes in 2 years

interest what they have received' (47:2). Dryden's own career 'depended less on his personal qualities than on the circumstances in which he was placed' (47:1); as a poet he is a representative not of the 'creative school', which belongs to the early period of a culture's development when imagination is dominant, but to 'the age of critical poetry', when 'the judgment, and the wit, contribute far more than the imagination' (47:12). Certain refinements are made to the basic theoretical outline in order to take into account circumstances peculiar to seventeenth-century England – for example, the closing of the theatres and the restoration of a monarch whose tastes were largely French – and in this way both the general theory about the development of poetry and the particular demonstration of Dryden as the product of his age are made conformable to each other.

Macaulay's general theory of imaginative decline obviously became less satisfactory the more highly he learned to value the work of the Romantic poets. Only a little more than two years separates the essay on Dryden from that on Byron, but Macaulay has in the meantime considerably shifted his theoretical ground. Byron is a near contemporary, and the closeness of the perspective in combination with the vivid individuality of the subject's personality would seem to militate against too simple a presentation of him as a product of his era. But this is still insisted upon at certain points in the essay: 'He was the creature of his age', that is, 'he was the man of the last thirteen years of the eighteenth century, and of the first twenty-three years of the nineteenth century'; as such, he belonged 'half to the old, and half to the new school of poetry' (53:564). The difficulty here is that Macaulay now recognizes the new school as superior to the old. The acknowledgment, however unenthusiastic, of the greatness of Wordsworth, the far warmer response to Scott and to 'the magnificent imagery and the varied music of Coleridge and Shelley' (53:556), the generosity with which Shelley is again celebrated in (of all places) the 1831 *Edinburgh* essay on *The Pilgrim's Progress* – these new perceptions play havoc with the historical theory of imaginative decay paradoxically fused with technical and experiential advance which had sufficed to put Dryden so neatly in his place. Clearly no mere bending of the rules will make room for a whole school of major Romantic poets.

Most of the theorizing in the Byron essay itself is devoted to questions of correctness and realism, and Macaulay is again treading fairly familiar Romantic critical ground when he insists that it is not adherence to metrical rules or traditional conventions which makes a poem

17

correct, but rather 'conforming to rules which have their foundation in truth, and in the principles of human nature' (53:553). The discussion of imitative realism – deliberately ahistorical in its reference to Aristotle and its invocation of Homer, Dante, Shakespeare, and Milton as 'in one sense, and that the best sense, the most correct of poets' (53:553) – sets up a standard by which the poets of the new nineteenth-century school can be judged: 'Sir Walter Scott, Mr Wordsworth, Mr Coleridge, are far more correct writers than those who are commonly extolled as the models of correctness, – Pope, for example, and Addison' (53:554). The emphasis now is on the 'eternal and immutable principles' (53:558) of poetry rather than on literary history, and Dr Johnson is implicitly criticized for the temporal blindness of his declaration 'that since the time of Dryden, English poetry had shown no tendency to relapse into its original savageness; that its language had been refined, its numbers tuned, and its sentiments improved' (53:559). There is, of course, nothing in this view of Johnson's incompatible with the theories Macaulay had propounded in his own essay on Dryden, nor is Johnson directly contraverted in the Byron essay itself, but the belittling comments on eighteenth-century poetry which follow the Johnson quotation, and the assertion that 'Men became tired of an insipid conformity to a standard which derived no authority from nature or reason', serve alike to prepare the way for a view of the Romantic literary revolution as a moment when 'The eternal laws of poetry regained their power, and the temporary fashions which had superseded those laws went after the wig of Lovelace and the hoop of Clarissa' (53:560). Byron can now be presented positively as one who, despite his own preference as a critic for 'the school of poetry which was going out', played a crucial role as a poet in the new movement: 'During the twenty years which followed the death of Cowper, the revolution in English poetry was fully consummated. None of the writers of this period, not even Sir Walter Scott, contributed so much to the consummation as Lord Byron' (53:562).

Byron is none the less criticized, and especially for the lack of realism which Macaulay finds in his dramatic verse: 'Lord Byron, like Mr Wordsworth, had nothing dramatic in his genius' (53:565); his portraits are always of the same few human types; he depends much too heavily on the satirist's method of exhibiting characters in a 'sharp antithetical way' (53:566). 'A dramatist', Macaulay declares, 'cannot commit a greater error than that of following those pointed descriptions of character in which satirists and historians indulge so much. . . .

If the dramatist attempts to create a being answering to one of these descriptions, he fails, because he reverses an imperfect analytical process' and produces 'not a man, but a personified epigram' (53:566). Byron failed to create his characters dramatically because he 'exhibited them in the manner, not of Shakespeare, but of Clarendon. He analyzed them. He made them analyze themselves, but he did not make them show themselves' (53:567). Ironically enough, one might make the same complaint of Macaulay's presentation of Byron. It is of course true that he is writing an essay, even something of a Clarendonian 'character', and not a play; even so, the portrait of Byron near the beginning of that essay is so much the 'personified epigram' as to become not just a paradigm but almost a parody of the method subsequently attributed to satirists and historians:

> In the rank of Lord Byron, in his understanding, in his character, in his very person, there was a strange union of opposite extremes. He was born to all that men covet and admire. But in every one of those eminent advantages which he possessed over others, there was mingled something of misery and debasement. . . . The young peer had great intellectual powers; yet there was an unsound part in his mind. He had naturally a generous and tender heart; but his temper was wayward and irritable. He had a head which statuaries loved to copy, and a foot, the deformity of which the beggars in the streets mimicked. Distinguished at once by the strength and by the weakness of his intellect, affectionate yet perverse, a poor lord, and a handsome cripple, he required, if ever man required, the firmest and the most judicious training. . . . He came into the world, and the world treated him as his mother treated him – sometimes with kindness, sometimes with severity, never with justice. It indulged him without discrimination, and punished him without discrimination. He was truly a spoiled child, – not merely the spoiled child of his parent, but the spoiled child of nature, the spoiled child of fortune, the spoiled child of fame, the spoiled child of society. (53:564)

The Byron essay, says Christopher North in *Noctes Ambrosianae* for August 1831:[48]

> is an exceedingly clever thing, and you ought to glance your eye over it. The Edinburgh has had nothing so good these several

> years past. In fact, it reads very like a paper in one of their early
> numbers – much the same sort of excellencies – the smart, rapid,
> popgun impertinence – the brisk, airy, new-set truisms,
> mingled with cold, shallow, heartless sophistries – the conceited
> phlegm, the affected abruptness, the unconscious audacity of
> impudence – the whole lively, and amusing, and much
> commended among the dowagers –.

Macaulay perhaps found himself in some agreement with this damning praise. On 8 June 1831, before the article was even completed, he wrote to his sister, Hannah, that it was 'without exception, the worst thing I ever wrote in my life',[49] and the exaggeration in this statement perhaps indicates his uneasy awareness of the lack of congruence between his theory and his practice.

In the early critical essays Macaulay is feeling his way towards a new form, a kind of sub-genre which he was to make peculiarly his own – the narrative essay, a merging of history and biography with those more static forms of characterization, related to the seventeenth-century 'character', which set out to capture the essence of a personality or the fundamentals of an achievement. What in the highly successful essays of the early 1840s was to emerge as a fruitful tension between dynamic and static impulses remains at this stage a series of unresolved conflicts, the failure of resolution made all the more obvious by the simultaneous presence of dogmatically advanced theories of history and literature. In the Byron essay he defined the difference between the methods of the dramatist and the historian in terms of an opposition between the manner of a Shakespeare and that of a Clarendon, while from other essays of the 1820s we know that the writing of history seemed to him to have veered too far not merely in the direction of analysis but of polemic, and that his own impulse was to bring into history proper some of the dramatic realism he found in Scott's historical fiction. If his own essays were to contribute to such an endeavour he had clearly to find new ways of presenting the protagonists, and yet in evoking Byron the man – as later in evoking Boswell the man – he found himself employing those very methods of analytical and antithetical portraiture for which he had berated Byron the dramatist.

Macaulay had tried his hand at fiction and drama in *Knight's Quarterly* and failed to endow his personages with life. In analysing other men's achievements in this same creative sphere he found his various theories about cultural history, poetic development, and the permanent truths of art brought into an uncomfortable proximity which served only to reveal their incompatibility. When the new poets of the nineteenth century presented him with a particularly intransigent critical problem, his solution was to stop writing about them, and indeed about critical questions in general, for almost the whole of the next decade – the essay on Johnson forming only half an exception. He turned instead to political and historical subjects, perhaps in the hope of salving the wounds he had sustained on the field of critical theory with some practical victories in the arena of polemical argument. When he returned to literary subjects in the essays of the 1840s Macaulay avoided head-on confrontations with questions of general critical theory and side-stepped the problem of the relationship of the man of the highest literary genius to the age in which he lived: he contented himself with an Addison rather than a Milton, a Fanny Burney rather than a Byron, and he did not extend his historical range beyond the end of the eighteenth century. This may suggest that the lessons of the 1820s were purely negative, but that is not in fact the case. What is demonstrated by all the later narrative essays, both critical and historical, as by the *History of England* which followed them, is that Macaulay had arrived by experience if not by theory at what was for him an effective balance in handling the interconnection over an extended period of time between the patterns of a man's life and the changing course of public events. These same works also show that Macaulay had learned to use a variety of conventions in the shaping of narrative, and they suggest that those abortive attempts at fiction and drama in *Knight's Quarterly* had at least taught him that the ironies of history and the structures of drama or romance can be made to work in fruitful combination. If he did not master that combination in his first attempts, that was because he was searching for theories which would explain the successful creative achievements of others in a coherent, historically describable way, invoking either the pattern of progress or that of decline, or some simple combination of the two. He never lost his taste for dogmatic assertions of theory as well as of fact, but he did learn in the course of time the wisdom of following his narrative instincts rather than his theoretical concepts when actually engaged in his tasks as historian and essayist.

2

Apprenticeship in Polemics

The Essays on Southey and Croker's Boswell

On 1 October 1824 Macaulay wrote to tell his father that he had that morning been elected a Fellow of Trinity College. For seven years from the date of his obtaining his M.A. the following June, he explained, the Fellowship would make him 'almost an independent man'.[1] The financial consideration was important, and would become even more so. Macaulay himself had little prospect of early reward as a barrister, and although he was called to the bar in 1826 his short career on the Northern Circuit and later in chambers in London was to be distinguished neither by industrious study nor by professional engagements. His father meanwhile was losing during the 1820s the substantial fortune he had built up in the course of the previous thirty years. In 1823 Zachary Macaulay decided to devote himself even more exclusively to the Anti-Slavery movement and to withdraw, therefore, from active participation in the firm of Macaulay and Babington which he had set up in partnership with his nephew, Thomas Gisborne Babington. The Macaulays had earlier moved from Clapham to a more comfortable and elegant house in Cadogan Square when the Clapham group began to break up, following the deaths of Henry Thornton and his wife in 1815; because he felt his reduced contribution to the firm ought to be reflected in his taking a smaller share of the profits Zachary Macaulay now moved his family to the less fashionable area of Great Ormond Street. By 1826 Thomas Babington's mismanagement had brought Macaulay and Babington to the point of ruin, and while Zachary was never actually forced into bankruptcy he was henceforward in constant financial difficulty. These disasters were to have a profound effect on his son's career: he could now have no expectation of that financial security on which he had once depended, and he would be obliged instead to contribute whatever he could to the depleted resources of his younger brothers and sisters. He seems, however, to have accepted the situation without complaint, and certainly his sister, Hannah, was to recall the middle and late 1820s as 'years of intense happiness',[2] largely because of Macaulay's almost daily presence in the family circle at Great Ormond Street.

By the late 1820s Tom Macaulay was famous – not, of course, as a lawyer but as a contributor to the *Edinburgh Review*, the greatest of the great journals of that period. Although it is not quite clear how he was first approached by the editor, Francis Jeffrey, it is not surprising that his name should have reached Jeffrey's ears. His Cambridge reputation, especially after his success in the Trinity Fellowship examinations, was very considerable, and both his speech before the Anti-Slavery Society and his pieces for *Knight's Quarterly* had attracted some notice. More-over, Henry Brougham, one of the *Edinburgh*'s chief contributors, had recently become associated with Zachary Macaulay in the Anti-Slavery movement, and he seems to have been at least partly instrumental in introducing Zachary's son to the pages of the Review. Hannah's account was that when *Knight's Quarterly* ceased publication 'Jeffrey who was always on the lookout for fresh hands asked him [Macaulay] to write for the E.R. He gratified his Father by writing his first article in 1825 on West Indian Slavery. His second the Review on Milton at once established his reputation as a first rate Essayist.' The Milton essay was, of course, printed anonymously, but the secret of its author-ship was soon out. 'In Byron's words,' Hannah adds, 'he might have said he woke one morning & found himself famous. I shall never forget Jeffrey's glowing exulting letter on reading it.'[3]

The *Edinburgh Review* was dedicated wholeheartedly to the promotion of the Whig cause, and although Macaulay's first great success had been with a literary essay he was to serve during his first five or six years as a contributor to the Review an essentially political apprenticeship – one which brought in due time the rewards of a post as Commissioner of Bankruptcy, a seat in parliament, and a place at the Holland House dinner table. In the several political essays of the late 1820s he played to the utmost the role expected of him, that of the bright and aspiring young man, the contentious gadfly who did not hesitate to attack the enemies of the Review and of the Whig party with every weapon of fact, argument, and rhetoric which came to hand. He was not required to propound fundamental theories about politics, since the empirical Whig tradition set little store by metaphysics, but he was implicitly charged with hitting out at the Tories on the right and the Benthamites on the left, and with advancing during intervening moments such favoured causes as Catholic emancipation and reform of the franchise.

He performed his task with great vigour and enthusiasm, and with considerable effect, but the essays in question are likely to hold little interest or attraction for twentieth-century readers. This is in part natural enough, since the concern is with specific men and issues of the late 1820s: the 1827 article on 'The Present Administration', for instance, was so entirely partisan in argument, so unpleasantly violent in tone, and so completely tied to a particular moment in the parliamentary battle that it was never reprinted by Macaulay and was even excluded from the catch-all collection published by his executors under the title *Miscellaneous Writings*. The following attack on the *New Anti-Jacobin Review*, the ostensible occasion of the article, represents one of the lowest of the numerous low points to which the writing sinks:

> It is not a very cleanly, or a very agreeable task, to rake up from
> the kennels of oblivion the remains of drowned abortions, which
> have never opened their eyes on the day, or even been heard to
> whimper, but have been at once transferred from the filth in
> which they were littered, to the filth with which they are to rot.
> But unhappily we have no choice. Bad as this work is, it is quite
> as good as any which has appeared against the present
> administration. We have looked everywhere, without being
> able to find an antagonist who can possibly be as much ashamed
> of defeat as we shall be of victory. (46:245)

But there are more general reasons why these early political pieces should have so little to offer later readers. Even the best of them – the essays on James Mill and the Utilitarians and on Michael Sadler, the Tory campaigner[4] – can best be characterized negatively. They are almost entirely given over to refutation and, indeed, demolition, and offer nothing very substantial in the way of constructive counter-argument. In the three Utilitarian essays Macaulay himself insists again and again that his concern is not to advance alternative theories, and although Malthusian doctrines are implicitly present as a counter to Sadler's ideas on population they are nowhere explicitly expounded or defended. In the two Sadler essays, in fact, Macaulay contents himself with demonstrating his victim's logical inconsistencies, statistical *naïveté*, and general mathematical incompetence; the resulting tone of vaunting cocksureness is gratingly unattractive, even if individual feats of swashbuckling and knockabout comedy manage to sustain a certain vitality for a page or two here and there.

The attacks on the Utilitarian followers of Bentham are as destructive in tone as those on Sadler and the Tories, but the energy with which they are mounted may perhaps betray an underlying realization on Macaulay's part that in terms of actual practice – as opposed to formulated theory – some of the political and administrative reforms he himself might favour were not unrelated to the ends pursued by the Benthamites. Certainly the tests of common sense, enforcibility, and fairness he was later to invoke in his development of an Indian Penal Code had much in common with the more moderate of the Utilitarian positions, and in 1843, when he issued his essays in collected form, his work in India had given him good reason to admire James Mill as a man and be grateful to him as an ally. That more relaxed assurance, very different from his earlier self-assertiveness, which Macaulay achieved in his forties also enabled him to combine opposition to Mill's political theories with a tribute to his work in other spheres, and in the preface to the 1843 edition of the *Essays* he gives the following explanation of the omission of the Utilitarian articles: 'Serious as are the faults of the Essay on Government, a critic, while noting those faults, should have abstained from using contemptuous language respecting the historian of British India.' He continues with more specifically personal amends to Mill: 'It ought to be known that Mr. Mill had the generosity, not only to forgive, but to forget the unbecoming acrimony with which he had been assailed, and was, when his valuable life closed, on terms of cordial friendship with his assailant.'[5]

If the fire in Macaulay's attacks on the Utilitarians gradually subsided, it was never entirely extinguished from his confrontations with the Tories. The long - smouldering animosity to Croker first exposed during the Reform Bill debates flares up occasionally in letters to Macvey Napier in the early 1840s and in comments on Croker's review of his *History* at the end of the same decade; it also makes its contribution to the famous article on Croker's edition of Boswell which Macaulay published in 1831. But once Macaulay was in parliament he had a more immediate outlet for his attacks on Toryism, another field on which to deploy his talents for argument and the marshalling of evidence, for finding small holes in the opposing case and transforming them into yawning gaps, and for exploiting all the devices of rhetoric not merely to demolish a theory he believed unsound but to convey the impression of having achieved a moral no less than an intellectual victory. Those early speeches, especially on the Reform Bills, confirmed a fame already well established by the articles in the *Edinburgh Review*; they also supplied him with a public persona he could adopt within the palace of Westminster and on the hustings.

The problem of evolving a satisfactory literary persona within the essays was not so easily solved, for while the Sadler and Utilitarian essays and the other political pieces of the 1820s revealed a distinctive authorial personality, it was not a particularly engaging one; politically, too, it had the disadvantage of being vulnerable to the attacks of Professor Wilson and his *Blackwood's* cronies. The 'Noctes Ambrosianae' section of that journal specialized in an insidious brand of belittling mockery combined with unpleasantly personal recrimination which did much to harass the Whigs during the 1820s. The tactics were designed to distract the attention of the Whig polemicists from major issues and embroil them in minor skirmishes, and each Whig sprat was greedily pounced upon as it swam into view. Macaulay was a particularly obvious prey, not only because he and his family were the beneficiaries of various forms of Whig patronage but because his performances in the *Edinburgh Review* suggested an ambition and assertiveness which demanded a rapid cutting down to size. Macaulay was quickly assigned in the *Blackwood's* mythology the role of the bumptious boy who didn't know his own place and who showed no signs of ever growing up. Of the article on 'The Present Administration' David Robinson wrote in the October 1827 issue of *Blackwood's*: 'We scarcely ever met with a more striking specimen of frothy, shallow, pointless, feeble declamation – of puerile, low, scurrilous "sound and fury, signifying nothing".'[6] John Wilson himself, attacking Macaulay's Sadler articles in the February 1831 issue, called him 'the little Cockney-champion' who is 'on the wrong side of five-and-twenty, by a good many years – and yet "destined to be a boy all his life"; for what have his best compositions been, but a tawdry bedizenment of flower, froth, fume, foam, flash, flutter, and feather of speech.'[7] Macaulay's difficulties with mathematics while a Cambridge undergraduate were brought up by way of undermining the attack on Sadler, and he was perhaps lucky to escape with this: Professor McCulloch, the *Edinburgh*'s chief writer on economics, had the lowliness of his origins dragged out against him in the same *Blackwood's* piece and found himself scorned for having once been 'a common day-labourer' who not many years before might have been seen 'digging and ditching, if not with much skill or alacrity, at least with that dogged perseverance, for which, more than by any higher quality, he is still distinguished'.[8] At the time of the Southey essay in 1830 the Ettrick shepherd speculated on Macaulay's likely fate should Southey be roused to respond: 'Only suppose Soothey to stir in his sleep – but to gie a sneeze or a snore – and hoo the bit barrister – for I remember what the bit body is noo – would wriggle awa like a worm, and divin' intill some dung, hide himsell amang the grubs.' On the same page Zachary Macaulay was characterized as 'The Sierra Leone Saint, who has been the means of sendin' sae mony sinners to Satan through that accursed settlement.'[9]

If the venom of the later attacks is in part attributable to a recognition that Macaulay was not going to be easy to dispose of, the consistent association of him with a juvenile role and personality shows a good deal of shrewdness. As his father had feared, the young Macaulay had undoubtedly failed to disguise a self-satisfied confidence in his own powers; he revealed too openly his delight in his logical thrusts and stylistic panache, and the general impression of youthful arrogance makes itself felt as much in the literary essay on Milton as in the political attack on Sadler. In moving into the 1830s – the decade which coincided with his own thirties – Macaulay was faced with the problem of developing some kind of mask, structure, or manner which would mitigate the impression of arrogance and allow him to maintain the allegiance of his readers even while he assembled a devastating battery of arguments and instances, exposed fallacies and follies, and demonstrated the superiority of his own intelligence and information. He developed the necessary techniques in essays which, while still largely polemical in form and manner, and still aimed at well-known Tory spokesmen, none the less went beyond the stage of simple destructiveness. The first of these was the review – of Southey's *Sir Thomas More: or Colloquies on the Progress and Prospects of Society* (1829) – which provoked the Ettrick shepherd to the riposte already quoted. But if Macaulay could succeed in establishing his new authorial persona and the relationship with his audience it implied, he would be able in future to shrug off such attacks, confident that they could have only a minimal effect on his readers.

That the composition and publication of the Southey essay had a direct relevance for the progress of Macaulay's political career there can be little doubt. The review appeared in the January 1830 number of the *Edinburgh*; in February 1830 Macaulay's sister, Hannah, later recalled, Lord Lansdowne wrote to tell Macaulay 'how much he had been struck by his articles on Mill & that finding his character was high and his talents were great he wished to be the means of first introducing him into the House of Commons'[10] – specifically, by inviting him to stand for the vacant seat at Calne, his pocket borough in Wiltshire. Macaulay was duly elected for Calne – that 'villanous hole', as William Cobbett called it in one of his frequent tirades against Whig–controlled boroughs[11] – and while the articles on Mill were those specifically mentioned by Lansdowne, his confidence in Macaulay's party loyalty must have been significantly strengthened by the celebration of Whig views and values at the conclusion of the Southey essay. The representativeness of that essay as a youthful expression of Whig dogma was perhaps one of the reasons why Macaulay chose to reprint it in later years even while omitting several others among the early argumentative pieces. He may have taken a certain satisfaction in reissuing what *Blackwood's* had so strongly attacked, and he had, in any case, no personal reason for sparing Southey of the kind which led him, out of deference to the memory of James Mill, to refuse to republish the three essays on Utilitarianism.

In choosing to write about Southey Macaulay was ranging himself against a formidable antagonist, one whose position as Poet Laureate and the author of popular works in verse and prose gave added force to his expression, in the pages of the *Quarterly Review* and elsewhere, of the doctrines of Tory paternalism. Macaulay could of course assume among the *Edinburgh*'s predominantly Whig audience a general sympathy for his own position and a revulsion from Southey's Toryism, but it was none the less necessary to make allowance for Southey's occupation of the Poet Laureateship and for the pleasure which some of his early works would have given to many in this same audience. It would be bad tactics, psychologically and rhetorically, to take hostility to Southey and sympathy with the reviewer too obviously for granted. The problem provides Macaulay with an excellent opportunity for exercising his talent for paradox, and by opening the essay with an overview of Southey's whole *oeuvre* he is able to mingle praise with blame in judicious quantities while still leaving open the option of an entirely critical treatment of the specific work under review. The opening pages thus serve to establish the reviewer's fairness – and, of course, the breadth of his knowledge – and by confining praise almost exclusively to Southey's poetry they create a strong if as yet unfocused impression that the author of the *Colloquies* is somehow unfitted for the harsher realities of prose. It is, indeed, by the praise of Southey's imaginative powers as much as by the criticism of his reasoning faculties that Macaulay seeks to undermine his opponent's position before mounting his main attack – which, like most of the others in these early polemical essays, will be a direct frontal assault energetically prosecuted.

By far the most striking feature of these early pages is the introduction of a comparison with Burke. The great statesman's conduct at the time of the Hastings impeachment – especially his oratorical evocation of 'Hindostan, with its vast cities, its gorgeous pagodas, its infinite swarms of dusky population' (50:529) – is presented with a vitality and independence, a brilliance amounting to the flashy, which seems at first glance out of place, or at least out of proportion; at the same time, like other extended allusions and passages of brilliantly 'got up' tangential material in Macaulay's essays, it performs something of the function of an epic simile. Such excursions give to the essays an additional richness of an occasionally over-coloured kind; more immediately they serve to expand or elevate a particular point in the discussion or narrative, and to fix that point firmly in the reader's mind. Like epic similes they are required to operate analogically only at the point of departure and possibly that of return, having meanwhile a quite proper and often spectacular life of their own. By the change of subject or tone which they introduce, passages of this kind can also function as an effective disguise for some lacuna in the argument or narrative structure – even while their very specificity seems to be giving support and illustration of the most concrete kind – and their vitality may extend these effects beyond the immediate context in which they occur. In this particular instance the support given by the Burke comparison to the assertion of Southey's inability to reason does not seem to justify either its length or its tone; the chief function of the passage, however, has been to impress the reader by its very brilliance and thus to establish the credentials of the reviewer still more firmly in the reader's mind.

The central part of the essay is devoted to a direct refutation by argument of Southey's views, and here Macaulay's fecundity in illustration and historical reference comes powerfully and persuasively to his support. He does not rest, however, in the negativity of refutation: the basic movement of the essay is from the negative to the positive, from the exposure of the inadequacies of Southey's position to the optimistic assertion of Macaulay's own beliefs, reaching its climax in the famous final pages – virtually a manifesto of Whig concepts of self-reliance and *laissez-faire* capitalism:

If we were to prophesy that in the year 1930, a population of fifty millions, better fed, clad, and lodged than the English of our time, will cover these islands, – that Sussex and Huntingdonshire will be wealthier than the wealthiest parts of the West-Riding of Yorkshire now are, – that cultivation, rich as that of a flower-garden, will be carried up to the very tops of Ben Nevis and Helvellyn, – that machines, constructed on principles yet undiscovered, will be in every house, – that there will be no highways but rail-roads, no travelling but by steam, – that our debt, vast as it seems to us, will appear to our great-grandchildren a trifling encumbrance, which might easily be paid off in a year or two, – many people would think us insane. We prophesy nothing; but this we say – If any person had told the Parliament which met in perplexity and terror after the crash in 1720, that in 1830 the wealth of England would surpass all their wildest dreams – that the annual revenue would equal the principal of that debt which they considered as an intolerable burden – that for one man of L.10,000 then living, there would be five men of L.50,000; that London would be twice as large and twice as populous, and that nevertheless the mortality would have diminished to one-half what it then was, – that the post-office would bring more into the exchequer than the excise and customs had brought in together under Charles II, – that stage-coaches would run from London to York in twenty-four hours – that men would sail without wind, and would be beginning to ride without horses – our ancestors would have given as much credit to the prediction as they gave to Gulliver's Travels. Yet the prediction would have been true; and they would have perceived that it was not altogether absurd, if they had considered that the country was then raising every year a sum which would have purchased the fee-simple of the revenue of the Plantagenets – ten times what supported the government of Elizabeth – three times what, in the time of Oliver Cromwell, had been thought intolerably oppressive. . . . On what principle is it, that when we see nothing but improvement behind us, we are to expect nothing but deterioration before us?

It is not by the intermeddling of Mr Southey's idol – the omniscient and omnipotent State – but by the prudence and energy of the people, that England has hitherto been carried forward in civilisation; and it is to the same prudence and the same energy that we now look with comfort and good hope. Our rulers will best promote the improvement of the people by strictly confining themselves to their own legitimate duties – by leaving capital to find its most lucrative course, commodities their fair price, industry and intelligence their natural reward, idleness and folly their natural punishment – by maintaining peace, by defending property, by diminishing the price of law, and by observing strict economy in every department of the state. Let the Government do this – the People will assuredly do the rest. (50:563–5)

The tone here is undoubtedly over-confident; the colours are too bright, the outlines too definite. Yet within the context of the essay itself these stridencies have a kind of rightness. Whatever intellectual doubts one may have about them in retrospect, it is hard while actually reading the essay to resist the emotional force which derives from their structural and rhetorical inevitability. For they rest not only upon the apparent destruction of Southey's argument in the central part of the essay but, far more importantly, upon the creation from the beginning of a kind of *dramatis personae* comprising the figures of the reviewer, the reader, and Mr Southey.

In an anonymous review the author has no identity independent of the review itself or of the 'personality' – in the case of the *Edinburgh*, a very powerful one – of the journal in which the review appears. The reader may make guesses, informed or otherwise, as to who the author may be, but any such conception is itself a product of the review. In works where the author is named, even if the name itself means nothing to the reader its very presence may provide some external impression, and it serves, at the very least, to put a stop to speculation. Anonymity, on the other hand, can seem positively to invite the reader to create an authorial personality, and this is particularly so when what is in question is primarily the expression of opinions and attitudes. In all of Macaulay's essays the personality of the author is not far to seek: it makes its presence felt from the outset in the clear, authoritative, often brilliant prose style, and in the firmness and directness of the statements. In the Southey essay, however, the process of continuous consideration of the work under review provides us with a second created figure, that of the author of the *Colloquies*, and the trio is completed by the impression of the reader himself which the essay implies. The relationship between these three figures provides the emotional ambience within which a logical refutation of Southey's views can receive a sympathetic hearing – and also a camouflage for any flaws in the reviewer's own logic.

The Burke comparison had affirmed by its manner the reviewer's distinction as a man of creative imagination, and by its matter his authority as one who understands and appreciates the power of reason as well as that of the imagination – to such an extent, indeed, that Southey suffers in comparison not only with Burke but with the implied figure of the reviewer. But an equally important aspect of the passage is the way it works together with the many minor allusions in the essay to create the figure of the reader – who is, quite simply, a person to whom such allusions will be meaningful. The impression of such a figure is sustained by ensuring that the real, the flesh-and-blood reader will not be alienated or discouraged by having undue demands made upon his knowledge. Almost all the allusions are self-contained, carrying with them basic information as to their source or significance: the emotions 'which have consecrated the shades of Vaucluse and the rocks of Meillerie' (50:532) have already been identified as those of love; mention of Uncle Toby in one sentence is followed in the next by a reference to him as Captain Shandy (50:533), lest anyone should have let slip from mind the title of the book in which he figures. Sometimes the gloss is even more direct: 'He has passed from one extreme of political opinion to another, as Satan in Milton went round the globe, contriving constantly to "ride with darkness"' (50:534). Occasionally, information as to source is offered quite explicitly, as in the quotation from *The Relapse* (50:550). Although such references may function immediately to diminish the figure of Southey – who is identified with Uncle Toby, Satan, and Vanbrugh's shoemaker – they also serve to elevate the figure of the reader, who is able so comfortably and so knowingly to recognize them and appreciate their significance. The reader, in short, joins the reviewer in the company of the knowledgeable and well-read.

These figures of author, reviewer, and reader are all essentially fictional, elements in the essay's rhetoric, and they have no necessary identity with any reality outside the essay. Yet the reader tends inevitably to assume that the 'Mr Southey' of the essay is identical with the Poet Laureate, just as he tends unconsciously to accept the flattering portrait of himself which emerges and the picture of the reviewer which has also been created in his mind. The essay depends in large measure upon this transference of the truths of fiction to life itself: rejection of paternalistic Toryism and acceptance of individualistic

Whiggism arises at least in part from the reader's impression of the figures represented as respectively holding such views. The whole strategy of the essay revolves upon its *dramatis personae* and upon the drama in which they are engaged: the reviewer debates with Mr Southey while the reader provides a sympathetic audience. What Macaulay presents, in fact, is virtually his own 'Colloquy', and while his protagonists may seem at first sight to be distinctly less fanciful figures than that ghost of Sir Thomas More with whom Southey represents himself as conversing they are none the less fictional creations, susceptible of infinite manipulation in order to advance both the design of the essay itself and the Whig propaganda which the essay embodies.

The attack on John Wilson Croker's edition of Boswell's *Life of Johnson*, published in the September 1831 issue of the *Edinburgh*, seems at first sight a mirror image of the Southey article: an assault on a literary man for his political thinking is replaced by the pillorying of a politician for his inadequacies as editor, scholar, and stylist. But whereas Southey's literary achievements are discussed in the earlier essay and play some part in its rhetorical strategy, Croker's politics are not so invoked, even though the animus with which he is treated almost certainly owes something to the tensions of Reform Bill England and Croker's position as one of the leading Tory spokesmen in the House of Commons. Although in both essays Macaulay is attacking what he sees as fundamentally the same failing – incompetence accompanied, indeed produced, by arrogance – the Croker review remains a very different affair from the Southey. The criticism is fiercer, the tone angrier, the ridicule turned to bitterness. The article takes the offensive immediately; it insists not only on the failings of the nineteenth-century editor but on the personal weaknesses of the eighteenth-century subject and his biographer; and there is nothing to match the hymn to progress by which the Southey is eventually transposed from critique to celebration.

If there is, none the less, a modulation from the negative to the positive, it is one in which the positive elements are always controlled by criticisms or qualifications. The structure of the essay depends for both its large and its small effects on the pervasiveness of paradox, the framing irony being that of Croker's failure to appreciate the greatness and organic unity of the *Life of Johnson*. The initial impact is completely negative – 'This work has greatly disappointed us' (54:1) – yet the criticisms of the editor are followed by praise of Boswell's famous biography as 'assuredly a great – a very great work' (54:16). Amplification of the opening statement is supplied in the enumeration of Croker's editorial sins and errors, culminating in the central offence of 'mangling' Boswell by incorporating into his narrative all manner of alien material selected chiefly from other memoirists of Johnson: 'We have half of Mrs Thrale's book, scraps of Mr Tyers, scraps of Mr Murphy, scraps of Mr Cradock, long prosings of Sir John Hawkins, and connecting observations by Mr Croker himself, inserted into the midst of Boswell's text' (54:13). The second part of the essay evokes Boswell, Johnson, and their world with a vitality which testifies to the power and excitement of the experience of reading the *Life of Johnson* and underlines, by that same token, the failure of sensitivity which resulted in the dismemberment of the very work whose classic status the whole editorial endeavour was designed to establish.

Discussions of this essay in the past have focused primarily on Macaulay's motives in attacking Croker's edition and on the practical results of that attack;[12] the reader of Macaulay's essay, however, is concerned not so much with the biographical facts as with the literary effects, the part played by the criticisms of Croker's editorial performance in the overall strategy of the essay. These criticisms are, in fact, crucial to Macaulay's central point – the affirmation of the unity and greatness of Boswell's book, and of its uniqueness as a product of Boswell's personality:

There is scarcely, in the whole compass of literature, a book which bears interpolation so ill. We know no production of the human mind which has so much of what may be called the race, so much of the peculiar flavour of the soil from which it sprang. The work could never have been written if the writer had not been precisely what he was. (54:16)

To interpolate Mrs Thrale, Hawkins, Cradock and the others is to destroy.[13] To demonstrate multiple errors as a means of strengthening the case against an editor who engages in such destruction is a valid rhetorical procedure, and it is made by Macaulay to seem almost a necessary moral procedure as well.

The major sections devoted to Boswell and Johnson supply the positive element in the essay, but even these are hedged about with all kinds of restrictions, criticisms, and condemnations, so that a combination of negative and positive provides not merely the structural outline of the essay but a kind of central motif. 'The work could never have been written if the writer had not been precisely what he was', but what worries Macaulay is precisely the manner of man he conceived Boswell to be. This, indeed, is what has struck readers most forcibly ever since the article first appeared – the insistence on the discrepancy between the stature of Boswell the man and that of the biography he wrote:

> We are not sure that there is in the whole history of the human intellect so strange a phenomenon as this book. Many of the greatest men that ever lived have written biography. Boswell was one of the smallest men that ever lived; and he has beaten them all. (54:16)

It is very easy, with the hindsight of Malahide, to attack Macaulay for his failure to perceive the artistry of Boswell's achievement and thus separate Boswell's stature as an artist from the personality of the man himself. But even without such fuller knowledge of Boswell's powers of selecting, arranging, and shaping, the limitations of Macaulay's approach are readily apparent.

In this essay, at least, Macaulay comes very close to matching the *Blackwood's* image of him as the clever boy led astray by his own brilliance. Writing to Napier on 25 January 1830 about some passages omitted from his last essay, on 'Utilitarian Theory', Macaulay had remarked:[14]

> The passages omitted were the most pointed and ornamented sentences in the review. Now for high and grave works, a history for example or a system of political or moral philosophy, Doctor Johnson's rule that every sentence which the writer thinks fine – ought to be struck out, is excellent. But periodical works like ours, which unless they strike at first reading are not likely to strike at all, – whose whole life is a month or two, may, I think, be allowed to be sometimes even viciously florid. Probably, in estimating the real value of any tinsel which I may put upon my articles, you and I should not materially differ. But it is not by his own taste, but by the taste of the fish, that the angler is determined in his choice of bait.

It must be said that Macaulay's view of the periodical essay was developing rapidly at this time, and that in the eighteen months between this letter and the Croker article his judgment as to the admissibility of the 'viciously florid' had undergone some modification; he had also shown himself much more willing to submit to Napier's emendations.[15] Even so, the paradoxes about Boswell are allowed to take on a life of their own, each generating the next in a manner spectacularly cumulative but hardly capable of withstanding close, logical examination. Macaulay is here at his prestidigitatory best; the concrete details which recreate the experience of reading Boswell's book are chosen with an unerring eye, and give the appearance of leading almost inevitably to the antithetical climax: 'If he had not been a great fool, he would never have been a great writer' (54:18). Yet the cause and effect relationship Macaulay asserts is nowhere logically demonstrated: everything depends upon the whole rhetorical strategy of large and small paradoxes, and upon the steady bombardment of selected details. The reader's attention is deflected. Instead of demonstration he is given dazzling antithesis and contradiction:

> He had, indeed, a quick observation and a retentive memory. These qualities, if he had been a man of sense and virtue, would scarcely of themselves have sufficed to make him conspicuous; but, as he was a dunce, a parasite, and a coxcomb, they have made him immortal. (54:18)

The quickness of the hand deceives the eye, but the conjurer ends up by misleading even himself.

Macaulay comes very close at one point to an important perception about Boswell's relationship to his book. A key to the apparent Boswell/Bozzy contradiction is in his hands, but he tosses it away:

> Those parts of his book which, considered abstractedly, are most utterly worthless, are delightful when we read them as illustrations of the character of the writer. Bad in themselves, they are good dramatically, like the nonsense of Justice Shallow, the clipped English of Dr Caius, or the misplaced consonants of Fluellen. (54:18)

Macaulay here hovers on the edge of grasping the essentially 'dramatic' nature of the 'character' of Boswell as he appears in the *Life of Johnson*, but he fails to make the transition from the creation of non-authorial characters like Fluellen to that of an authorial persona. The book's statements remain, for Macaulay, 'illustrations of the character of the writer' rather than the very stuff out of which the figure of Boswell is created. Macaulay, indeed, conceives of the problem too simply. He was too good an historian not to have compared the impression of Boswell he got from reading the *Life* with the view of Boswell given in contemporary accounts – he speaks earlier both of Boswell's 'own account' and of 'the united testimony of all who knew him' (54:16), and Croker's mish-mash afforded a good opportunity for refreshing his memory of the various sources. But, despite the Shakespearian comparison, it seems never to have occurred to him that the figure in the book, while closely resembling a flesh-and-blood person, might none the less be an artistic creation, functioning dramatically or, to be more precise, fictionally, and demanding consideration by the critic in terms of the achieved work of art rather than of historical or biographical fact.

As Macaulay drifts away from one incipient perception he touches on another; once again, however, he fails to grasp the full implication of his own statement that 'Of all confessors, Boswell is the most candid' (54:18). To see the *Life* as a member of the genus 'confession' with Boswell as its protagonist, as well as of the genus 'biography' with Johnson as its subject, is to go a long way towards understanding the book's unique power, and Macaulay is surely on potentially fruitful lines in comparing Boswell with Byron and Rousseau. But his conception of what Boswell is doing remains too rigidly realistic. Boswell 'is' the most 'candid' of all confessors, and the question of how far the 'is' of history can be assimilated to the 'seems' of fiction within the art of biography is not considered. The artistic consequences of Boswell's frankness are ignored, and we are left only with a somewhat hollowly paradoxical assertion of Boswell's foolish honesty:

> He was perfectly frank, because the weakness of his understanding and the tumult of his spirits prevented him from knowing when he made himself ridiculous. His book resembles nothing so much as the conversation of the inmates of the Palace of Truth. (54:19)

Macaulay's assurance prevents him from seeing that a slight shift of his own position might transform the Palace of Truth into something not unlike the Palace of Art, and his smoothly turned summary loses all sight of the possibility that Boswell might be the anti-hero of his own confessions. From so devoted a reader of *Tristram Shandy* we might have hoped for something more than this.

The treatment of Johnson which occupies the final section of the essay offers almost a paradigm of Macaulay's early *Edinburgh Review* method and manner. Boswell's Johnson is first of all recreated through a series of brilliantly selected details, and the reader is thus established in a comfortably familiar relationship with the subject under discussion. Then comes the indication of what this picture, for all its richness, lacks: 'But we have no minute information respecting those years of Johnson's life, during which his character and his manners became immutably fixed' (54:20). The lacuna once indicated, the essay proceeds immediately to supply it with a swiftly sketched history of the state of literary affairs and the mode of life of writers during Johnson's youth – a procedure which not only provides that element of fresh narrative which Macaulay seems increasingly to have regarded as an essential feature of the periodical essay but brings this particular essay satisfyingly full circle: the peculiarities noted in the opening sketch of Johnson become explicable in terms of the account of Grub Street now offered, and Johnson is seen as an antediluvian survivor, 'the solitary specimen of a past age' (54:25).

As Macaulay goes on to consider Johnson's views on religion, the supernatural, manners, human nature, and politics, paradox once more takes control. 'The characteristic peculiarity of his intellect', we are told, 'was the union of great powers with low prejudices' (54:27), and the account continues in the same aphoristic vein: 'He began to be credulous precisely at the point where the most credulous people begin to be sceptical' (54:28). Within the context of the essay this way of discussing Johnson's views operates very fruitfully. The insistence on peculiarity, the frequent resort to paradox, the reassuring concreteness of the numerous details, anecdotes, and pieces of dialogue – all provide a satisfactory fulfilment for an audience whose confidence in the reviewer's authority has already been completely established by the demolition of Croker and the vividness of the evocation of Boswell and Johnson as personalities. That Macaulay is shallow in his judgments and fails to glimpse even a shadow of Johnson's true greatness is beside the rhetorical point. The essay works out its own brilliant pattern; though obviously susceptible of many criticisms, it remains somehow impervious, secure in the possession of a life and logic of its own.[16]

Brilliant as the success of Macaulay's early essays undoubtedly was, the articles themselves represent an achievement of a strictly limited kind: they contain too much confrontation and display too little intrinsic substance to be capable of a continuing life beyond their original moment, other than as examples of youthful bravura. But they already display a keen awareness of audience and an ability to manipulate illustrations, arguments, and structures in such a way as to win that audience and make it responsive to the reviewer's intention, receptive to his views. Macaulay's limitation – despite the temporary political effectiveness of some of the essays – is that he has not yet perceived the literary uses to which this sensitivity to audience might best be put. It was only when he found his proper form through a shift of emphasis from argument to narration that he was able to bring the perspective implied by a constant awareness of his nineteenth-century readers into a coherent relationship with his material, discovering in the process that the satisfactions of leading those readers to right judgments through the experience of concrete narrative were far superior to those of dazzling them by illustration and paradox into a delighted but temporary and sometimes confused adherence to his views on particular political or literary issues. Already in the early essays it is possible to detect the first signs of that shift to historical narrative and the portrayal of individual men which was to characterize Macaulay's later career: even the paradoxical structure of the Croker piece yields those memorable portraits of Boswell and Johnson – outrageous caricatures, no doubt, but now identifiable as the prototypes of a long line of major historical characterizations. From the fabrication of temporary images of himself, his subject, and his reader – always ready, for all their rhetorical vitality, to merge back into the insubstantial air from which he had called them into being – Macaulay turned to the presentation of specific figures from the past, attempting to endow these creations of the historian with a sense of actual life.

3

Reform, Revolution and Party

The Years of Confidence

Macaulay took his seat in the House of Commons early in 1830, at a moment of great significance in British history and especially in the history of the parliamentary system itself. The long rule of the Tories, stretching back over forty years to the time of the French Revolution, was at last coming to an end amid considerable public restlessness and a general sense of the urgent need for reform in the area of parliamentary representation. On 5 April Macaulay made his maiden speech in support of a bill (subsequently defeated) for the Removal of Jewish Disabilities; he created a favourable impression but spoke only once more in the House before the death of George IV at the end of June was followed, as contemporary custom demanded, by the dissolution of parliament and the calling of a general election. Early in the campaign news arrived of the French Revolution of July 1830, and the expulsion of the Bourbons gave a fresh impetus to the cause of reform in England and a warning of the possible consequences of reform too long deferred. Macaulay, assured of re-election by Lord Lansdowne's pocket borough, spent the summer travelling in France, enjoying the excitement of the Revolution's immediate aftermath and meeting some of the leading figures involved – notably the Duc de Broglie, long a friend of Zachary Macaulay's, and the Marquis de Lafayette.

Parliament assembled in October 1830, and although the election itself had been inconclusive there was wide agreement among both parties that some measure of electoral reform must soon be introduced. When the Duke of Wellington, who was again Prime Minister, declared his absolute resistance to any such step, the government collapsed and, in November, resigned, leaving the way open for a Whig administration under Lord Grey. This was very much a government of the aristocratic Whig oligarchy, but on 1 March 1831 it none the less introduced, in the shape of the first Reform Bill, a more far-reaching proposal than had generally been anticipated. Although Macaulay's own seat at Calne was one of those destined for abolition, he was enthusiastic in his support for the Bill and made, on the second day of the debate, a speech which was greeted with unusually high praise from all sides. Even the 'Noctes Ambrosianae' section of *Blackwood's* for August 1831, while criticizing the content of Macaulay's early speeches, was willing to acknowledge their effectiveness:[1]

> What he says is substantially, of course, mere stuff and nonsense; but it is so well worded, and so volubly and forcibly delivered – there is such an endless string of epigram and antithesis – such a flashing of epithets – such an accumulation of images – and the voice is so trumpetlike, and the action so grotesquely emphatic, that you might hear a pin drop in the House. . . . It is obvious that he has got the main part at least by heart – but for this I gave him the more praise and glory.

From this time onwards Macaulay was increasingly acknowledged as one of the outstanding speakers of his day: when he began to speak, G. H. Francis later reported in *Orators of the Age* (1847), 'the House becomes, as if by magic, as much crowded as when the leader for the time being is on his legs.'[2] This oratorical success seems the more remarkable in that Macaulay's speaking manner was too hurried and too high-pitched to be absolutely effective. After his second speech his sister, Selina, noted in her diary that it 'was extremely admired as to matter, but all who heard it agree in saying that he speaks far too rapidly, & thus weakens very much the effect of what he says',[3] while the description of a typical Macaulay speech in *Orators of the Age* suggests that this rapidity of delivery, attributed by Francis to Macaulay's having memorized the entire speech in advance, was never corrected:[4]

> An opening is made in the discussion, and he rises, or rather darts up from his seat, plunging at once into the very heart of his subject, without exordium or apologetic preface. In fact, you have for a few seconds heard a voice, pitched in alto, monotonous, and rather shrill, pouring forth words with inconceivable velocity 'ere you have become aware that a new speaker, and one of no common order, has broken in upon the debate. A few seconds more, and cheers, perhaps from all parts of the House, rouse you completely from your apathy, compelling you to follow that extremely voluble and not very enticing voice in its rapid course

through the subject on which the speaker is entering with a resolute determination, as it seems, never to pause. You think of an express train which does not stop even at the chief stations.

On 23 March 1831 the first Reform Bill passed the Commons by a single vote – an occasion which Macaulay described to his friend Thomas Flower Ellis as 'like seeing Caesar stabbed in the Senate House, or seeing Oliver taking the mace from the table, a sight to be seen only once and never to be forgotten'.[5] The crisis, however, was only just beginning. In April the Whigs were defeated and the King dissolved parliament; the election brought the Whigs back with an increased majority, and in June a second Reform Bill, only slightly different from the first, was introduced. Macaulay's speech of 5 July, on the occasion of the second reading, was again enthusiastically received. By this time he was very much a social as well as a political lion, and he was able to write to Hannah a few days later that he had met Lord and Lady Holland at a dinner at the Prime Minister's official residence and that Lady Holland, in inviting him to Holland House, 'shook my hand very warmly, and told me, in her imperial decisive manner that she had talked with all the principal men on our side about my speech – that they all agreed that it was the best that had been made since the death of Fox, and that it was more like Fox's speaking than anybody's else.'[6]

The Bill passed the Commons, but its rejection by the Lords early in October was the occasion of great public unrest, including meetings and riots sufficiently violent to prompt real fears of revolution or civil war. Macaulay, to judge from a letter to Hannah of 13 September, had been vehement in urging the ministers not to back down in the face of 'the bigotry of the Lords',[7] and on 10 October, after the defeat in the Lords, he strongly supported a Commons motion of confidence in the administration. In the event, Grey did not resign but chose instead to bring in a third Reform Bill, incorporating minor concessions, in December 1831. Passage of the Bill through the Commons was assured – Macaulay making important speeches on the second reading on 16 December and again on the third reading on 19 March 1832 – and in mid-April it passed second reading in the Lords by nine votes. During the committee stage in the Lords the government suffered defeat on a procedural motion and decided that the King must be asked to create fifty new peers to ensure the Bill's safe passage. Upon William IV's refusal the government resigned amid renewed public commotion and threats of civil war. The Duke of Wellington, summoned to form a Tory government, could not do so, and when the Whigs declined to return to power without the assurance that new peers would be created at need, William IV gave way. The Lords, intimidated by the mere threat of new creations on such a scale, allowed the Bill to pass its third reading on 4 June 1832. Three days later it became law.

Nothing is more remarkable in Macaulay's essays, speeches, and letters of this period than his vivid sense of the long-term historical significance of the contemporary political events in which he was himself playing so notable a role. He saw the passing of the Reform Act not as an isolated victory but as yet another contribution to that long sequence of Whig achievements which included as its particular glory the Revolution of 1688. Once more, in 1831 and 1832, the Whigs were acting to bring about change, but change which would be the means of preserving the British constitution and of saving it from the violent disruption which had occurred in France in July 1830 or, more devastatingly, in the France of 1789. Macaulay's constant themes at this period are change, particularly revolutionary change, and party, more especially the history of the Whig party, and while these themes were to recur throughout his career what gives a distinctive note to his public and private utterances of the early 1830s is his enormous confidence in himself and in the causes with which he is identified – the assurance and even joyfulness with which he embraces change and glories in his party.

Macaulay had a ready appetite for political and intellectual conflict and was eager to take on all those who opposed the Whigs in Parliament or in the pages of the Tory newspapers and reviews. This was a time, as G. O. Trevelyan remarks, when his spirit was high and 'his pen cut deep':[8]

> He was too apt to undervalue both the heart and the head of those who desired to maintain the old system of civil and religious exclusion, and who grudged political power to their fellow-countrymen, or at any rate to those of their fellow-countrymen whom he was himself prepared to enfranchise. Independent, frank, and proud almost to a fault, he detested the whole race of jobbers and time-servers, parasites and scandal-mongers, led-captains, led-authors, and led-orators.

He exulted in the confidence that he had given Croker a trouncing, and would willingly face him on political, literary, or any other grounds.

In the Leeds election of 1832 he confronted Michael Sadler with an enthusiasm only whetted by memories of their earlier encounters in print. But there is a very real sense in which Macaulay's major argument was not with the Tories or even with the Utilitarians. At a deeper level, so that it appears only rarely on the surface of his speeches and essays, he was engaged in a persistent debate with the shade of Edmund Burke and with those elements in the Whig tradition – above all, the attitudes to revolutionary change and to the role of party in relation to the English Constitution – which Burke had so powerfully expressed and embodied.

Macaulay had a deep and ever-growing admiration for Burke, whose works he read again and again, and whom he eventually described in his *Journal* in 1853 as 'The greatest man since Milton'.[9] It seems peculiarly regrettable, therefore, that for one reason and another he never wrote the articles on Burke he planned on several occasions.[10] They would have provided fascinating documentation for his views on reform, revolution, and the place of party in English politics. Certain other documents are also lacking. Macaulay was prevented from completing an account of the French Revolution of July 1830 for the *Edinburgh* by Brougham's insistence on reserving the subject for himself. Deeply angered by this intervention, Macaulay contemplated severing his connection with the Review altogether, but the editor, Macvey Napier, was able to soothe his feelings sufficiently to prevent such a rupture. Macaulay then decided to draw upon his French material in writing a history of the events of 1830 for a volume in one of the Longman's series edited by Dionysius Lardner. A substantial portion of this history was completed, and as late as 1866 eighty-eight pages of proof survived in Spottiswoode's printing house; unfortunately, these have since disappeared, apparently without trace. In projecting the *History of England* to Napier in July 1838 Macaulay spoke of dispatching events from the beginning of Walpole's long administration to the 1770s 'concisely', but went on: 'From the commencement of the American war it will again become necessary to be copious.' Later in the same letter he suggested that the work might best end with the death of George III: 'The History would then be an entire view of all the transactions which took place between the revolution, which brought the crown into harmony with the parliament and the revolution which brought parliament into harmony with the nation.'[11] Burke would certainly have received full treatment in any account of the American Wars and of the response of England to the French Revolution, and by carrying his narrative up to the eve of Reform Macaulay would have had a chance to explore fully as an historian the potentially revolutionary situation which prevailed at the time of his own entry into active politics. In the event he lived to complete only his account of that other great Whig triumph, the Glorious Revolution of 1688.

In the absence of any full treatments by Macaulay of the eighteenth-century revolutions in America and France, of the events of the July Revolution of 1830, or of the Reform Bill crisis, the essays of the early 1830s, particularly those on Hampden, Lord Burleigh, and Mirabeau written in the first half of 1832, take on an especial importance for the reader interested in Macaulay's ideas on reform and revolution and in his response to that particular combination of Whig ideas – inherited on the one hand from Burke and on the other from Sir James Mackintosh and the followers of Charles James Fox – which profoundly affected his thinking both on the politics of his own day and on the major crises of English history.

The Hampden essay, published in the December 1831 issue of the *Edinburgh*, offers in the main a straightforward account of Hampden's life and the events leading to the Civil War, and embodies the generally accepted Whig view of the seventeenth-century English revolutions. Elizabeth is praised for her responsiveness to the pressures against authoritarianism, the Stuarts criticized for taking the opposite stand: 'The whole principle of [Charles I's] government was resistance to public opinion' (54:515). The Stuarts attempted to destroy the traditional balance of English government by annexing to the crown powers and privileges belonging to the parliament, and in the 1640s, as later in 1688, the necessity of defending the constitution justified resistance: 'The attainder [of Strafford] was, in truth, a revolutionary measure', but it is seen as warranted by 'the public danger' and as forming 'part of a system of resistance which oppression had rendered necessary' (54:533). Macaulay again advances here the view he had expounded in his 1828 essay on Hallam's *Constitutional History*: that it had been essential in the 1640s to violate one part of the constitution, the prerogative of the crown, in order to preserve the spirit of the constitution as a whole.

Macaulay does not confine himself in the Hampden essay to analogies with 1688 but employs a technique he was to use throughout his career – the deployment of a set of mutually supportive or illuminatory episodes. One historical crisis throws light on another and in combination they serve to reveal the existence of underlying historical principles.

45

In this essay, for example, Macaulay compares the possibilities open to those who resisted the King in the 1640s to other occasions of conflict between subjects and monarchs in English history: 'The best course which the Commons could have taken would perhaps have been to depose the King; as their ancestors had deposed Edward the Second and Richard the Second, and as their children afterwards deposed James' (54:543). He even introduces a contemporary analogy of a speculative kind when he touches upon the possibilities of resistance to the despotic Ferdinand VIII of Spain, and he ends by invoking the name of George Washington as a way of defining the qualities of constructive leadership which were lost to the Parliamentarians on Hampden's death.

A similar if less wide-ranging set of analogies is employed in the Burleigh essay, which appeared in the *Edinburgh* for April 1832. Elizabeth is once more praised because 'she avoided with care, or retracted with speed, every measure which seemed likely to alienate the great mass of the people' (55:294), and the relevance of this lesson is not restricted to Charles I, who is again cited, but extended to those who are still in a position to benefit from it – the parliament of England engaged in March and April 1832 in the final details of Reform legislation. Many passages in the Burleigh essay seem clearly designed to encourage the supporters of Reform and sustain the climate of opinion favourable to the accomplishment of its final stages, and although the main body of the essay is concerned with the effects of the Protestant Reformation, parallels are frequently drawn with more recent events, above all with the French Revolution of 1789:

> The Reformation is an event long past. That volcano has spent its rage. The wide waste produced by its outbreak is forgotten. The landmarks which were swept away have been replaced. The ruined edifices have been repaired. The lava has covered with a rich incrustation the fields which it once devastated; and, after having turned a garden into a desert, has again turned the desert into a still more beautiful and fruitful garden. The second great eruption is not yet over. The marks of its ravages are still all around us. The ashes are still hot beneath our feet. In some directions, the deluge of fire still continues to spread. Yet experience surely entitles us to believe that this explosion, like that which preceded it, will fertilize the soil which it has devastated. Already, in those parts which have suffered most severely, rich

cultivation and secure dwellings have begun to appear amidst the waste. The more we read of the history of past ages, – the more we observe the signs of these times, – the more do we feel our hearts filled and swelled up with a good hope for the future destinies of the human race. (55:279)

And in the Mirabeau essay – finished in June and July 1832 in the weeks following the passing of the Reform Act and completing the series of three essays with which Macaulay punctuated his efforts in the great parliamentary debates – the favourite set of mutually illuminating instances is once more brought into play:

> Why was the French Revolution so bloody and destructive? Why was our revolution of 1641 comparatively mild? Why was our revolution of 1688 milder still? Why was the American Revolution, considered as an internal movement, the mildest of all? There is an obvious and complete solution of the problem. The English under James the First and Charles the First were less oppressed than the French under Louis the Fifteenth and Louis the Sixteenth. The English were less oppressed after the Restoration than before the great Rebellion. And America, under George the Third, was less oppressed than England under the Stuarts. The reaction was exactly proportioned to the pressure, – the vengeance to the provocation. (55:560–1)

Both the strengths and the limitations of Macaulay's gift for historical generalization are fully evident here. The practitioners of Whig history, of which Macaulay is reckoned the first great exponent, are always accused – and often with justice – of deriving their historical patterns from the last item in a sequence of events, of tracing a line backwards from a particular crisis such as 1688 or 1789 and disregarding all occurrences which that line does not intersect. But no simple process of endowing temporal sequence with the appearance of a causal chain can account for the clarity and authority which Macaulay's patterning of history conveyed to his audience. The sense the reader has of shape and design in Macaulay's work comes from his combination of the linear pattern of chains of events with an insistence on recurrent historical phenomena, situations separated in time whose similarities imply the existence of underlying laws. Macaulay does not spell out these things in theoretical terms, but again and again the analogical schema recur: 1641, 1688, 1789, and even 1832 fall into place in a

E

series of related and comparable revolutionary situations, each reinforc-
ing the evidence for the existence of certain simple and almost mechanical laws – for instance, the law that repression and resistance to change
will lead, unless relieved by compromise, to a violent reaction. In his
speech of 16 December 1831 Macaulay declared:[12]

> In peace or in convulsion, by the law, or in spite of the law,
> through the Parliament, or over the Parliament, Reform must be
> carried. Therefore be content to guide that movement which you
> cannot stop. Fling wide the gates to that force which else will
> enter through the breach. Then will it still be, as it has hitherto
> been, the peculiar glory of our Constitution that, though not
> exempt from the decay which is wrought by the vicissitudes of
> fortune, and the lapse of time, in all the proudest works of human
> power and wisdom, it yet contains within it the means of self-
> reparation.

Images of destruction characteristically generate countervailing images
of renewal in Macaulay's mind – as in that reference in the Burleigh
essay to the 'eruption' of the French Revolution which promises to
'fertilize the soil which it has devastated' – so that his imagination
habitually translates linear sequence into forward motion and trans-
forms change into progress. This makes possible that acceptance of
revolution which brings into his Reform speeches the special excitement produced by tension between horror of anarchy and commitment
to the dynamics of change. By 1834 he was willing to assert as part
of his defence of Sir James Mackintosh: 'It is our deliberate opinion
that the French Revolution, in spite of all its crimes and follies, was a
great blessing to mankind' (61:276). He could not, on the face of it,
have set himself more firmly apart from the views of his hero Burke.

Macaulay's assertion in the Hallam essay of 1828, 'We know of no
great revolution which might not have been prevented by compromise
early and graciously made' (48:169), is in line with Burke's view of the
seventeenth-century English revolutions and the American Revolution,
and with Burke's judgment that the open break with the American
colonies could have been avoided by flexible interpretation of the
English constitution.[13] Where Macaulay openly differs from Burke is
in viewing the French Revolution in similar terms. He remarks in the
Mirabeau essay:

When Mr Burke was reminded in his later years of the zeal

which he had displayed in the cause of the Americans, he vindicated himself from the charge of inconsistency, by contrasting the wisdom and moderation of the colonial insurgents of 1776 with the fanaticism and wickedness of the Jacobins of 1792. He was in fact bringing an argument *a fortiori* against himself. The circumstances on which he rested his vindication, fully proved that the old government of France stood in far more need of a complete change than the old government of America. (55:561)

For Macaulay the violence of the reaction which overthrew the *ancien régime* in France proved how urgently change had been required, and he goes on to argue that the relative mildness of the 1830 revolution is evidence that the French have lived 'for seventeen or eighteen years under institutions which, however defective, have yet been far superior to any institutions that had before existed in France' (55:562).

Macaulay, as he well knew, had over Burke the great advantage of hindsight. Even so, his quarrel with Burke about the French Revolution, had he ever fully articulated it, would presumably have been that while Burke was well-informed about the events leading up to the Revolution, and while he was capable of perceiving in history both analogical patterns and fundamental laws (such as that repression breeds revolution), he none the less turned his face away from these truths and allowed passion to cloud his judgment. Something of this kind of charge is in fact advanced in the Hastings essay, published in October 1841, when Macaulay compares Burke's response to injustice in India, as manifested in the speeches he made during the Hastings impeachment, with his reaction to the French Revolution as embodied in such passages as that on Marie Antoinette in the *Reflections on the Revolution in France* of 1790:

> Those who think that he was more violent and acrimonious in debates about India than on other occasions, are ill-informed respecting the last years of his life. In the discussions on the Commercial Treaty with the Court of Versailles, on the Regency, on the French Revolution, he showed even more virulence than in conducting the impeachment. Indeed it may be remarked, that the very persons who represented him as a mischievous maniac for condemning in burning words the Rohilla war, and the spoliation of the Begums, exalted him into an inspired prophet as soon as he began to declaim, with greater vehemence, and not with greater reason, against the taking of the Bastile, and the

49

insults offered to Marie-Antoinette. To us he appears to have been neither a maniac in the former case, nor a prophet in the latter; but in both cases a great and good man, led into extravagance by a tempestuous sensibility, which domineered over all his faculties. (74:233–4)

Given Macaulay's essential sympathy with Burke, a sympathy which was to amount in later years to something close to identification, it is perhaps not surprising that he should be so critical of a failure to recognize in the case of France the working out of laws which he believed Burke himself to have perceived in other revolutionary situations. Macaulay was himself willing to extend the implications of these laws to the widest range of circumstances, and he saw Burke's attitude to the American Revolution of the 1770s as relevant not only to events in France in the 1780s but to the continuing and apparently very different problems of Ireland or even British India. It is conceivable that Burke's own demonstrated anger at injustice and mismanagement in Indian affairs may have encouraged Macaulay in his readiness to apply Burke's thinking on the American colonies to the Indian situation and to envisage – albeit after a long period of education and development – the prospect of ultimate self-government there, and perhaps even of independence:[14]

> It may be that the public mind of India may expand under our system till it has out grown that system; that by good government we may educate our subjects into a capacity for better government; that, having become instructed in European knowledge, they may, in some future age, demand European institutions. Whether such a day will ever come I know not. But never will I attempt to avert or to retard it. Whenever it comes, it will be the proudest day in English history.

At the same time, the clear echoes in this famous 1833 speech on India of Macaulay's speeches on Reform – 'It is precisely because our institutions are so good that we are not perfectly contented with them; for they have educated us into a capacity for enjoying still better institutions'[15] – amount to an insistence on the necessity of change which becomes hard to distinguish from an advocacy of change, and which certainly seems very different from Burke's essential conservatism.

Burke himself did not entirely rule out change in the system of government. At the end of *Reflections on the Revolution in France* he wrote: 'I would not exclude alteration neither; but even when I changed, it should be to preserve.'[16] This concept of preserving change, particularly as it applied to the events of 1688, became standard Whig doctrine in the late eighteenth and early nineteenth centuries; and Mackintosh, who had once sought to vindicate the French against Burke, provided in his posthumously published *History of the Revolution* (1834) a definition with which his old opponent could not have quarrelled: 'A defensive revolution, of which the sole purpose is to preserve and secure the laws, has a fixed boundary, conspicuously marked out by the well-defined object which it pursues, and which it seldom permanently over-reaches; and is thus exempt from that succession of changes which disturbs all habits of peaceable obedience, and weakens every authority not resting on mere force.'[17] Macaulay's famous speeches on Reform were to expound this idea and inject it with a new urgency; the first, made on 2 March 1831, incorporated it in its peroration an emotional plea for preservation through change:[18]

> Renew the youth of the State. Save property, divided against itself. Save the multitude, endangered by its own ungovernable passions. Save the aristocracy, endangered by its own unpopular power. Save the greatest, and fairest, and most highly civilised community that ever existed, from calamities which may in a few days sweep away all the rich heritage of so many ages of wisdom and glory. The danger is terrible. The time is short. If this bill should be rejected, I pray to God that none of those who concur in rejecting it may ever remember their votes with unavailing remorse, amidst the wreck of laws, the confusion of ranks, the spoliation of property, the dissolution of social order.

In the *Reflections* Burke had followed up his statement on alteration by insisting: 'I should be led to my remedy by a great grievance. In what I did, I should follow the example of our ancestors'[19] – an example seen as embodying a 'politic caution', an awareness of human fallibility, a practical political sense quite distinct from the 'desperate flights' of the 'aëronauts of France'.[20] Macaulay could readily share all Burke's respect for their joint political ancestors, the great Whigs who had made the preserving revolution of 1688, and his own distrust of theoretical solutions as opposed to those based on the practical wisdom of experienced leaders led him to declare in the House of Commons, 'I rest my opinion on no general theory of government. I distrust all general theories of government',[21] and to praise in the Mirabeau essay the leadership of 'practical statesmen' (55:572) which had made possible the recent non-violent achievement of Reform:

> Some orators have described the reform of the House of Commons as a revolution. Others have denied the propriety of the term. The question, though in seeming merely a question of definition, suggests much curious and interesting matter for reflection. If we look at the magnitude of the reform, it may well be called a revolution. If we look at the means by which it has been effected, it is merely an act of Parliament, regularly brought in, read, committed, and passed. In the whole history of England, there is no prouder circumstance than this, – that a change which could not, in any other age, or in any other country, have been effected without physical violence, should here have been effected by the force of reason, and under the forms of law. The work of three civil wars has been accomplished by three sessions of Parliament. An ancient and deeply rooted system of abuses has been fiercely attacked and stubbornly defended. It has fallen; and not one sword has been drawn; not one estate has been confiscated; not one family has been forced to emigrate. (55:563)

Macaulay thus explained the apparent conflict between himself and Burke on the issue of Reform, as on that of the French Revolution, by a version of the 'more Catholic than the Pope' argument. He insisted on the essential conformity of his own position with the true Whig principles as expounded by Burke, even though Burke himself had opposed extension of the franchise on the grounds that the connection between the people and the parliament was not a matter of simple representativeness and that while parliament depended upon the people for its authority the members of that parliament were in no sense to be regarded as delegates. On the latter point Macaulay was in total agreement, declaring in a speech of February 1832 that it was 'a bad thing, I fully admit, that a Member of Parliament should be a mere delegate',[22] and while he maintained a healthy respect for the capacity of his constituents to make their views known and, indeed, to influence his own, his basic attitude to the electors of Leeds and later of Edinburgh and his conception of an M.P.'s rights of individual conscience were not so very different from the position Burke had adopted in his relations with the electors of Bristol.[23] But Macaulay believed, along with most of his party colleagues, that by 1831 circumstances had changed so completely that the authority which parliament derived from the people had been dangerously eroded by the failure to recognize in electoral terms the presence of new and powerful elements wielding major social and economic influence. In Macaulay's case this belief amounted to a passionate certainty; he was absolutely convinced that the need for Reform constituted a Burkean 'great grievance' and necessitated the immediate initiation of the processes of preserving change.

It is very clear from the essays and speeches of the early 1830s that the assimilation of the thinking of both Burke and Fox involved in the transition from eighteenth- to nineteenth-century Whiggism made it possible for Macaulay to combine in his own political creed views which forty years earlier had divided and almost destroyed his party. He could express all the horror of Fox against tyranny and enslavement while echoing at the same time, with all the force which his own dread of anarchy inspired, Burke's celebration of the institutions and traditions by which the English constitution had sustained itself through the ages. He could advocate that reform of the franchise which Burke had opposed, and advocate it as the only means of saving the established constitution in whose defence Burke had exercised all his magnificent eloquence. The combining of these opposed elements in the Whig tradition seemed to Macaulay clear evidence in itself of the continuing vigorous life of the party, and it provided, in the years immediately preceding his departure for India, the basis for a celebration of party scarcely less enthusiastic than his espousal of the cause of Reform.

Once the Reform Act had become law, Macaulay could turn his attention to other topics, but while the three essays written mainly in 1833 – those on the War of the Spanish Succession, on Horace Walpole, and on Chatham – may seem at first sight to represent a turning aside from contemporary politics and an escape into the world of the eighteenth century, they in fact represent, at least in part, a further exploration of the ideas and issues which had preoccupied Macaulay during the previous five years and which would continue to recur throughout the remainder of his *Edinburgh* career and on into the pages of the *History of England*. There is an interesting passage in the War of the Spanish Succession essay, published in the January 1833 issue of the *Edinburgh*, on the 'progressive' nature of the science of government (56:536), and the Horace Walpole essay of October 1833 incorporates an account of pre-Revolutionary intellectual stirrings in France; but it is the Chatham essay of January 1834, with its tracing of the Great Commoner's early career and his refusal to combine consistently with

53

any single party, which points most clearly to the underlying concern in all three essays with the history and constitutional significance of the English party system. The Chatham essay pauses at that illusively peaceful period after the victories of 1759 and 1760 when the elder Pitt was at the height of his career. The disturbances and humiliations to come are alluded to at the end of the essay, and there is a half-promise to deal with them at some later date, but for the moment Macaulay stops short in the middle of the eighteenth century – just before the party disputes of the 1760s and the open conflict with the American colonies. The three essays thus culminate at – and to some extent explore the pre-history of – one of the most crucial moments in the history of party government in England, a moment which Burke had analysed in one of his most influential pamphlets – *Thoughts on the Cause of the Present Discontents* (1770) – and a moment to which Macaulay repeatedly returned in the course of his reflections on the significance of party and the role of the Whigs.

In the 1828 Hallam essay he had described the situation in 1760:

> During the reign of George the Second, things were evidently tending to repose. At the close of it, the nation had completed the great revolution which commenced in the early part of the sixteenth century, and was again at rest. The fury of sects had died away. The Catholics themselves practically enjoyed toleration; and more than toleration they did not yet venture even to desire. Jacobitism was a mere name. Nobody was left to fight for that wretched cause; and very few to drink for it. The constitution, purchased so dearly, was on every side extolled and worshipped. Even those distinctions of party which must almost always be found in a free state, could scarcely be traced. The two great bodies which, from the time of the Revolution, had been gradually tending to approximation, were now united in emulous support of that splendid administration which smote to the dust both the branches of the House of Bourbon. The great battle for our ecclesiastical and civil polity had been fought and won. The wounds had been healed. The victors and the vanquished were rejoicing together. (48:163–4)

In the succeeding paragraph of the same essay Macaulay goes on to describe 'How soon faction again began to ferment' (48:164), and he specifically refers to Burke's *Thoughts on the Cause of the Present Discontents*. The analysis just quoted coincides almost exactly with

Burke's account of the peaceful state of affairs in 1760, particularly in its insistence on the virtually unanimous acceptance of the revolutionary settlement by the time of George III's accession in that year and the resulting breakdown of the old party structure – what Burke called the 'great parties',[24] Macaulay the 'great bodies' – developed from the two sides which had fought the Civil War.

Burke was concerned in the *Thoughts* to advocate both the necessity for the kind of political parties which were growing up in the 1770s and the respectability of the idea of party in general.[25] He argued that the great parties of the seventeenth century with their major disputes about religion and the constitution had become obsolete, but that the existence of smaller parties of men united by shared principles and by the ties of friendship was the only way of assuring stability of government and the achievement of particular goals without placing excessive dependence on individual great men. The people could easily perceive when a man deserted his party, but the changes of course of a host of independent politicians were far less easy to recognize and evaluate. Burke was thus advancing an argument for responsibility through party which seems very familiar to a twentieth-century reader – 'Party is a body of men united, for promoting by their joint endeavours the national interest, upon some particular principle in which they are all agreed'[26] – and which certainly provided the basis for Macaulay's conception of party in the 1830s and 1840s. In the last article he wrote for the *Edinburgh Review*, the second Chatham essay of October 1844, Macaulay paid direct tribute to the view of party propounded by Burke and embodied in the conduct of the Rockingham Whigs in the 1760s; the passage, indeed, is virtually an epitomization of *Thoughts on the Cause of the Present Discontents*:

> The Rockingham party was, in our view, exactly what a party
> should be. It consisted of men bound together by common opinions,
> by common public objects, by mutual esteem. That they desired
> to obtain, by honest and constitutional means, the direction of
> affairs, they openly avowed. But, though often invited to accept
> the honours and emoluments of office, they steadily refused to do
> so on any conditions inconsistent with their principles. (80:572)

There was, however, one significant distinction between Macaulay's view of the development of the parties and Burke's. While Macaulay agreed with Burke about the dying down of the religious and constitutional issues which had dominated seventeenth-century politics, he found less need to insist upon the more delimited nature of the kind of parties necessary to modern parliamentary government. The resistance to the French Revolutionary spirit in the 1790s, the victories in the Revolutionary and Napoleonic wars, the settlement of the Catholic question, the emergence of a clearly identifiable movement for Reform, made possible in the 1830s a resurgence of party activity on clearly defined principles which enabled politicians like Macaulay to fall heir to Burke's advocacy of party respectability without having to argue the issue of respectability themselves. Macaulay, therefore, did not need to follow Burke in making fundamental distinctions between modern Whigs and Tories and the seventeenth-century great parties, but could rather satisfy his persistent yearning to trace historical continuities by insisting upon a fundamental connection between the seventeenth and nineteenth centuries in the matter of parties as of everything else.

In his article on the War of the Spanish Succession Macaulay takes up Lord Mahon's observation on 'how much the course of a century has inverted the meaning of our party nicknames, – how much a modern Tory resembles a Whig of Queen Anne's reign, and a Tory of Queen Anne's reign a modern Whig' (56:535). Macaulay is prepared to accept the point about modern Tories resembling the Whigs of the early eighteenth-century but he challenges the rest of the statement. Since the 'science of government is a progressive science', it is natural for the Tories to stand where the Whigs once stood: 'Society, we believe, is constantly advancing in knowledge. The tail is now where the head was some generations ago. But the head and the tail still keep their distance' (56:536). Pursuing this last point, he goes on to assert the continuing existence of two distinct parties in the whole movement against absolutism from Magna Carta to the Reform Bill: 'there have been, under some name or other, two sets of men; – those who were before their age, and those who were behind it – those who were the wisest among their contemporaries, and those who gloried in being no wiser than their great-grandfathers' (56:536). Two years later, in the Mackintosh essay, he was to expand this idea in more dynamic terms:

> It is thus that we ought to judge of the events and the men of
> other times. They were behind us. It could not be otherwise. But
> the question with respect to them is not where they were, but
> which way they were going. Were their faces set in the right or

in the wrong direction? Were they in the front or in the rear of their generation? Did they exert themselves to help onward the great movement of the human race, or to stop it? (61:285)

The Whigs of the eighteenth century, he declares in the same essay, were as imperfect as other men and 'when they had power they sometimes abused it'; nevertheless, they held consistently to their fundamental theory that 'power is a trust for the people', a theory which was 'the badge of their party' (61:319–20).

It is this fundamentalist view of party which enables Macaulay to dismiss Horace Walpole's claims to be a Whig: 'He was a Whig by the accident of hereditary connection; but he was essentially a courtier' (58:230). Much of Macaulay's irritation with Horace Walpole is attributable not merely to his having to confront a temperament completely alien to his own, but to what he takes to be Walpole's trivialization of politics and belittling of the party to which he nominally belonged. Macaulay views Sir Robert Walpole with considerable respect and has no time for the *ad hoc* coalition of extreme Tories and disgruntled Whigs who banded together in the early 1740s to bring him down. In the 1844 Chatham essay he treats these self-styled Patriots more harshly still, calling them 'a reptile species of politicians' who were willing 'to coalesce with any party, to abandon any party, to undermine any party, to assault any party, at a moment's notice' (80:576), and blaming Pitt for failing, in his antipathy to the idea of party, to distinguish between 'gangs of knaves associated for the mere purpose of robbing the public, and confederacies of honourable men for the promotion of great public objects' (80:580). The language is Macaulay's but the sentiments are Burke's: neither could forgive Pitt for his failure to join with the Rockingham Whigs in the mid-1760s.

Party is thus for Macaulay at this period a kind of absolute. Whig and Tory correspond almost to distinct states of being, each developing and changing with the times but always maintaining the same distance from the other. To desert one's party for personal advantage seemed to him the worst of sins, involving not just disloyalty and greed but the betrayal of sacred principles. Party, in fact, was in some ways Macaulay's substitute for religion, and he undoubtedly found much satisfaction in tracing the genealogy of the Whigs, in almost Biblical fashion, back beyond Magna Carta, and in anticipating the continuation of the tradition on into the future. He could thus once again reconcile his yearning for permanence with his recognition of the need for development and change, and maintain the equipoise between admiration and disagreement in his attitude towards Burke and the Burkean tradition.

But this kind of balancing act proved more tenuous than Macaulay in these years of confidence seems ever to have anticipated. After his years in India, years of exile and of bitter personal experience, he was never to recapture that optimistic enthusiasm with which he had once set off to conquer the world from the pages of the *Edinburgh Review* and the benches of the House of Commons. It was a changed and chastened Macaulay who returned to London from Calcutta, one who, as the years went by, had an increasing tendency to live in the past and retreat from new personal involvements – one who still accepted intellectually the inevitability of change but who longed increasingly for permanence and stability. It was this Macaulay, his active political career at an end, the heat gone out of the causes for which he had once fought, who declared in his *Journal* in 1853 that Burke was the greatest man since Milton.

4

The Indian Years

Engagement and Withdrawal

Throughout the whole period of the Reform Bill crisis Macaulay, though so new to parliamentary affairs, was as deeply and as continuously involved as any member not actually holding ministerial office. He had deserved well of his party by the consistency of his attendance and his voting and by the universally acknowledged brilliance of his few but immensely effective speeches. In 1832 he received his reward in the form of appointments, first as one of the Commissioners of the Board of Control of the East India Company, and then as Secretary to the Board; places were also found for other members of his family. Political success had come rapidly and, as a result of Lord Lansdowne's interest, relatively smoothly, but the seat at Calne had now disappeared and before the end of 1832 Macaulay found himself fighting a long and arduous battle for one of the two parliamentary seats which had been given to the newly-enfranchised borough of Leeds.

The abrasiveness of the contest was not diminished by the fact that his opponent was Michael Sadler, whose ideas he had already attacked on two occasions in the pages of the *Edinburgh Review*, nor by the support given to Sadler by Richard Oastler, the formidable Tory radical. Something of the flavour of the campaign can be gained from the following anti-Macaulay verses, with their allusions to the £1,200 a year Macaulay received as Secretary to the Board of Control and to the government appointments as a Commissioner of Inquiry into the Administration of Public Charities and as Commissioner of Arbitration in Sierra Leone recently obtained by, respectively, his father and his brother:[1]

I beg of no man for a vote,
I always was timid and shy,

I merely presume to denote
That the 'trust is most solemn & high';
But the 'duty you have to perform,'
Electors, 'as the daylight is clear,'
In my snug little berth keep me warm,
To enjoy my TWELVE HUNDRED a year.

I got a snug THOUSAND for Dad,
With the saints he has still been a crony;
TWO THOUSAND for Henry, poor lad,
Who's just off for Sierra Leone;
Only think what a saving of pelf
To the People of England is here;
To get Henry, and Dad, and myself
And all for FOUR THOUSAND a year!

That Macaulay's response, though higher in tone, was not lacking in vigour is suggested by the address which he issued to the electors on 12 December 1832, at the end of the first, somewhat turbulent, day of voting:[2]

An attempt has been made to introduce into Leeds, all the corruption and intimidation which disgraced the elections of Newark [Sadler's former seat]; and an ingenious malevolence has employed against us arts, such as even Newark never witnessed. Slander and hypocrisy, threats and caresses, bludgeons and gin, have done their worst; and the result is that the cause of Reform has triumphed in this great community by means worthy of such a community and of such a cause. I have but one word to add. Let not the advantage which you have obtained induce you to relax in your exertions. Persist. Be firm. Be vigilant. Remember how desirable it is that your success should be complete and decisive. Be content with nothing short of a final victory over those who, having long misgoverned you by means of a vicious representative system, are now attempting to misgovern you by means of that franchise which you have at length acquired in despite of them.

'I despise myself', Macaulay wrote to Hannah that same day, 'for feeling so bitterly towards this fellow as I do.'[3]

Macaulay won his seat, issued a conciliatory address to all the electors of Leeds – 'The victorious and the vanquished party are equally now, my constituents'[4] – and in January 1833 attended the first session of the reformed parliament. Since the Whigs had been returned with a large majority, Macaulay retained his post as Secretary to the Board of Control; he played an active part in drafting and defending one of the session's chief measures, the Bill to renew the Charter of the East India Company, and on 10 July 1833 made one of his longest and most famous speeches on the occasion of the Bill's second reading. His financial situation, always delicate, became far more so at this period following the collapse of Macaulay and Babington, and it was therefore the more difficult for him to jeopardize the salary he received at the Board of Control by deciding to vote against the government on what he and his father agreed in regarding as an unacceptable aspect of the Bill providing for the emancipation of West Indian slaves – the culmination of the Anti-Slavery movement's long crusade. In the event, many members of the House voted with Macaulay on the issue, and the government instead of accepting Macaulay's proffered resignation, agreed on 25 July to an amendment which permitted him to satisfy his father, retain his post, and support the administration, all with a good conscience. That night he wrote to Hannah: 'I shall now certainly remain in office; and if, as I expect, the Irish Church Bill, passes the Lords, I may consider myself as safe till the next Session when Heaven knows what may happen. It is still quite uncertain when we may rise. I pine for rest, air, and a taste of family life, more than I can express. I see nothing but politicians, and talk about nothing but politics.'[5]

Within a month, however, he was writing to Hannah in very different terms, begging her to accompany him in a prolonged exile to India. 'By the new India Bill', he wrote on 17 August 1833, 'it is provided that one of the members of the Supreme Council which is to govern our Eastern empire is to be chosen from among persons who are not servants of the [East India] Company. It is probable, indeed nearly certain, that the situation will be offered to me.'[6] Macaulay's appointment, finally confirmed at the beginning of December, was as the so-called law or legislative member, charged with a special responsibility for the drafting of legislation, of the Governor-General's Supreme Council, established under the 1833 Charter Act (what Macaulay calls the 'India Bill') as the single legislative authority for all of Britain's Indian possessions. Under the Act the Governor-General was also to appoint a four-man commission to suggest revisions of the Indian legal system, and Macaulay later accepted voluntarily the additional task of heading this Law Commission.

Macaulay left England with Hannah in February 1834 and reached India in June, at the middle of the hot season – though he seems from the first to have been singularly unaffected by the notorious Indian climate. That he was moved emotionally and aesthetically by his first experience of India there can be no doubt: 'but to be in such a land!' he wrote to his sister, Margaret: 'dark faces and bodies with white turbans and flowing robes – the trees not our trees – the very smell of the atmosphere like that of a hothouse – the architecture as strange as the vegetation.'[7] At the same time, he was no stranger either to the history or to the problems of the sub-continent. His Evangelical background had long made him aware of India – seen by the Clapham-ites chiefly as a field for missionary endeavour – and since May 1832 he had, of course, been directly involved in Indian affairs at the Board of Control and had even played some part (though the major influence seems to have been that of James Mill, then the Chief Examiner of the Company) in framing the very Act which created the position he was now to occupy.

At the time of Macaulay's arrival in Calcutta in late September of 1834 a controversy was raging in the General Committee of Public Instruction about the future of government-supported higher educa-tion in India. On the one side were the Orientalists, who advocated that the limited funds available under an Act of the English parliament of 1813 should continue to be used, as they had been until that time, exclusively for the support of colleges for the teaching of Sanskrit and Arabic, for translations of works into those languages, and for the payment of stipends to students enrolled in the Sanskrit and Arabic colleges. The opposing view was that of the Anglicists, who urged that the money be used instead for the teaching of English, that no further stipends be paid, and that there be no further expenditure on transla-tions, since the works required for educational purposes were already available in English; their central position was that English was a much more useful language, providing access not merely to the literature of the past but to the whole range of modern knowledge. As Gerald and Natalie Sirkin have recently underlined in an important article, the debate was conducted in terms of a choice not between English and the Indian vernaculars, but between English and Classical Sanskrit and Arabic, which were for the natives of India dead languages, to be learned only by a process of arduous study:[8]

To the Indian students, Sanskrit and Arabic and English *were equally unknown*. But the useful knowledge to be studied was not to be found in Sanskrit and Arabic, and the prospect of translating Western learning into the classical Oriental languages was as pointless as it was overwhelming. The study of Sanskrit or Arabic merely inserted an additional, and a virtually insurmountable obstacle between the student and modern education. Clearly, if the curriculum was to be modern, the medium of instruction had to be English.

The decision of the Governor-General, Lord William Bentinck, was in favour of the Anglicist view, and there can be no doubt of its having been profoundly influenced by Macaulay's Minute of 2 February 1835. This impressive document, written in Macaulay's most trenchant manner, is wholly dismissive of the Orientalist position and of the notion of devoting public funds to the teaching of 'languages in which, by universal confession, there are no books on any subject which deserve to be compared to our own.'[9] Gerald and Natalie Sirkin attribute some of Macaulay's vehemence to his awareness of the argumentative skill and sophistication of his opponents, and they point out that the Orientalists chose not to argue against the view that 'the objective of higher education in India was the introduction of useful knowledge',[10] preferring instead to blur the issues somewhat by the invocation of terminology which tended to obscure the distinctions between the vernaculars and the classical languages they sought to protect. This strategy did not win the day in the Supreme Council, but it has served to confuse many subsequent commentators who have seen Macaulay as leading an attack not on classical Sanskrit and Arabic but on the principle of vernacular instruction. In point of fact, one of the arguments in the Education Minute to support the use of English for higher education is that those who had benefited from such an education would be in a position 'to refine the vernacular dialects of the country, to enrich those dialects with terms of science borrowed from the Western nomenclature, and to render them by degrees fit vehicles for conveying knowledge to the great mass of the population.'[11]

Once Bentinck had signified his acceptance of the Anglicist position early in March 1835, Macaulay took up the position – already assigned to him – of President of the General Committee of Public Instruction and entered energetically upon the task of administering and reforming Indian education. His subsequent career in the office can to some extent be followed in a series of economically and sometimes brusquely worded minutes which display him in his characteristic role of liberal pragmatist, capable of impatience and even insensitivity but always concerned to find and follow the course likeliest to prove equitable, humane, and workable. The inscription he composed in 1835 for the statue in Calcutta of his friend and ally, Lord William Bentinck, is eloquent of those standards, public and private, which Macaulay felt should ideally guide the British rulers of India, himself among them:[12]

TO
WILLIAM CAVENDISH BENTINCK,
Who, during seven years, ruled India with eminent
Prudence, Integrity, and Benevolence:
Who, placed at the head of a great Empire, never laid aside
The simplicity and moderation of a private citizen:
Who infused into Oriental despotism the spirit of
British Freedom:
Who never forgot that the end of Government is
The happiness of the Governed:
Who abolished cruel rites:
Who effaced humiliating distinctions:
Who gave liberty to the expression of public opinion:
Whose constant study it was, to elevate the intellectual
And moral character of the Nations committed to his charge.

These values, tinged as they are with Evangelicalism, with Utilitarianism, and with a kind of liberal paternalism, are certainly those which Macaulay attempted to pursue in his major work in India as President of the Law Commission. In the course of his famous speech of 10 July 1833 on the second reading of the 'India Bill' – a speech which an old member of the House assured him would console younger members for never having heard Burke[13] – Macaulay had declared that the necessary reconsideration of the Indian legal system would be better carried through by a 'quiet knot of two or three veteran jurists' than by a 'large popular assembly'.[14] Three and a half years later Macaulay, who could scarcely have thought of himself as a veteran jurist, found himself forced by circumstances to do much of the work of the Law Commission alone – in a minute of 2 January 1837 he explains that only he among the four commissioners had kept consistently well[15] – and his influence is everywhere visible in the proposed new Penal Code which the Commission eventually laid before the Governor-

General in May 1837. The Introductory Report and the Notes which accompanied the Code when it was published later that year seem to have been almost entirely Macaulay's work,[16] and the economy and force of the arguments, the use of particular illustrations, and the clarity and concreteness of the phraseology are all in his characteristic vein.

The whole document is a monument to common sense and liberal principles, and even today it does not seem hopelessly out-dated. Its provisions for speedy justice, its aim of treating all men as equally as the diversity of India would allow, its concern to limit the merely punitive aspects of its sanctions – all compare very favourably with the state of the penal law in England in the 1830s and for many decades afterwards. The Penal Code was attacked at the time, and has been attacked since, for its indifference to existing Indian laws, but while it was undoubtedly intended to be a very clean sweep, a new beginning on fresh principles, it not only took account of British law and the legal codes of France and Louisiana but was firmly grounded in the specifically Indian experience of the Commissioners and the civil servants who assisted them. Note E, for example, 'On the Chapter of the Abuse of the Powers of Public Servants', includes the following passage:[17]

In all states of society the receiving of a bribe is a bad action, and may properly be made punishable. But whether the giving of a bribe ought or ought not to be punished is a question which does not admit of a short and general answer. There are countries in which the giver of a bribe ought to be more severely punished than the receiver. There are countries, on the other hand, in which the giving of a bribe may be what it is not desirable to visit with any punishment. In a country situated like England, the giver of a bribe is generally far more deserving of punishment than the receiver. The giver is generally the tempter, the receiver is the tempted. The giver is generally rich, powerful, well educated, the receiver needy and ignorant. The giver is under no apprehension of suffering any injury if he refuses to give. It is not by fear, but by ambition that he is generally induced to part with his money. Such a person is a proper subject of punishment. But there are countries where the case is widely different, – where men give bribes to Magistrates from exactly the same feeling which leads them to give their purses to robbers, or to pay ransom to pirates, –

where men give bribes because no man can, without a bribe, obtain common justice. In such countries we think that the giving of bribes is not a proper subject of punishment. It would be as absurd, in such a state of society, to reproach the giver of a bribe with corrupting the virtue of public servants, as it would be to say that the traveller who delivers his money when a pistol is held to his breast corrupts the virtue of the highwayman.

The argument is typical of the way in which the central impulse of the Code towards unity and consistency and simplicity of administration is not allowed to override considerations of practical reality and everyday humanity.

There was something Utilitarian in the systematization and planned efficiency implicit in the very notion of creating a new body of law for a vast country, and Eric Stokes has amply demonstrated the extent to which many of the ideas informing the Code are derived from Bentham and, more immediately, from James Mill.[18] But the Code as a whole is founded not on exclusive concepts of the operations of human society but on a wide range of general ideas about social behaviour and morality tempered by a realistic appraisal of prevailing Indian customs and traditions. Macaulay's pragmatism was quite equal to adopting many practical aspects of the Utilitarian programme even while he remained intellectually and temperamentally opposed to what he regarded as the remote abstractions of Utilitarian theory. So much is clear even from those early essays written when his hostility to the Utilitarians was at its most intemperate. Before he left for India Macaulay had arrived at a much fuller appreciation of James Mill's work and ideas; he was touched by the news that Mill had supported his appointment as legislative member, and the two men soon became friends and allies. Indeed, as Chief Examiner, Mill was in a position to give strong support to Macaulay's reforming activities in India, and the difficulties and delays Macaulay experienced during his last two Indian years were in part a consequence of Mill's death in 1836.

Macaulay was also unfortunate in the departure of Lord William Bentinck in 1835 and his replacement by the Earl of Auckland – also a Whig, but less effective as an administrator and less dedicated as a reformer – and for these and other reasons Macaulay's immediate impact upon India was not great. The immense consequences of his influence upon Indian education were only to appear in the long term, and even the Penal Code did not become operative until 1860, the year following Macaulay's death. The only major piece of legislation he saw enacted before he left India was the so-called 'Black Act', a classic measure of liberal reform which made English residents living outside Calcutta subject to the same system of courts as the native inhabitants – and which made Macaulay himself highly unpopular with the English expatriate community. The optimism with which he originally confronted Indian affairs was soon tempered by encounters with the perennial Indian problems of climate and communications and with the opposition of colleagues on the Supreme Council and of those compatriots offended by the 'Black Act'. Macaulay was sufficiently resilient to survive vilification by the English press of Calcutta, but there seems little doubt that the setbacks he received in his public life in India served both to intensify the private sufferings of that time and to encourage his latent tendencies towards withdrawal.

In personal terms Macaulay's departure from England in 1834 had meant danger to health, separation from relations and friends, and exile from those political and literary worlds in which he had so recently begun to cut a very considerable figure. Only the most powerful motives could have induced him to take a step of this kind, but such motives were present, and very clear. Writing to his sister Hannah to ask her to accompany him to India, he explained that the great advantage of the post was that it carried a salary of ten thousand pounds a year, of which living costs would absorb no more than half. By saving the remainder, with interest, 'I may therefore hope to return to England at only thirty nine, in the full vigour of life, with a fortune of thirty thousand pounds. A larger fortune I never desired.'[19] At a time when a property qualification for members of parliament was still legally in effect, Macaulay was well aware both of the difficulties of making a political career without private means and of the suspicions to which a poor man occupying a government position was inevitably exposed. His Indian salary, he explained to Lord Lansdowne in December 1833, was important not for its own sake but because it would give him sufficient independence to avoid his present dire alternatives of becoming a hack writer or of clinging desperately to political office: 'Without a competence it is not very easy for a public man to be honest: it is almost impossible for him to be thought so.' Macaulay added:[20]

But this is not all. I am not alone in the world. A family which I love most fondly is dependent on me. Unless I would see my

father left in his old age to the charity of less near relations; my
youngest brother unable to obtain a good professional education;
my sisters, who are more to me than any sisters ever were to a
brother, forced to turn governesses or humble companions, – I
must do something, I must make some effort. An opportunity has
offered itself.

Faced with all these consequences of his father's financial losses, it was
an opportunity he felt bound to seize, but it was also one which
subsequent events were often to cause him to regret.

The four years between his election to parliament in 1830 and his
departure for India in 1834 had been for Macaulay the years of recognition and of confidence. His successes in the *Edinburgh Review* were
now matched by a series of oratorical triumphs in the debates on the
Reform Bill. His party was in the ascendant; he had access to its most
influential inner circles; he was fêted at Holland House. He was able to
please his father by his general success and by his conduct on the
slavery issue; his friends had found places for his father and for two of
his brothers. Above all, he was absolutely secure in the love and affection of his sisters – for in the end every public achievement was
measured by the domestic standard. In July 1831 he wrote to his sister,
Hannah:[21]

My greatest pleasure in the midst of all this praise is to think of
the pleasure which my success will give to my father and my
sisters. It is happy for me that ambition – the fiercest and most
devouring of all passions – has in my mind been softened into a
kind of domestic feeling, and that affection has at least as much
to do as vanity with my wish to distinguish myself. This I owe
to my dear mother and to the interest which she always took in my
childish successes. From my earliest years the gratification of those
whom I love has been associated with the gratification of my own
thirst of fame, until the two have become inseparably joined in
my mind.

But this great source of Macaulay's early strength – the absolute sense
of family love and loyalty which determined his decision to go to
India – was soon to prove the source of his greatest weakness. The
assurance of the early 1830s had fragile foundations, based as it was
upon a domestic affection and stability which he chose to view
as unchanging and unchangeable. The degree of his emotional,

and apparently quite asexual, dependence upon his sisters ('more to me than any sisters ever were to a brother') is the single most extraordinary thing in Macaulay's psychological make-up, and the note of near-hysteria which occasionally makes itself heard in his denunciations of political renegades[22] finds its counterpart in the tone of some of his letters to Margaret and Hannah. It is clear, for example, that their marriages affected him initially as acts of personal betrayal. In December 1833 he wrote to Hannah of how she must feel at the prospect of parting from Margaret, now Mrs Edward Cropper:[23]

> I well know, my darling, what your feelings must be now that you are on the eve of the most painful of all these painful separations, – the separation from our dear Margaret. I went through that misery a year ago [on Margaret's marriage]. To me the bitterness of that death is past. Whether I am in London or at Calcutta, she is equally lost to me. Instead of wishing to be near her, I rather shrink from it. She is dead to me: and what I see is only her ghost. But her marriage, which has set an impassable gulf between her and me, has united her to you more closely than ever.

Within another year Hannah herself became engaged to Charles Trevelyan, whom she had met since arriving in India, and near the end of her life she still recalled with considerable distress how Macaulay had responded to the news with 'the most fearful letter of misery & reproach, followed the next day by one begging me to forgive it'. After his death she found 'entries in his journals referring to this unhealed wound which were exquisitely painful to me to read & most of which I have erased!'[24] In a letter of 7 December 1834 Macaulay poured out to Margaret his feelings of isolation and loss:[25]

> I have reaped as I sowed. At thirty-four I am alone in the world. I have lost everything – and I have only myself to blame. The work of more than twenty years has vanished in a single month. She was always most dear to me. Since you left me she was everything to me. I loved her. I adored her. For her sake, more than for my own, I valued wealth, station, political and literary fame. For her sake far more than for my own I became an exile from my country. [In] her society & affection I found an ample

compensation for all that brilliant society which I had left. She
was everything to me: and I am to be henceforth nothing to
her – The first place in her affection is gone – Every year some
new object of love will push me lower and lower in the scale of
her regard till I am to her what our Uncles and Aunts were to
our Father and Mother.

I do not repine. Whatever I suffer I have brought on myself[.]
I have neglected the plainest lessons of reason and experience[.]
I have staked my happiness without calculating the chances of
the dice. I have hewn out broken cisterns, I have leant on a reed.
I have built on the sand. And I have fared accordingly. I must
bear my punishment as I can, and above all I must take care that
the punishment does not extend beyond myself.

Worse, however was to come. Margaret had died even before this
letter was written, and when the news reached Calcutta in January 1835
Hannah and her husband came hurrying back from their honeymoon
to give some comfort to a Macaulay overwhelmed by grief. He told
Ellis in a letter of 8 February 1835 that Margaret had been 'as dear to
me as one human being can be to another. Even now, when time has
begun to do its healing office, I cannot write about her without being
altogether unmanned.'[26]
In the same letter, Macaulay adds: 'That I have not utterly sunk
under this blow I owe chiefly to literature. What a blessing it is to love
books as I love them, – to be able to converse with the dead and to live
amidst the unreal.'[27] The longing to retreat into books and into the
past was to become very powerful from this time onwards and, as this
and subsequent letters to Ellis make clear, it took the immediate form
of immersion in the world of the classics and of classical scholarship.
One curious by-product – both of the classical reading and of the
whole instinct for withdrawal into the past – was to be the *Lays of
Ancient Rome*, substantially written at this time although not published
until 1842. Shortly before that first publication Macaulay described
their origin in a letter to Macvey Napier:[28]

You are acquainted, no doubt, with Perizonius's theory about the
early Roman History, – a theory which Niebuhr revived, and
which Arnold has adopted as fully established. I have myself not
the smallest doubt of its truth. It is that the stories of the birth
of Romulus and Remus, the fight of the Horatii and Curatii,
and all the other romantic tales which fill the first three or four

books of Livy, came from the lost ballads of the early Romans.
I amused myself in India with trying to restore some of these
long perished poems.

The inception of the *Lays* probably dates from about the time of
Macaulay's letter to Ellis of 29 May 1835 which reports that he is
engaged in a complete re-reading of Livy and a simultaneous reconsideration of Niebuhr's views on ancient Roman history.[29] Macaulay
deals somewhat severely in this letter with what he considers Niebuhr's
disregard for the laws of evidence, but, as the letter to Napier and the
general preface to the published *Lays* both show, he was to find in
Niebuhr's theory precisely the stimulus his imagination needed to
produce his own versifications of Roman legend.

Macaulay's early dramatic and fictional fragments had been historical,
and in the verse which he wrote for his sister's albums or for the pages of
Knight's Quarterly there is a striking preponderance of poems prompted
by particular occasions or by historical subjects. The poem contributed
to the *Friendship's Offering* for 1833 was on the Armada; a specific
contemporary event, the Leicester election of 1826, in which Macaulay
had participated in support of a friend, provided the subject-matter of
an imitation ballad which Macaulay, it appears, had printed like a
genuine broadside and then pasted into his personal collection of street
ballads;[30] one of his most interesting poems was occasioned by his
own defeat in the Edinburgh election of July 1847. All this suggests a
poetic imagination of secondary power, capable of launching itself only
from a firm basis of fact – as perhaps Leigh Hunt was suggesting when,
in a letter which gave Macaulay a good deal of amusement, he combined an appeal for a loan with an expression of regret that the recently
published *Lays* lacked 'the true poetical *aroma* which breathes from
Spenser's Faery Queen'.[31]

As first published by Longman in 1842, the four poems were
supplied with a general preface and with individual prefaces, and in
these Macaulay was chiefly concerned to explain how the *Lays* were
related both to the legends that supplied their narrative content and to
the contexts in which they were conceived to have been composed and
recited. Niebuhr's theory that the lost ballads were the means by which
certain legends found their way into early Roman history is first
summarized and then supported by the citation of specific references
made by later writers to the existence of such ballads, and by an appeal
to the history of ballads in general and the phenomenon of their survival

in the literature of other nations, particularly Britain and Spain. The suggestion as to the way they were transmitted is further supported by a discussion of the origins of certain legendary materials in Hume's *History of England*.

Of particular interest in this mixture of fact, theory, argument, and analogy is Macaulay's concern to place his ballads in an historical context. The poems themselves are ordered in historical sequence corresponding to their supposed date of composition, so that the last is specifically attributed to 'the latest age of Latin ballad poetry' and the reader required to assume that 'The minstrel who sang on that day might possibly have lived to read the first hexameters of Ennius, and to see the first comedies of Plautus.'[32] Such details are drawn from Macaulay's considerable knowledge of Roman history, politics, and social customs, and they create out of historical fact an essentially fictionalized context which, in its turn, provides the reader with a stepping-stone back into the world of legend. Towards the end of the general preface Macaulay explains his contextual method:[33]

> In the following poems the author speaks, not in his own person, but in the persons of ancient minstrels who know only what a Roman citizen, born three or four hundred years before the Christian aera, may be supposed to have known, and who are in nowise above the passions and prejudices of their age and nation.

The preface to 'Horatius' explains:[34]

> The following ballad is supposed to have been made about a hundred and twenty years after the war which it celebrates, and just before the taking of Rome by the Gauls. The author seems to have been an honest citizen, proud of the military glory of his country, sick of the disputes of factions, and much given to pining after good old times which had never really existed.

At the end of the preface to 'Virginia' the reader is urged to imagine himself a member of the audience of Plebeians to whom the poem is supposed to have been originally addressed, sharing those feelings of resentment against the Patricians which the ballad itself, recited at the height of an election, was intended to exacerbate.

It is tempting to ascribe these prefaces, and to a lesser extent the poems which they introduce, simply to Macaulay's delight in scholarly gymnastics – a delight which comes out most clearly in his letters to his friend, Ellis, with whom he shared his love of the classics and to whose judgment the *Lays* and their apparatus were repeatedly submitted during the final stages of composition. But while the prefaces are in some degree scholarly *tours de force*, they also represent an essential element in the production of the *Lays* themselves: their function as stepping-stones for the reader is far exceeded by their importance as stepping-stones for the author himself. Macaulay's concern to establish the precise historical context of each poem and to identify exactly the perspective of each narrator seems to be his way of taking bearings from the historically known before venturing into the unknown territory of legend and imagination; as such, it is akin to the process by which he feels his way into poetic expression not only by using an invented persona but by seeking reassurance in analogies with Homer, Scott, and the border ballads. Even after the *Lays* had been substantially finished, he took pleasure in finding confirmatory evidence for the appropriateness of his chosen method: on 22 August 1842 he writes to tell Ellis of remembering that the metre of the lost Roman ballads was probably Saturnian and of discovering Saturnian lines in his own versions of them.[35] It seems fair to say, indeed, that the prefaces belong more to the author and to the processes by which the *Lays* came into existence than they do to the reader. Macaulay is seeking, consciously or unconsciously, to justify the endeavour to himself, and there is perhaps an ironic justice in the fact that the prefaces have been so often ignored, especially by the generations of schoolboys who have taken the poems themselves all too literally to heart. Immediately the *Lays* were published they were found to satisfy to an extraordinary degree that need Macaulay himself described in the general preface: 'All human beings, not utterly savage, long for some information about past times, and are delighted by narratives which present pictures to the eye of the mind.'[36] Delighted by the pictorialism of Macaulay's verse narratives, the audience has been a good deal less concerned than the author to discriminate between the historical and legendary elements in their subject-matter.

Whatever the prefaces may reveal about Macaulay's attitudes to history, his concern with narrative perspective, and his need to dramatize an historical context for his poetic fictions, they still tell us very little about the poems themselves or about the reasons for their amazing popularity. G. O. Trevelyan eschews analysis but records that 'by June 1875, upwards of a hundred thousand copies had passed into the hands of readers.'[37] By the end of the century the figures must have been very much higher, and even beyond the middle of the twentieth century 'Horatius' has not entirely disappeared from the schools as a text for reading or recitation. The slightly jingoistic sentiments which Macaulay ascribed to his old Roman Tory – and which the forgotten preface sought to place in an historical context and distinguish from the views of author and reader – have certainly contributed to the continuing popularity of this particular poem, but a century of active life rests on something more than this. The speed and economy with which the action is portrayed, the clarity of the plot outline, the ease with which (despite the exotic and historical nature of the subject-matter) the heroes and the villains can be distinguished – these features have a permanent appeal to the youthful imagination, and the excitement of the actual narration is heightened by the colour and detail of the pictorial imagery and the roll-call of strange names. Above all, the patterns created by rhythm, rhyme, and the repetition of phrases and syntactic structures make the verses not just easy to remember but virtually impossible to forget. Perhaps only 'Hiawatha' has proved a match for 'Horatius' in this respect.

To read 'Horatius' today is an odd experience. The colours seem too bright, the characters and situations too crudely drawn, the sentiments too simplistic; and yet the excitement of the narrative and the sheer energy of the verse still have a certain mesmeric effect. There is about it no trace of Arnoldian 'high seriousness', but it remains a supreme example of that paradoxical form, the Philistine work of art. Macaulay had said of his imaginary bards: 'A man who can invent or embellish an interesting story, and put it into a form which others may easily retain in their recollection, will always be highly esteemed by a people eager for amusement and information, but destitute of libraries.'[38] With just one poem Macaulay succeeded in winning such a place for himself even in a world full of libraries and school anthologies.

Macaulay possessed to a remarkable degree the capacity to conjure up men and events out of the past, to carry himself back to particular moments in time, and to hold those moments in temporary stasis. Some of his later essays supply, like the *Lays* themselves, memorable examples of his ability to translate such experiences into written form: one thinks of the impeachment scene in Westminster Hall in the Hastings essay or, in a quieter vein, the description at the end of the Addison essay of the poet emerging from his library. During the Indian years such imaginative re-creations had their therapeutic value for Macaulay; even so, they could afford only a temporary respite from his awareness of time and change as seen in their traditional guise of transience and decay rather than in the more cheering form of progress or regeneration. Both aspects of change make themselves felt in a complexly moving passage from the tribute Macaulay wrote after his return from India to the memory of Lord Holland, in whose famous home he had savoured only a few years before the heady triumphs of the various battles for the cause of Reform. Holland House and the world which it represented, and which Macaulay so valued, are seen in this July 1841 *Edinburgh* article as threatened by a combination of urban expansion and the passage of time:

> Yet a few years, and the shades and structures may follow their illustrious masters. The wonderful city which, ancient and gigantic as it is, still continues to grow as fast as a young town of logwood by a water-privilege in Michigan, may soon displace those turrets and gardens which are associated with so much that is interesting and noble – with the courtly magnificence of Rich – with the loves of Ormond – with the counsels of Cromwell – with the death of Addison. The time is coming when, perhaps, a few old men, the last survivors of our generation, will in vain seek, amidst new streets, and squares, and railway stations, for the site of that dwelling which was in their youth the favourite resort of wits and beauties – of painters and poets – of scholars, philosophers, and statesmen. They will then remember, with strange tenderness, many objects once familiar to them – the avenue and the terrace, the busts and the paintings; the carving, the grotesque gilding, and the enigmatical mottoes. With peculiar fondness they will recall that venerable chamber, in which all the antique gravity of a college library was so singularly blended with all that female grace and wit could devise to embellish a drawing-room. (73:567)

Even in this context Macaulay cannot bring himself to view London as some kind of Cobbettian Great Wen; he still sees the city as possessing in its old age something of the essentially progressive vitality of younger settlements. Nevertheless, the passage is dominated by the sense of loss and regret as it flows on to the end of the article through nine more long sentences, each beginning 'They will remember' or 'They will recollect', each calling up the names of some of the many famous men who frequented Holland House during the lifetime of its late master. The burden of the final sentence is loyalty to mentors, to friends, and to party ties:

> They will remember that, in the last lines which he [Lord Holland] traced, he expressed his joy that he had done nothing unworthy of the friend of Fox and Grey; and they will have reason to feel similar joy, if, in looking back on many troubled years, they cannot accuse themselves of having done any thing unworthy of men who were distinguished by the friendship of Lord Holland. (73:568)

There is an elegiac note here which was never heard in the essays of the early 1830s – which is, in fact, distinctively the note of the years of exile and return. It is already present, together with a recurrent emphasis on the theme of loyalty, in the only two essays, those on Mackintosh and Bacon, which were actually completed while Macaulay was in India. Though less fraught with emotion than his feelings about his family, Macaulay's own loyalty to those who had helped and encouraged him was strong and prompt, and it was therefore particularly unfortunate that the editor of Sir James Mackintosh's unfinished *History of the Revolution* should have chosen to imply in his introductory memoir that Mackintosh's change of heart about the French Revolution amounted to little more than ratting for a place. Macaulay's response, published in the July 1835 issue of the *Edinburgh*, was an attack whose vehemence almost resulted in a duel on his return to England. But the essay raised other issues beyond those of loyalty. It made Macaulay turn his mind once more to the general problem of the best way of writing history, while the fact that Mackintosh and Fox – who is considered at some length in the opening pages of the essay – had both combined parliamentary careers with the writing of history but had both failed, though for different reasons, to produce a satisfying major history, raised the particular question as to whether a serious career in politics was compatible with substantial achievement as an historian. Macaulay must have wondered about the nine years of his life which Mackintosh had given to India. Although Mackintosh had left behind him at his death a moderate reputation as a parliamentarian and a certain fame for having once challenged the great Edmund Burke with his *Vindiciae Gallicae*, the crucial thing for Macaulay was the unfinished fragment of the major historical work Mackintosh had set himself to write, a work whose subject – the Revolution of 1688 – could have made it one of the Whig sacred books. The relevance of all this for the choices Macaulay would have to make about his own future was inescapable, and the writing of the article undoubtedly prompted an examination of his own situation. Written at a time when his feelings of exile and isolation had been increasingly exacerbated by the sense of having cut himself off in mid-career to come to a strange continent and face considerable opposition to his ideas on penal and educational reform, when the impending marriage of his sister, Hannah, was about to deprive him of his most precious possession, and when his deep feelings of personal and party loyalty were productive of nothing but anguish – it is perhaps understandable that the essay should be somewhat uneven in texture and in tone.

The essay on Bacon, which he commenced soon after the completion of the Mackintosh and which appeared in the July 1837 issue of the *Edinburgh*, seems to represent a deliberate withdrawal on Macaulay's part into historical narrative and analysis, and it contains an especially moving evocation of his increasingly powerful sense that permanent solace could only be found in literature and true happiness only in the company of men long dead. It is a passage to set alongside the long lists of books he read in India, and alongside the dates written into some of those books which indicate two or even three readings during that relatively short period:

> These friendships are exposed to no danger from the occurrences
> by which other attachments are weakened or dissolved. Time
> glides by; fortune is inconstant; tempers are soured; bonds which
> seemed indissoluble are daily sundered by interest, by emulation,
> or by caprice. But no such cause can affect the silent converse
> which we hold with the highest of human intellects. That placid
> intercourse is disturbed by no jealousies or resentments. These are
> the old friends who are never seen with new faces, who are
> the same in wealth and in poverty, in glory and in obscurity.
> With the dead there is no rivalry. In the dead there is no change.
> Plato is never sullen. Cervantes is never petulant. Demosthenes
> never comes unseasonably. Dante never stays too long. No
> difference of opinion can alienate Cicero. No heresy can excite
> the horror of Bossuet. (55,ii:3)

This is clearly the public – and, for Macaulay, extraordinarily naked – expression of a deeply felt private experience. During the Indian years the forces of time and mutability began to take on for him a more threatening aspect than they had ever worn before. In his public life his enthusiasm had been blunted by the experience of opposition and defeat, and he had perhaps begun to see something two-edged in that weapon of change which he had previously advocated as the only sure preserver of traditional institutions. In his private life he was from time to time overwhelmed by a profound sense of helplessness in the face of processes of change which carried away from him the things he loved and deprived him of the stability for which he longed. Exiled in India, surrounded by an alien culture and unsympathetic colleagues, his family circumstances rapidly and disastrously transformed, it is less surprising than might at first appear that Macaulay - in his middle thirties already famous as a man both of letters and of affairs, as an acclaimed orator, and as an administrator of prodigious energy and influence – could none the less declare: 'Books are becoming everything to me. If I had at this moment my choice of life, I would bury myself in one of those libraries that we saw together at the universities, and never pass a waking hour without a book before me.'[39]

5

Time of Decision

The Essays on Temple and Clive

The temptation to retreat into the world of literature and the dead remained one of the alternatives before Macaulay when he arrived back in England in 1838, and it cannot have been lessened by the fact that he was greeted by the news of his father's death. Although Macaulay was now much more affluent than he had been before leaving England, he was also much sadder, less confident and optimistic. He had gone to India to make himself independent. Now, with his father and Margaret both dead, Hannah married, and the possibility that he would himself ever marry becoming more and more remote, he found himself independent to a degree and in a sense that he had never envisaged. The fortune accumulated in India, together with £10,000 left him by his uncle, General Colin Macaulay, gave him financial freedom, but the lack of a family home and of close personal ties gave him freedom of quite another kind. The opportunity for political eminence was clearly open to him; rumour was soon at work putting him back in office, and the Whig government, currently in some disarray, would have welcomed so stalwart a recruit. 'They are going to bring in Mcauley [sic] into Cutler Ferguson's situation', Sydney Smith confided to Lady Grey on 15 November 1838, adding: 'Mcauley had resolved to lead a Literary Life but cannot withstand the temptation – like Ladies who resolve upon celibacy if they have no offers.'[1] But Smith was proved wrong when Macaulay refused the offer of Ferguson's former position of Judge Advocate. Literary opportunity in the pages of the *Edinburgh Review* was even more immediately available, since the Bacon essay, published during his absence, had considerably enhanced ced his fame, helping to make him, according to Sydney Smith, 'incomparably the first lion in the Metropolis'.[2]

Back in a London much changed during his four years in India, with no permanent home and no public duties, with a new sovereign on the throne and new faces in the ministry, Macaulay found himself faced with a decision which he had contemplated but not resolved during the years of exile. His letter to Napier of 26 June 1838 suggests that he saw in the turmoil of the streets of a pre-Coronation London an apt image of his own disturbed state:[3]

> I am quite unsettled – Breakfasts every morning – dinners every evening and calls all day prevent me from making any regular exertion. My books are at the baggage warehouse. My book-cases are in the hands of the cabinet-maker. Whatever I write at present I must, as Bacon somewhere says, spin like a spider, out of my own entrails. And I have hardly a minute in the week for such spinning. London is in a strange state of excitement. The western streets are in a constant ferment. The influx of foreigners and rustics has been prodigious, and the regular inhabitants are almost as idle and curious as the sojourners. Crowds assemble perpetually, nobody knows why, with a sort of vague expectation that there will be something to see, and after staring at each other, disperse without seeing anything. This will last till the Coronation is over. The only quiet haunts are the streets of the city. For my part I am sick to death of the turmoil, and almost wish myself at Calcutta again, or becalmed on the Equator.

Macaulay seems to have been more and more attracted at this time by the idea of leaving London and abandoning all thought of a return to politics. He wrote to Napier on 20 July 1838:[4]

> Whether I shall continue to reside in London seems to me very uncertain. I used to think that I liked London. But in truth I liked things which were in London and which are gone. My family is scattered. I have no parliamentary or official business to bind me to the capital. The business to which I propose to devote myself is almost incompatible with the distractions of a town-life. I am sick of the monotonous succession of parties, and long for quiet and retirement. To quit politics for letters is, I believe, a wise choice. To cease to be a member of parliament only in order to become a diner out, would be contemptible: and it is not easy for me to avoid becoming a mere diner-out if I reside here.

The 'business' to which he proposed to devote himself was, of course, the *History of England*. This scheme had been mooted to Ellis in a letter from Calcutta as early as December 1835, and at that time Macaulay had seen withdrawal from politics as the necessary condition for the writing of such a work:[5]

> What my course of life will be when I return to England is very doubtful. But I am more than half determined to abandon politics, and to give myself wholly to letters – to undertake some great historical work which may be at once the business and the amusement of my life, and to leave the pleasures of pestiferous rooms, sleepless nights, aching heads, and diseased stomachs, to greater men, – to Roebuck and Praed.

Macaulay spent the summer of 1838 making up his mind. He did not recoil from the turmoil of London back to Calcutta or to a ship becalmed on the equator, but he did leave in the middle of October for a tour of Italy. Ostensibly this was the reward for the long years of Indian exile, a gift to Macaulay the scholar and historian. But while he devoted much of his time to Classical and Renaissance art, toyed with his *Lays of Ancient Rome*, and confined his reading almost entirely to guide books and bad novels, he was in fact settling the future course of his life. The offer of the Judge Advocateship was declined from Florence in November without much difficulty, but a letter to Lord Lansdowne of 19 December 1838 shows that even while declining office Macaulay was not averse to the idea of returning to parliament, apparently in the belief that he could make a useful contribution as a private member and still have time to work on his projected *History*.[6] His *Journal*, which makes clear the firmness of his refusal of office in December 1838,[7] also shows that he actually began writing the *History* in the early months of 1839 and that he spent much of April collecting material in the British Museum.[8] At the same period he began work on an essay of the old controversial type, though without the old virulence – the review, published in April 1839, of a book by a rising young Tory, William Ewart Gladstone's *The State in its Relation with the Church*. In fact, by the time Macaulay returned to London in February 1839 the question of remaining in the capital had been resolved, or had resolved itself, and he seemed to have taken up the threads, both literary and political, of his former life very much where he had dropped them in February 1834. May saw him standing as a candidate at Edinburgh, and once he was back in parliament he inevitably came under greater pressure to join the Whig administration in its time of trouble. His sense of the need for party loyalty was as strong as ever – 'these are not times for flinching from the Whig banner',[9] he had declared in his 19 December letter to Lord Lansdowne – and he no doubt found it more and more difficult to justify his somewhat wishful assumption that he could best serve his party from the back benches, without too much interruption of his historical labours. It is therefore no great surprise to find him reluctantly setting the *History* aside and returning after all to office, this time with Cabinet rank, by accepting the Secretaryship at War in September 1839.

Before this, however, at the moment when the commitment to politics or to literature was in the balance, when a deliberate personal choice seemed to be necessary, Macaulay had written one of his most important essays – the October 1838 *Edinburgh* article on the relatively insignificant figure of Sir William Temple. Proposed in India, completed shortly before he left for Italy, the article belongs squarely to the months of the winding up of his affairs in India, of the journey home, of the turmoil of London – the months of indecision.

Writing to Napier from Calcutta on 15 June 1837, Macaulay had announced:[10]

> I will try my hand on Temple and on Lord Clive. Shaftesbury
> I shall let alone. Indeed his political life is so much connected
> with Temple's that, without endless repetition, it would be
> impossible for me to furnish a separate article on each.

If the juxtaposition of the names of Sir William Temple and Clive of India is in itself a little unexpected, still more curious, at first glance, is Macaulay's simultaneous selection of these two figures as subjects for *Edinburgh Review* essays – especially at a stage in his relationship with that journal when his freedom to choose his subjects was entirely unrestricted. That Macaulay, after his years in India, should have been fascinated by Clive is not surprising, nor, in view of his ambition to write a *History of England from the Accession of James II*, is his interest in late seventeenth-century English politics. But Temple seems a pale companion for Clive, and, in the context of the *Essays* volumes, for such men as Milton, Johnson, and Warren Hastings; and if Macaulay wanted to write on a seventeenth-century subject one might well wonder why he preferred to focus on Temple rather than on the more arresting figure of Shaftesbury. The solutions to these difficulties relate in part to the circumstances of Macaulay's life at this period; they also relate to his development as a narrative artist and to the way in which he shaped in the essays the techniques which found in the *History* their richest fulfilment.

The aspect of Temple's career which receives most attention in the essay is his habit of leaving public life, or avoiding being drawn into it, at moments of particular danger or crisis. It is almost as though Macaulay, himself considering the abandonment of politics for literature, wishes to test his own action by comparing it with an extreme case. By examining what he clearly considers to be excessive and illegitimate retreat Macaulay is perhaps seeking to define the kind of withdrawal which could be justifiable:

> Of course a man is not bound to be a politician any more than he is bound to be a soldier; and there are perfectly honourable ways of quitting both politics and the military profession. But neither in the one way of life, nor in the other, is any man entitled to take all the sweet and leave all the sour. (68:117)

Macaulay had drawn the same comparison between the political and the military life in a letter to William Empson of 19 June 1837. Speaking specifically of his own doubts about re-entering public life on his impending return from India, he had declared:[11]

> It is in my power to determine not to go into parliament. But it will not be in my power whenever a crisis comes which separates me from my most valued friends, to retire to private life. . . . It is a man's business to consider before he engages in politics whether he is prepared to make all the sacrifices of private feelings wh are likely to be required by his public duty.

This necessity for a clear choice of mode of life is emphasized throughout the essay in many different ways. Courtenay, the author of the book on Temple under review, may have wondered why his own departure from politics was made a matter of comment at the beginning of an essay which elsewhere found little space for references either to him or to his book. For readers of Macaulay's letters, however, this is familiar ground:

> We are truly glad that Mr Courtenay is so well satisfied with his new employment, and we heartily congratulate him on having been driven by events to make an exchange which, advantageous as it is, few people make while they can avoid it. He has little reason, in our opinion, to envy any of those who are still engaged in a pursuit, from which, at most, they can only expect that, by relinquishing liberal studies and social pleasures, – by passing

nights without sleep, and summers without one glimpse of the
beauty of nature, – they may attain that laborious, that invidious,
that closely watched slavery which is mocked with the name of
Power. (68:114)

Mr Courtenay, whose borough of Totnes lost one of its seats as a result
of the Reform Bill, may have suspected a certain irony in the congratu-
lations of the Whig reviewer, and no doubt he would have been right.
Macaulay was not himself considering the possibility of compulsory
political retirement any more than he was contemplating a retreat from
high office at a time of great crisis. His own position lay mid-way
between the relatively obscure political role of a Courtenay and the
eminence of a Temple, and if he gave up politics it would be for the
sake of a literary work differing considerably from the writings of
either of these men.

Macaulay had little time for Courtenay's achievements as an
historian, criticizing him briefly for not having 'sufficiently studied
the arts of selection and compression' (68:114) and for allowing
contemporary political feeling to intrude too forcibly into his historical
narrative. It is perhaps more surprising to find that scarcely greater
attention is given to Temple's own writings, apart from a single aspect
of the *Essay on Ancient and Modern Learning*. Clearly Macaulay felt that
although Temple might have written memoirs and essays – and good
ones – at Sheen or Moor Park, these could not be regarded as the reason
for his leaving political life, any more than Courtenay could be said to
have left parliament in order to write about Sir William Temple. This
perception may have been arrived at during the course of writing
the essay, since in the preliminary sketch made for Napier in
June 1837 'Temple's life and works' had formed the first item,
with the clear implication that the 'works' would be given ample
attention:[12]

> Temple's life and works, – the part which he took in the
> controversy about the Ancients and Moderns, – the Oxford
> confederacy against Bentley, – and the memorable victory which
> Bentley obtained will be good subjects. I am in good training for
> this part of the subject, as I have twice read through the Phalaris
> controversy since I arrived in India.

Temple's retreat, as Macaulay saw it, from responsibility, his
retirement to the delights of gardening and literature, helped to make

him interesting to Macaulay at a crucial moment in his own career; it also supplied a shaping emphasis for the management of the whole essay. Temple's involvement in the Phalaris controversy gave Macaulay a chance to write about an area of literature in which he moved easily and with great personal delight. Finally, Temple was especially associated with the relations between England and Holland, and for a prospective historian whose admiration for William of Orange dated from undergraduate days such a connection was of profound interest. In the Temple essay, as in the later *History*, Macaulay was concerned to demonstrate the importance of relations between England and Holland both before and after the Glorious Revolution, and Temple's Dutch associations were of themselves probably sufficient reason for Macaulay to prefer him to Shaftesbury as his subject. There is also a glance forward towards the *History* in the way in which Macaulay uses major episodes in Temple's life as occasions for explorations of the nature of historical writing and historical explanation.

All Macaulay's historical essays consider the central figure in intimate relation to his times, and the Temple essay affords an extreme example of this emphasis. The times themselves are as much the subject as Temple himself, but his life provides a framework which structures the essay and connects its various parts. We are given an account of Temple's youth and courtship, his early political and diplomatic career, the triumphant achievement of the Triple Alliance, and at appropriate points the background is filled in : the state of Ireland, the leading political figures of the day, the position of Holland, the character of De Witt. This background material is, however, so closely integrated into the body of the narrative that it is hard to say whether it is designed to fill out the life of Temple or whether that life is being recounted in order that its historical context may be described. The light shines on Temple, but as we follow the progress of his career various areas of seventeenth-century history are momentarily illuminated, certain figures come temporarily into focus. At the same time Temple himself is presented as typifying certain essential features of his age, so that the very concentration on a central figure becomes virtually another means of defining the historical moment.

The movement of the essay follows that of Temple's career – upwards to the Triple Alliance, then a brief plateau at the time of the formation of the Council of Thirty, followed by a steady downward movement which begins perceptibly in the account of the latter episode, continues through the withdrawal to Moor Park, and concludes with the Phalaris controversy. Counterpointed against this downward movement is Temple's personal contentment, his apparent lack of any sense that he may have failed to live up to his moment, and his final elderly vanity as he sets himself up as an authority on Greek literature. But beyond this limited ironic pattern is the larger one of the narrative's overall structure. For the detailed account of Temple's career is preceded by a preliminary survey of his life and character which establishes both the main outline of his achievement and a moral or evaluative attitude towards that achievement. Aware of the shape of Temple's life and provided with an attitude towards it, the reader watches as Macaulay conducts in the body of the essay a weighing and assessing of his subject almost in the manner of an experiment – a testing of the preliminary assertions and an expanded examination of the supporting evidence. The effect is of a judgment being continually strengthened and confirmed.

Temple's virtues are presented from the first as being hedged about not, perhaps, with vices – though it sometimes seems as though the reviewer would have preferred this – but certainly with restrictions and qualifications. The tone is always less than enthusiastic, the syntax often hesitant, and the positive statements tend to be couched in negative forms:

> Yet he is not without fair pretensions to the most honourable place among the statesmen of his time.

*   *   *

> To say of a man that he occupied a high position in times of misgovernment, of corruption, of civil and religious faction, that, nevertheless, he contracted no great stain, and bore no part in any great crime; – that he won the esteem of a profligate Court and of a turbulent people, without being guilty of any disgraceful subserviency to either, – seems to be very high praise; and all this may with truth be said of Temple. (68:115)

Despite these qualities Temple 'is not a man to our taste' (68:115); the movement of the essay is designed to expand the reference of that 'our' until it includes not simply the reviewer but his readers as well. This process of winning the audience's consent can be seen at work in the stress laid on Temple's 'caution', and 'moderation', on his lack of 'warmth', his unwillingness to 'risk' anything, and his concern not to 'give offence' (68:115–16). The nub of the matter, in Macaulay's view, was Temple's refusal to take a commanding role and his withdrawal from the national scene at times of peril:

> He avoided the great offices of State with a caution almost
> pusillanimous, and confined himself to quiet and secluded
> departments of public business, in which he could enjoy moderate
> but certain advantages without incurring envy. If the circumstances
> of the country became such that it was impossible to take any
> part in politics without some danger, he retired to his Library and
> his Orchard; and, while the nation groaned under oppression, or
> resounded with tumult and with the din of civil arms, amused
> himself by writing Memoirs and tying up Apricots. (68:116)

The moral judgment here is clear enough, and the reader's sympathy with it is reinforced by the analogy with Louis XIV's generalship which immediately follows. The comparison with Louis is set within the description of Temple, not given separately or even at the end of a paragraph, so that the disapproval it evokes carries over to the presentation of Temple, and especially to the juxtaposed account of his valetudinarianism.

The essay moves on to consider the degree to which Temple was a product of the age. A brief survey of the conditions of mid-seventeenth-century public life serves both as a means of further defining Temple's character in terms of contemporary behaviour and as an historical sketch in its own right. The skilful manner in which Macaulay interweaves background and foreground can be seen at its best in the final paragraph of this section of the essay – a paragraph in which generalizations take on all the clarity and force of the particular:

> This character is susceptible of innumerable modifications,
> according to the innumerable varieties of intellect and temper
> in which it may be found. Men of unquiet minds and violent
> ambition followed a fearfully eccentric course – darted wildly
> from one extreme to another – served and betrayed all parties in
> turn – showed their unblushing foreheads alternately in the van
> of the most corrupt administrations and of the most factious
> oppositions – were privy to the most guilty mysteries, first of the
> Cabal, and then of the Rye-House Plot – abjured their religion
> to win their sovereign's favour, while they were secretly planning
> his overthrow – shrived themselves to Jesuits with letters in cipher
> from the Prince of Orange in their pockets – corresponded with

the Hague whilst in office under James – began to correspond with St Germains as soon as they had kissed hands for office under William. (68:120–1)

'But Temple was not one of these' (68:121), we are firmly told; nevertheless he forms the subject of the second part of the same paragraph, and the structure thus implicitly asserts a connection which the statements of that second part rapidly confirm. Temple was no Shaftesbury or Sunderland, but he suffered from the malady of the age:

> His mind took the contagion, but took it *ad modum recipientis*; – in a form so mild that an undiscerning judge might doubt whether it were indeed the same fierce pestilence that was raging all around. The malady partook of the constitutional languor of the patient. (68:121)

The whole central narrative is rendered strangely negative by this initial presentation of Temple: Macaulay apparently did not want a figure to dominate the narrative, but rather one to give it continuity – a man whose life would legitimately bring into focus certain aspects of seventeenth-century history and certain problems in historiography.

The Dorothy Osborne episode, for example, allows Macaulay to issue what amounts to a personal manifesto on the importance to the historian of minor social details as well as major public events:

> There is a vile phrase of which bad historians are exceedingly fond – 'the dignity of history.' . . . How should a writer, who can talk about senates, and congresses of sovereigns, and pragmatic sanctions, and ravelines, and counterscarps, and battles where ten thousand men are killed, and six thousand men, with fifty stand of colours and eighty guns taken, stoop to the Stock-Exchange, to Newgate, to the theatre, to the tabernacle?

* * *

> That a historian should not record trifles, that he should confine himself to what is important, is perfectly true. But many writers seem never to have considered on what the historical importance of an event depends. (68:125–6)

Macaulay concludes his long and amply illustrated exposition of this point by returning to the question, raised originally by Courtenay, of the propriety of including a large number of Dorothy Osborne's letters in an historical work:

> The mutual relations of the two sexes seem to us to be at least as important as the mutual relations of any two governments in the world; and a series of letters written by a virtuous, amiable, and sensible girl, and intended for the eye of her lover alone, can scarcely fail to throw some light on the relations of the sexes; whereas it is perfectly possible, as all who have made any historical researches can attest, to read bale after bale of despatches and protocols without catching one glimpse of light about the relations of Governments. (68:127)

For Macaulay whatever illuminates a society 'politically, intellectually, and morally' is 'the really precious part of history, – the corn which some threshers carefully sever from the chaff, for the purpose of gathering the chaff into the garner, and flinging the corn into the fire' (68:127). In essence he is setting out here one of the major tenets which he would follow in writing his own *History*.

It was for no arbitrary reason that Macaulay chose to criticize Courtenay at the very beginning of the review for his failings as an historian. The lengthy treatment Macaulay gives to historical problems in this essay, handling certain episodes as exercises in historical explanation,[13] can be linked with his brilliantly economical narration of large segments of seventeenth-century history as pointing to a central concern as much with the nature of history as with the nature of Sir William Temple – or rather, since Macaulay was no philosopher of history, it might be better to speak of his being concerned with the business of the historian. Towards the end of the essay, the long section on the Phalaris controversy develops into a digression on the subject of scholarship in general, providing Macaulay with the opportunity of celebrating in a brilliantly narrated episode the shining virtues of genuine scholarship and the foolish vanity of those who claim expertise in matters of which they have in fact no command.[14] This is, of course, a favourite theme: he could not tolerate ignorance masquerading as authority, and again and again he would deploy his army of all-knowing schoolboys to rout by the example of their superior information the forces of the would-be eminent.

The Phalaris section is handled primarily as an episode in the life of Temple, and as such it serves finally to confirm the adverse impression Macaulay intends his readers to receive: that Temple, who was no scholar, should have set himself up as an authority on Greek literature was almost as great a sin in Macaulay's eyes as his having, without political courage, set up as a man of affairs. But the section also permits the exploration of yet another aspect of late seventeenth-century life and the introduction into the narrative of the splendid figure of Dr Richard Bentley. Macaulay's account of Bentley's *Dissertation on the Epistles of Phalaris* gradually expands into an evocation of Bentley the man and of his whole career as a scholar:

> His spirit, daring even to rashness – self-confident, even to negligence – and proud, even to insolent ferocity, – was awed for the first and for the last time – awed, not into meanness or cowardice, but into wariness and sobriety. For once he ran no risks; he left no crevice unguarded; he wantoned in no paradoxes; – above all, he returned no railing for the railing of his enemies.
> In almost every thing that he has written we can discover proofs of genius and learning. But it is only here that his genius and learning appear to have been constantly under the guidance of good sense and good temper. Here, we find none of that besotted reliance on his own powers and on his own luck, which he showed when he undertook to edite Milton; – none of that perverted ingenuity which deforms so many of his notes on Horace; – none of that disdainful carelessness by which he laid himself open to the keen and dexterous thrust of Middleton; – none of that extravagant vaunting, and savage scurrility, by which he afterwards dishonoured his studies and his profession, and degraded himself almost to the level of De Paucs [sic]. (68:185)[15]

The deliberately heightened style of the passage fittingly conveys the turbulent life and powerful personality of the great classicist. For a moment another window is opened on the late seventeenth-century, early eighteenth-century world. Even so, the sketch is consciously limited in scope: Bentley the classical scholar can be included within the framework of the essay, but no discussion is offered of his even more violent career as Master of Trinity.

It is tempting to see in the account of Bentley a personal relevance for Macaulay himself. Clearly he did not think of himself as another Bentley, and his own youthful sins of controversy could not match the lurid hue of Bentley's achievements in 'railing', 'vaunting', and 'scurrility'. Yet he may well have been aware of his own natural predisposition to wanton in a paradox and rely too confidently on his own powers. At this moment in his career it is interesting to find Macaulay discussing such aspects of the writing of a man whose intellect he enormously admired, especially since the discussion occurs in an essay which reveals other evidence of concern with his own decisions about a future career.

It was Temple himself, of course, who provided Macaulay with the clearest basis for meditations on his own position, and at the end of the discussion of the Phalaris controversy Macaulay returns, as though irresistibly drawn, to that aspect of Temple's life which fascinates him personally. Temple's supporters had likened him to Memmius, and this allusion enables Macaulay to link his account of the controversy to the central issue of his essay:

> In Boyle's book, Temple was praised in the highest terms, and compared to Memmius – not a very happy comparison; for the only particular information which we have about Memmius is, that in agitated times he thought it his duty to attend exclusively to politics; and that his friends could not venture, except when the Republic was quiet and prosperous, to intrude on him with their philosophical and poetical productions.

*   *   *

> This description is surely by no means applicable to a statesman who had, through the whole course of his life, carefully avoided exposing himself in seasons of trouble; who had repeatedly refused, in most critical conjunctures, to be Secretary of State; and who now, in the midst of revolutions, plots, foreign and domestic wars, was quietly writing nonsense about the visits of Lycurgus to the Brahmins, and the tunes which Arion played to the Dolphin. (68:185–6)

The essay thus comes full circle as the central topic of Temple's rejecting perilous responsibility is once more brought forward. The ironic structuring of the article by that initial survey and evaluation of Temple has never really allowed us to lose sight of his habits of withdrawal, but with the presentation of the *Essay on Ancient and Modern Learning* as the final product of Temple's leisure the evidence is complete. In the last two paragraphs Temple is allowed to merge back into his age – his possible free-thinking another symptom of a general malady which affected others more severely – and the estimate of him advanced from the beginning is again rehearsed. Appropriately, the final sentence of the essay is typical of the whole: it functions both to define Temple and, at the same time, to look outwards to larger concerns and to the work which lies in Macaulay's own future:

> But we must own, that he seems to us to sink into littleness and meanness when we compare him – we do not say with any high ideal standard of morality, – but with many of those frail men who, aiming at noble ends, but often drawn from the right path by strong passions and strong temptations, have left to posterity a doubtful and checkered fame. (68:187)

Macaulay was almost certainly thinking here of Lord Clive. Temple and Clive had been proposed as topics in that same letter to Napier of June 1837, and the essays may be said in certain respects to complement each other, the positive emphases of the Clive article reversing the negative impressions of the earlier piece on Temple. In dealing with the life of Clive[16] Macaulay had a freer hand than in writing about Temple, since he was unlikely to reach the story of eighteenth-century British India in his proposed *History* for some time; but the impression of unity, clarity, and almost free-wheeling ease produced by the Clive essay arises primarily from reasons more intrinsic to the work itself.

It is clear that Macaulay had mastered the history of British India as part of the preparation for his duties in Calcutta, and while his interpretations and evaluations of that history have been questioned, such doubts generally relate to the Warren Hastings essay rather than to that on Clive.[17] In addition to factual knowledge derived from written sources, Macaulay could draw upon his personal experience of India and Indian problems, and convey very powerfully the texture and excitement of things Eastern.[18] If the immediacy and sense of relaxed assurance rest upon personal knowledge, the effect of unity and completeness derives from the essay's conception and organization. That tension between content and form which Macaulay had exploited so skilfully in the Temple essay is again sustained, but whereas the movement had then been constantly outward from the biographical line, it is now essentially centripetal, always curving back to the central figure of Clive. 'The subject is a grand one, and admits of decoration and illustrations innumerable',[19] Macaulay had told Napier, but while he did not stint himself when it came to evoking the brilliant background or citing historical analogies, the grand subject is essentially Clive himself, and his portrait as a man of action is quite large enough to dominate the foreground. The major thrust of the essay is towards the exploration of the contradictions in Clive's story, the examination of the causes of his 'doubtful and checkered fame'; it seeks both to present Clive's career and to place it in relation to the present moment, so that the nineteenth-century reader is put in a position where he can take 'a fair and enlightened view' (70:297) not only of Clive but of other figures like him, not only of past events but of present circumstances.

The concern in Macaulay's biographical and historical essays with arrangement, perspective, illustration, and style is partly directed towards achieving a narrative vitality and interest which will make for surface attractiveness to the reader. It is also to be associated with a desire to make the past seem relevant to a contemporary audience – and the extent to which Victorian readers did indeed see Macaulay's historical essays in this way is suggested by G. O. Trevelyan's statement that at the time of the Indian Mutiny sales of the Warren Hastings essay doubled and those of the Clive trebled.[20] The Clive essay, in fact, provides a particularly good example of Macaulay's fusion, within the conventions of a review article, of the impulse to entertain with the impulse to instruct, and the opening discussion of the historians of India serves both as an indirect citation of authorities and as an indication of Macaulay's own narrative intentions. He means, in contrast to Mill, to be 'animated and picturesque' (70:296); to match Orme's 'style and power of painting' (70:296) while avoiding his excessive minuteness; to improve on Malcolm in matters of organization, condensation, and impartiality. This statement of his ambitions is completed by a sketching-in of the outlines of the picture of Clive which will emerge from such treatment – a picture which includes the warts but also suggests the finer qualities:

> Clive, like most men who are born with strong passions, and
> tried by strong temptations, committed great faults. But every
> person who takes a fair and enlightened view of his whole career
> must admit, that our island, so fertile in heroes and statesmen,
> has scarcely ever produced a man more truly great either in arms
> or in council. (70:296–7)

The polarities thus established shape the narrative which follows: on the one hand the passions, temptations, and faults; on the other, the heroic and statesman-like actions – with a secondary antithesis between the spheres of arms and council. Macaulay often seems happiest when working in terms of paired opposites, and the figure of Clive provides him, in that respect, with an ideal subject. The pattern is, however, worked out within the dynamic shape of Clive's life, and because that shape is both single and complete – from obscurity, to greatness, to suicide – there is an effective built-in control of any tendency to excessive antithesis and paradox.

This basic biographical framework affects all questions of arrangement and perspective. Events and figures having the greatest significance for Clive's life are singled out for treatment, but they are so selected as to represent other figures and actions, larger patterns of Indian, French, and British history, which must remain subordinate because of the limitations of the essay length. The career of Surajah Dowlah, himself both an individual and a type of the oriental despot, is illustrative of the breakdown of the Mogul empire. The defence of Arcot must represent other military successes for whose full treatment no place can be found. Labourdonnais stays a shadowy figure while Dupleix comes forward not merely as the greatest of Clive's European opponents but as the representative, in his cleverness, subtlety, ambition, and vaingloriousness, of a whole set of forces over which the British in India must triumph before empire can be achieved. The final behaviour of the French government toward Dupleix serves indirectly to reveal the English parliament's treatment of Clive as a gesture in the direction of generosity, sanity, and the long historical view.

It is on such a view that Macaulay insists as he moves towards an overall assessment of Clive's career. The account of the Battle of Plassy, the defeat of Surajah Dowlah, and the deception of Omichund is framed by a discussion of Clive's subsequent financial and diplomatic dealings in which his actions are judged in terms of the standards which have characterized later British achievements in India:

> During a long course of years, the English rulers of India,
> surrounded by allies and enemies whom no engagement could
> bind, have generally acted with sincerity and uprightness; and the
> event has proved that sincerity and uprightness are wisdom.
> (70:330)

This is the perspective of history, enabling the past to be judged in the light of subsequent experience, and the reader, aided by frequent references to the present situation in India as well as to the past, is invited throughout the essay to see Clive's career from precisely the same standpoint. If the judgment thus made is inevitably severe,

Macaulay is at the same time careful to familiarize his readers with all
the circumstances of corruption, avarice, and treachery which surrounded those actions of Clive's which fail to meet these wise standards
of 'sincerity and uprightness', and to set such episodes as the deception
of Omichund in the context of Clive's astonishing military victories
and his achievements as a great reforming administrator: though
'Ordinary criminal justice knows nothing of set-off' (70:357), the long
view of history may well do so. The essay further insists on the necessity
of attempting to arrive at this kind of balanced view of great men even
during their lifetime, and the decision of parliament not to proceed
against Clive is seen as a movement, no matter how stumbling and
illogical, in the direction of such wisdom and discrimination: 'Such
men should be judged by their contemporaries as they will be judged
by posterity' (70:357).

The last action is reserved for Clive himself. In the great general and
statesman we see once more the obscure and gloomy boy, and the
earlier attempts at suicide are fulfilled by the final gun shot. Self-made,
self-destroyed: the pattern is almost too perfect, and Macaulay wisely
allows it to speak for itself, turning instead to an assessment of Clive's
life in terms which go beyond the personal. In this final survey Clive's
individual achievement is interwoven with the larger patterns of
British history and then with those of world history, so that references
to Napoleon and the spread of the Roman Empire fall appropriately
into place. Finally, even the pantheon of warriors is transcended:

> His name stands high on the roll of conquerors. But it is found in
> a better list – in the list of those who have done and suffered much
> for the happiness of mankind. (70:362)

It is perhaps unfortunate that Macaulay felt it necessary to include his
admired friend, Lord William Bentinck, in this group of larger heroes
and round off the essay with his name. But this somewhat abrupt
return to the present moment, and even quite specifically to Scottish
politics,[21] serves once again to underline the essay's narrative standpoint. It is a story told from a modern angle for a modern audience
who – through experience of past events vividly felt and intellectually
known, and awareness of the connection between those events and the
present situation – will be capable of that 'fair and enlightened view'
both of historical figures such as Clive and of contemporary statesmen
as well.

If the final reference to Bentinck has the effect of somewhat restricting the referential potentialities of Clive's story, Macaulay has earlier insured against too great a limitation of that kind. The essay contains a wealth of references which, instead of narrowing down from Clive to the particular modern situation, open outwards to encompass other conquerors and other empires, to associate with the story of eighteenth-century India the glamour and excitement of other continents and campaigns. By invoking Mexico, the Roman Empire, feudal Europe, and a series of great heroes from Bruce of Scotland to Peter the Great of Russia, Macaulay places Clive in a universal context, inviting the reader to see him not simply as the maker of modern British India but in another dimension altogether.

These larger references establish a network of fixed historical points against which Clive's career can be charted. They form part of that technique of analogy, depending as much upon emotional as upon intellectual responses, by which Macaulay leads his readers from the known to the unknown. In the opening paragraph of this particular essay a few bold strokes and exotic names give the reader an impression of the history of the Conquests of Mexico and Peru, even if he has forgotten or never known many of its details.[22] 'Every schoolboy knows' is here a strategy to give the reader easy confidence, not to irritate him by the realization of his own ignorance.[23] The sketch of Spanish conquests, like the later evocation of Europe in the Dark Ages, persuades the reader by the sprinkling of vaguely familiar names and by the sheer pace of the prose, and so prepares him for an easy transition to the next stage of the proposition – that an interesting comparison can be made between Mexico and India, and that he should know about India as well. For the reader to know too much about Mexico might, in fact, interfere with the effect, since the transfer Macaulay intends him to make is essentially that of an excited and interested response rather than of concrete knowledge.

The weaving together of Mexico and India in the opening paragraph, suggesting as it does a profusion of strange and romantic detail to come, may well have been an element in that prospect of 'decoration and illustrations innumerable' which Macaulay had recognized from the first in the grand subject of Clive; the paragraph ends, however, on a more admonitory note, reminding readers of their strange ignorance of a most heroic part of their country's history. The romance of the subject on the one hand and, on the other, the feeling that Indian history had been too much neglected: these were undoubtedly important factors in Macaulay's decision to write about Clive. Another powerful impulse derived, of course, from his own situation as one newly returned from India thoroughly informed about its history and its customs.

It is perhaps perverse, in these circumstances, to look for further reasons for the choice of subject, to ask 'Why Clive?' as one asks 'Why Temple?' Yet if one does ask the question and tries to answer it by setting the name of Clive alongside the names of Macaulay's other heroes, the men he admired or was fascinated by, an interesting family resemblance begins to emerge. Temple, Addison, Bentley, Clive, and Warren Hastings must certainly figure in the list, and perhaps Bacon and Frederic the Great; it is also necessary to add two men, Swift and Burke, about whom he knew almost too much and whom he never fully treated in an essay, and finally Johnson, the writer to whom he returned near the end of his life. Few of these figures would rank high on a conventional list of heroes. Some of them lack powerful or exciting personalities, while those who display some flamboyance, or careers of a more traditionally heroic kind – Bentley and Johnson, Clive and Hastings – are all flawed in some way: 'there were dark spots on his fame', says Macaulay of Hastings (74:161), and he could equally have said it of the 'checkered' reputations of several of the others.[24] Macaulay set out, not with that surpassing love of the biographer which he attributed to Sir John Malcolm and others whose books he reviewed, but with the intention of painting these flawed or unexciting beings precisely as they were, balancing the good points against the bad, emphazising greatness where it could be found. It is very tempting to see them all essentially as apprentice work for that portrait of William the Third he had always in his mind's eye, a portrait which would give his readers 'a fair and enlightened view' of the true greatness of an ugly, ailing, foreign, little-known, and apparently unremarkable prince. A few years later, Thackeray would be writing a novel without a hero, Macaulay a history with the same striking omission.

6

Biography, History, Criticism
The Life and Times Formula in the Addison Essay

The parliamentary scene to which Macaulay returned in 1839 was very different from the one he had left six years earlier. The Whigs, under Lord Melbourne, were in power, but their position was not secure, they were under general suspicion of exploiting for political and personal ends the young Queen's dependence upon their leader, and they had lost both the capacity and the ambition to pursue further programmes of reform. Macaulay's acceptance of the Secretaryship at War represented, as we have seen, a reversal of a previously expressed reluctance to return to office, and he seems indeed to have joined the Cabinet almost exclusively from motives of loyalty to his party at a time when it was in severe difficulties. His first act upon going to Windsor to kiss hands was not a happy one: writing to his Edinburgh constituents to inform them of his acceptance of office, he dated the letter from Windsor Castle itself. This mild indiscretion was seized upon by *The Times*, already critical of Macaulay's Indian career, as an act of intolerable presumption, and while the incident caused Macaulay no serious political harm, references to Windsor Castle as his little place in the country were to haunt him for many years to come.

He seems, as always, to have taken little account of such attacks but to have proceeded quietly with his administrative and parliamentary duties. The War Office, at a time of peace, did not demand a great deal of his time and energy, apart from the preparation and introduction of the annual army estimates. Politically, however, the period remained a troubled one, and his relative serenity in coping with its tensions seems to have been very largely a consequence of Charles Trevelyan's appointment as Assistant Secretary to the Treasury. Hannah and her husband had come home from India with Macaulay, and he had dreaded the prospect of their going back; now he could hope to have his sister always near by. For a short time the Trevelyans shared a house with him in Great George Street, but in late 1840 they moved to Clapham and he took the rooms in the Albany which he was to occupy for the next fifteen years. On 11 June 1840, after a stormy day in the Commons, Macaulay remarked in his *Journal*: 'I went home with a headache and not in high spirits – But how different my frame of mind from what it was two years ago. How much domestic happiness has altered my whole way of looking at life. I have my share of the anxieties and vexations of ambition. But it is only a secondary passion now.'[1]

On 4 June 1841 the Whigs were defeated by a majority of one on a direct vote of no confidence. There was a general election and the Tories under Peel came in with a substantial majority. Macaulay, returned at Edinburgh without opposition, was not sorry to lose his place at the War Office. On 27 July he was able to write to Napier:[2]

> In India I was an exile. When I came back, I was for a time at liberty. But I had before me the prospect of parting in a few months, probably for ever, with my dearest sister and her children. That misery was removed. But I found myself in office, a member of a government wretchedly weak and struggling for existence. Now I am free. I am independent. I am in parliament, as honourably seated as man can be. My family is comfortably off. I have leisure for literature. Yet I am not reduced to the necessity of writing for money. If I had to chuse a lot from all that there are in human life, I am not sure that I should prefer any to that which has fallen me. I am sincerely and thoroughly contented.

In opposition Macaulay remained scrupulous in the performance of his parliamentary duties. He attended regularly and was able to exert considerable influence on a number of measures, most notably the Copyright Act of 1842. He spoke infrequently, but on a wide range of topics which included India, Chartism, relations with the United States, freedom of worship, slavery, and the affairs of Ireland. In the speech of 3 May 1842 on the People's Charter Macaulay made a fresh assertion of his belief in an essentially preserving process of reform in terms of opposition to what he saw as the unduly radical principle of universal suffrage: 'My firm conviction is that, in our country, universal suffrage is incompatible, not with this or that form of government, but with all forms of government, and with everything for the sake of which forms of government exist; that it is incompatible with property, and that it is consequently incompatible with civilisation.'[3] His major intervention, however, and certainly the one that was to assume the greatest importance in his own subsequent career, was in the matter of the government's decision to make an increased grant to the Catholic college of Maynooth, in Ireland. Having first condemned the Tories for their change of direction on Irish affairs since coming into office, he then declared his own intention of remaining consistent by voting with them in support of the bill, even if the action should cost him his seat at the next election.

It was, in fact, at the next election but one that Macaulay was to discover what his Maynooth vote had cost him. In the meantime, he remained in the Commons but out of office – despite his willingness to become Paymaster-General of the Army at the time of Lord John Russell's abortive attempt to form a government in December 1845 – for a five-year period ending in June 1846. During these years the *History*, postponed but by no means abandoned in 1839, was taken up again with great energy. Before long it was absorbing all the time Macaulay could spare from the House of Commons, and although he never formally broke his relationship with the *Edinburgh Review* the flow of his contributions eventually ceased:[4]

> As to the Review, you must really go on, as you well can, without me [he wrote to Napier on 11 August 1845]. I have made my arrangements for working with vigour and with scarcely any interruption during the next six months. I shall probably go down to Cambridge in the course of the autumn to rummage the Pepysian Library. But I shall at no time intermit my work for more than a day or two now and then. The truth is that I begin to fear the fate of poor Mackintosh. Unless I make some strenuous exertion I shall, like him, be pointed at as a man who began to build and was not able to finish.

The death of Napier in 1847 was probably the decisive factor in bringing the *Edinburgh* connection finally to a close.

The constant juxtaposition of politics and literature at this point in Macaulay's career perhaps played some part in his selection of Joseph Addison as the subject of one of his last essays for the *Edinburgh Review*. There are inevitable analogies to be drawn between the eighteenth-century Whig man of letters and his nineteenth-century counterpart, and the latter could hardly fail to be aware of them. Different though the two men were in the kinds of writing they produced, in their skill as orators, and, above all, in their personalities, Macaulay must have recognized in his predecessor's career anticipations of his own. Both owed their first opportunities to a political situation in which the aid of literary men was sought by politicians; both later held high offices of state; but for both literature remained the major interest. Macaulay's affection for his own college and its distinguished past enabled him to respond to Magdalen's reverence for its eminent Fellow; he shared Addison's keen interest in Latin scholarship; on his visit to Italy in 1838 he saw many of the scenes described in Addison's *Travels*, and his sense of their excitement for a man of mature years soaked in the literature and legends of Rome informs his evocation of that period in Addison's life.[5] At many points throughout the essay Macaulay must have felt, with personal acuteness, the links between Addison's situation and his own, and this no doubt increased his desire to convey something of the same feeling to his audience in the more general terms of an account of his subject's life and times.

The Addison essay provides an interesting example of a late Macaulay treatment of a literary subject and marks, in particular, just how far its author had come since the Milton essay of eighteen years earlier. Apart from the absence of that 'gaudy and ungraceful ornament'[6] which the Macaulay of 1843 himself criticized, the stress on biography and the absence of general critical theorizing are perhaps the most obvious differences between this late literary essay and its predecessor, and sufficient explanation for these can no doubt be found in the opportunity afforded by the numerous intervening articles for recognizing his own talents, and for giving them practice. But other factors also affected the essay. Since it was written in 1843, after the appearance of the first collected edition of the *Essays*, Macaulay was necessarily aware that it might subsequently appear in volume form; and since he was already at work on his *History* he was further aware that its appearance in such a volume would inevitably invite comparison with his own formal historical treatment of the period covered by Addison's life. If he was himself to determine the terms of such a comparison he had to be quite clear about the nature of the genre to which the essay belonged, and he had to make its methods and structure manifest that nature as fully as possible.

The Milton essay had about it very little of the review; it was the brilliant set-piece in which a young man displayed his talents. But it was followed by a series of essays in which Macaulay learned his trade as a reviewer, and evolved – in such articles as those on Sadler and on

Southey's *Colloquies* – the technique of developing a structural frame-work out of direct and continuous confrontation with the work under discussion. In the movement away from polemic in the direction of greater narrative continuity which marked his later career, Macaulay gave his essays more of an independent structure – often, as in the Addison essay itself, a firmly biographical one – but he never lost sight of the specific reviewing situation. Even Gleig, whose *Life* of Warren Hastings Macaulay described to Napier as 'the worst book that I ever saw',[7] still gets some mention in the course of the 1851 'Traveller's Library' edition of the article on Hastings, despite the fact that Macaulay charitably omitted the first two paragraphs of the *Edinburgh* version which had so wounded Gleig's feelings. Macaulay's *Journal* records his decision in March 1851 to remove the paragraphs; it also includes an account of his embarrassment on accidentally meeting Gleig on 19 June 1851: 'he thanked me for taking him out of the pillory – I had rather that he had left his thanks unuttered. I did not know how to look.'[8]

Macaulay's constant awareness of the review article as a definite genre whose conventions he could use both to shape his essays and to mark their distinction from formal history is seen especially in his treatment of Lucy Aikin and her *Life of Joseph Addison*. G. O. Trevelyan, stressing the effect which the likelihood of volume publication had upon the essays written after 1842, slightly misrepresents Macaulay's decision to handle Miss Aikin's numerous and egregious errors in footnotes rather than in the essay itself:[9]

> Macaulay was now no longer able to conceal from himself the
> fact, that, whether he liked it or not, his Essays would live; and
> he accordingly took pains to separate the part of his work, which
> was of permanent literary value, from those passing strictures upon
> his author which as a Reviewer he was bound to make, in order
> to save himself the trouble of subsequent revision and expurgation.

Macaulay's *Journal*, in passages which Trevelyan later quotes, shows quite clearly that Macaulay had not originally thought of making the illustrative footnotes a separable element; their omission from the article when it was included in later editions of the *Essays* seems simply to have been a means of reprinting the piece while yet moderating the affront to Miss Aikin's feelings.

Macaulay, who disapproved strongly of Croker's treatment of Madame D'Arblay and other women writers,[10] found the task of reviewing Miss Aikin somewhat distasteful: as he told Napier in a letter of 15 June 1843, 'it goes much against my feelings to censure any woman even with the greatest lenity. My taste and Croker's are by no means the same. I shall not again undertake to review any lady's book, till I know how it is executed.'[11] His embarrassment was not decreased by the fact that Longman had shown him the proof sheets of the book before publication; on 19 April 1843 he told Napier what had followed:[12]

> I was vexed at observing, in a very hasty perusal of the sheets, a great number of blunders, any of which singly was discreditable, and all of which united were certain to be fatal to the book. To give a few specimens, the lady called Evelyn Sir John Evelyn, transferred Christ Church from Oxford to Cambridge, confounded Robert Earl of Sunderland James the Second's Minister with his son Charles Earl of Sunderland George the First's Minister, confounded Charles Montague Earl of Halifax with George Savile Marquess of Halifax, called the Marquess of Hertford Earl of Hereford, and so forth. I pointed the grossest blunders out to Longman, and advised him to point them out to her, without mentioning me. He did so. The poor woman could not deny that my remarks were just. But she railed most bitterly both at the publishers, and at the Mr Nobody who had had the insolence to find any blemishes in her writings.

In February 1849 Longman told Macaulay that Miss Aikin, still smarting from the review of her Addison, was abusing the first two volumes of the *History* 'like a fury'. Noting this in his *Journal*, Macaulay recalled how she had refused to let him 'save her from exposing herself' on that earlier occasion, and added: 'Even now I do not reprint one of my best reviews for fear of giving her pain.'[13] By April he had decided that he would, after all, reprint the essay, but without the footnotes: 'Corrected my article on Addison – I shall leave out all animadversions on Miss Aikin's blunders. She has used me ill; and this is the honourable & gentleman-like – not to say Xtianlike – revenge.'[14] In the *Edinburgh Review* Miss Aikin's mistakes had been exemplified in footnotes simply because it was not part of this particular essay's strategy to engage in continuous dispute with the author of the work under review. Miss Aikin was no Croker, and her errors marred no one's work but her own; Addison's writings had not suffered the fate of Boswell's. Serious criticisms are none the less made of her in the actual text of the essay, both at the beginning and in the course of the main narrative, and these marks of review origin are retained in the volume version.

Far from engaging in that process of 'revision and expurgation' which Trevelyan posits, Macaulay shunned radical changes or omissions and restricted corrections of his essays to occasional errors and to infelicities of phrasing. He commented in the Preface to the 1843 edition:[15]

> The blemishes which have been removed were, for the most part, blemishes caused by unavoidable haste. The author has sometimes, like other contributors to periodical works, been under the necessity of writing at a distance from all books and from all advisers; of trusting to his memory for facts, dates, and quotations; and of sending manuscripts to the post without reading them over. What he has composed thus rapidly has often been as rapidly printed. His object has been that every Essay should now appear as it probably would have appeared when it was first published, if he had then been allowed an additional day or two to revise the proof-sheets, with the assistance of a good library.

There was no essential distinction in Macaulay's mind between an essay's origin as review and whatever it might possess 'of permanent literary value'. Although he might remove such easily detachable specific matter as the Aikin footnotes or the preliminary remarks on the total incompetence of Gleig on Warren Hastings, he made no attempt to conceal the origin of any of his essays in the collected editions published during his lifetime. Macaulay was in fact anxious that his readers should understand the exact status of his essays. Having always viewed the periodical article as something ephemeral, designed to attract and hold the attention for only a brief period, he was unwilling, even when American piracies compelled him into collected editions, to advance any higher claims for his own achievements in the genre. On 24 June 1842 he wrote a long letter to Napier, explaining his reluctance to publish his essays in volume form:[16]

> But, on the whole I think it best that things should remain as they are. The public judges, and ought to judge indulgently of periodical works. They are not expected to be highly finished. Their natural life is only six weeks. Sometimes the writer is at a distance from the books to which he wants to refer. Sometimes

he is forced to hurry through his task in order to catch the post. He may blunder; he may contradict himself; he may break off in the middle of a story; he may give an immoderate extension to one part of his subject, and dismiss an equally important part in a few words. All this is readily forgiven if there be a certain spirit and vivacity in his style. But as soon as he republishes, he challenges a comparison with all the most symmetrical and polished of human compositions. . . . My reviews are generally thought to be better written, and they certainly live longer than the reviews of most other people. And this ought to content me. . . . What the Yankees may do I cannot help. But I will not found any pretensions to the rank of a classic on my reviews.

If, however, the retention of review features on republication was partly motivated by Macaulay's desire to claim even for his final essays a lower status than the *History*, it was also motivated by reasons more organic to their structure and technique. Macaulay always placed great emphasis on establishing defining contexts for his essays, and in the essay on Addison, as in that on Clive, these took the form both of placing the narrative in relation to earlier treatments of the subject and of making connections between the nineteenth-century audience and the historical events and personages he was presenting. The reviewing situation thus performs an important rhetorical function. The opening strictures on Miss Aikin allow the reviewer to indicate the intentions of his own presentation, while her life of Addison falls into place alongside those of Thomas Tickell, Eustace Budgell, Dr Johnson, and the *Biographia Britannica* to supply the backdrop against which that presentation is acted out.

The most important of these names is, of course, that of Dr Johnson, who represented for Macaulay a predecessor in the Addison field far more significant than Miss Aikin herself. When writing of Clive Macaulay could use, quite simply and directly, the histories of Orme and Mill as a means of defining his own very different intentions – since he was operating in terms of a narrative mode quite distinct from theirs. But Johnson inevitably loomed large across the path of any essay-length literary biography of Addison, and it was no easy task for Macaulay to make a distinctive imprint of his own. Certainly Johnson's life of Addison, not Miss Aikin's inaccurate volume, supplies the standard against which Macaulay matches himself,[17] and it is of some interest that he does not follow Johnson's division of his essay into a biographical section and an entirely separate section devoted exclusively to literary criticism.

To compare the methods of Johnson and Macaulay is to set a generalizing technique against one of deliberate specificity. Macaulay everywhere invokes examples and illustrations, sketches in concrete details, attempts to make the reader hear and see as well as judge; while Johnson, in the narrative portion of his 'Life of Addison', prefers summary, generalization, and judgments interspersed with occasional anecdotes. It is true that at the very end of his essay, in a conclusion which echoes very closely the sentiments if not the phrasing of Johnson's account of Addison's life, Macaulay himself seeks an effect of finality almost in the Johnsonian manner:

> It [the memorial in Westminster Abbey] was due, above all, to the great satirist, who alone knew how to use ridicule without abusing it, who, without inflicting a wound, effected a great social reform, and who reconciled wit and virtue, after a long and disastrous separation, during which wit had been led astray by profligacy, and virtue by fanaticism. (78:260)

But earlier in the same paragraph he had used a description of Addison's memorial to evoke the figure of the essayist himself in wholly particular and concrete terms:

> It represents him, as we can conceive him, clad in his dressing-gown, and freed from his wig, stepping from his parlour at Chelsea into his trim little garden, with the account of the Everlasting Club, or the Loves of Hilpa and Shalum, just finished for the next day's Spectator, in his hand. (78:260)

It is in passages such as this, in which the distance between Macaulay and Johnson is most apparent, that Macaulay's intentions – narrative as opposed to critical – can be most clearly perceived. His comment on Addison's Angel simile puts the matter well:

> The popularity which the simile of the angel enjoyed among Addison's contemporaries, has always seemed to us to be a remarkable instance of the advantage which, in rhetoric and poetry, the particular has over the general. (78:218)

For Macaulay this advantage undoubtedly extended into the area of biography and the historical essay, and in the Addison essay itself he was consistently concerned not merely or even principally to evaluate Addison's work but to bring before the reader's eye a picture, sharply drawn and brilliantly coloured, of the man himself and the times in which he lived. It is thus hardly surprising that he should complain of Miss Aikin's material that it seemed to have been deliberately got up in order to make a book and that, since 'she is not well acquainted with her subject' (78:193), the general effect was of men and things described without 'either a correct or a vivid idea of them' (78:194). Quite simply: 'No person who is not familiar with the political and literary history of England during the reigns of William III., of Anne, and of George I., can possibly write a good life of Addison' (78:193). This conception of the interdependence of a man's actions and the circumstances of his time was fundamental to all Macaulay's writing, and it controls both content and technique in the account of Addison which follows.

In establishing contact between his audience and the story of Addison Macaulay was faced with what seems at first sight a simpler problem than that which confronted him in the Clive essay. Since there is no need to inform readers about the history of a distant and foreign land, there are no initial references to Mexico or other exotica to alert them to the strangeness of what is to follow. Yet despite the fame of some of Addison's works Macaulay believed that the period in which they were written was unknown territory; on 5 November 1841 he wrote to Napier: 'English history from 1688 to the French revolution is even to educated people, almost a *terra incognita*.'[18] In interweaving history, biography, and critical discussion he must therefore supply information, but at the same time take care not to insult an audience familiar with Addison's *Tatlers* and *Spectators*. The essay seems, in fact to presume a much more sophisticated and literate audience than the one to which Macaulay had directed such early pieces as that on Southey's *Colloquies*, and this was no doubt an effect of writing consciously for posterity as well as for the six-week life of a review: one notes a much wider range of reference, both literary and political, and considerable use of classical details, involving unglossed quotation of both Latin and Greek. The intention, nevertheless, is still to build a bridge between the essay's readers and its subject-matter, so that while the point of the narrative or argument can be taken without recognizing every allusion, the account of the relatively unknown world of the early eighteenth century is interspersed – through references to the classics, English literature, and nineteenth-century events, as well as to topics treated in Macaulay's own earlier essays[19] – with evocations of a cultural world with which readers can be expected to be familiar. What Macaulay seeks once more is that comforting effect, long recognized and exploited, of establishing firm interconnections between reviewer, audience, and subject.

As an additional means of maintaining the reader's sense of assurance Macaulay is careful to subordinate the recounting of eighteenth-century history to the narration of Addison's life. He restricts himself to those figures, events, and circumstances which are of crucial relevance to Addison so that everything is brought to bear on the biography as illumination or explanation, or is shown to be the product of Addison's actions or influence. Connections are constantly made with larger areas outside the essay's focus, but the narrative itself remains cohesive and firmly biographical. By adopting this method, and by choosing, further, to place special emphasis on Addison's public life, Macaulay showed that by this point in his career he was fully aware both of his talents as an essayist and of his limitations. He can now, if he so wishes, approach Addison's writings obliquely rather than by direct critical confrontation. Obviously these writings are too important to be consigned to that outer darkness beyond the narrative glow to which he had earlier dispatched those lesser-known achievements, the works of Sir William Temple, but they are discussed within the narrative framework of Addison's political as well as his literary career, and various kinds of knowledge and approach beyond the specifically critical are brought into play.

Macaulay's success in making the reader feel that he knows just where Addison belongs depends above all upon a full and vivid sense of the historical moment. By making history illuminate literature Macaulay seeks to unify Addison's public and literary careers and thus weld into a single account the literary, biographical, and historical aspects of the essay as a whole. His discussion of *The Campaign*, for example, invokes the great storm of 1703 by way of a gloss on Addison's famous Angel simile:

> The extraordinary effect which this simile produced when it first appeared, and which to the following generation seemed inexplicable, is doubtless to be chiefly attributed to a line which most readers now regard as a feeble parenthesis –
> 'Such as, of late, o'er pale Britannia pass'd.'
> Addison spoke, not of a storm, but of *the* storm. The great tempest of November 1703, the only tempest which in our latitude has

equalled the rage of a tropical hurricane, had left a dreadful recollection in the minds of all men. No other tempest was ever in this country the occasion of a parliamentary address or of a public fast. Whole fleets had been cast away. Large mansions had been blown down. One Prelate had been buried beneath the ruins of his Palace. London and Bristol had presented the appearance of cities just sacked. Hundreds of families were still in mourning. The prostrate trunks of large trees, and the ruins of houses, still tattested, in all he southern counties, the fury of the blast. (78:218)

Dr Johnson had taken the same image as the starting point for a fine discussion of the nature of simile, but where Johnson's concern was to connect his view of Addison with issues of general critical theory, Macaulay's was to set Addison's work in the framework of history. In so doing he was able to move beyond his general dependence upon secondary sources to make his own contribution to Addison's biography. Other such contributions include his remarks on the Italian Cato play (78:209), some of the details of Addison's Irish career (78:227), and the suggested explanations for Addison's not contributing to the early numbers of the *Guardian* (78:239) and for his use of the name 'little Dicky' (78:257). Although these were not major additions to contemporary knowledge of Addison, they show clearly that in writing his essays Macaulay was not content merely to rehash the work under review. He was accustomed to 'get up' the subject with considerable care, if it was one of which he was not already a master, and sometimes a new piece of information would be added at quite a late stage in an essay's composition: the passage on Addison's Irish career, for instance, is written on a separate page of manuscript, marked for insertion at the appropriate point; the identification of 'little Dicky' was not completed until after the essay had appeared in the *Edinburgh*, and Macaulay had a note inserted in the next issue naming the actor who played Gomez as Henry Norris (78:550).[20]

At the point when Macaulay came to discuss Addison's periodical essays, he clearly warmed to his task. If there is a suggestion of brilliant evasion about the accounts of Addison's earlier works, when the *Tatlers* and *Spectators* are under discussion the reader gets a firm impression of the reviewer's genuine desire to celebrate their greatness. Even here, however, Macaulay moves at first by indirection, invoking Addison's style by contrast with the 'half French style of Horace Walpole', or 'the half Latin style of Dr Johnson', or 'the half German jargon of the present day' (78:229). Similarly, Addison's wit is not discussed by itself but placed in relation to Cowley's, while his humour is compared with that of Swift and Voltaire in a passage of what might almost be called definition by characterization. But then, for Macaulay, neither style, wit, nor humour is the essential element in the greatness of Addison's periodical essays; what places Addison 'in the first class' is his perceptiveness 'As an observer of life, of manners, of all the shades of human character' (78:229).

Johnson had earlier spoken of Addison's verisimilitude in precisely similar terms:[21]

> As a describer of life and manners, he must be allowed to stand perhaps the first of the first rank. His humour, which, as Steele observes, is peculiar to himself, is so happily diffused as to give the grace of novelty to domestick scenes and daily occurrences. He never *outsteps the modesty of nature*, nor raises merriment or wonder by the violation of truth. His figures neither divert by distortion, nor amaze by aggravation. He copies life with so much fidelity, that he can be hardly said to invent; yet his exhibitions have an air so much original, that it is difficult to suppose them not merely the product of imagination.

There is a dilemma here which Macaulay, with the hindsight of the 1840s, is able to resolve by making praise of Addison's realism into an historical rather than a critical statement: while Addison was writing his *Spectators*, 'Richardson was working as a compositor. Fielding was robbing birds' nests. Smollett was not yet born' (78:236) – but they would soon begin to fill those ranks behind the great essayist. Macaulay, indeed, sees Addison's observations of life in the *Spectator* essays as cohering into something closely akin to the novel:

> Every valuable essay in the series may be read with pleasure separately; yet the five or six hundred essays form a whole, and a whole which has the interest of a novel. It must be remembered, too, that at that time no novel, giving a lively and powerful picture of the common life and manners of England, had appeared. (78:236)

He continues this paragraph by picking out selected characters and incidents, recalling the *Spectator* to the reader's mind by a method he had developed as early as his essay on *Pilgrim's Progress*. The members of Addison's famous club are brought forward, with just enough of an outline of their doings to support the claim being advanced for the existence of a rudimentary plot in the series taken as a whole:

> Such events can hardly be said to form a plot; yet they are related with such truth, such grace, such wit, such humour, such pathos, such knowledge of the human heart, such knowledge of the ways of the world, that they charm us on the hundredth perusal. We have not the least doubt that, if Addison had written a novel, on an extensive plan, it would have been superior to any that we possess. As it is, he is entitled to be considered, not only as the greatest of the English Essayists, but as the forerunner of the great English Novelists. (78:237)

Even if Macaulay perceives more unity and structure in the *Spectator* essays than they really possess and places Addison too directly in the main line of the development of the English novel, his seeing the *Spectators* in this light has interesting implications for his own conceptions of narrative and his sense of the interrelationship of history and fiction. The warm appreciation of Addison's fictional 'picture of the common life and manners of England' was no doubt the product, in part, of Macaulay's own concern to present such a picture in historical terms; he retained, nevertheless, a clear sense of the distinction between the contemporary view of Addison and the great eighteenth-century novelists and the longer perspectives of the historian or the historical novelist. The historian writing of 'then' has a task quite different from that of the novelist writing of 'now', and Macaulay's handling of the time perspective in the Addison essay is of direct relevance to his later *History*.

Central to the essay are its evocations of historical continuity. Of Addison's career at Magdalen, Macaulay writes:

> His college is still proud of his name; his portrait still hangs in the hall; and strangers are still told that his favourite walk was under the elms which fringe the meadow on the banks of the Cherwell. (78:197)

Later in the essay we read of Addison's return to Rome by water:

> The felucca passed the headland where the oar and trumpet were placed by the Trojan adventurers on the tomb of Misenus, and anchored at night under the fabled promontory of Circe. The voyage ended in the Tiber, still overhung with dark verdure,

and still turbid with yellow sand, as when it met the eyes of Æneas. (78:210–11)

Finally, we may set beside these two passages a third rather different in its emphasis, the account of Naples as Addison must have seen it:

> Naples was then destitute of what are now, perhaps, its chief attractions. The lovely bay and the awful mountain were indeed there. But a farm-house stood on the theatre of Herculaneum, and rows of vines grew over the streets of Pompeii. The temples of Paestum had not indeed been hidden from the eye of man by any great convulsion of nature; but, strange to say, their existence was a secret even to artists and antiquaries. (78:210)

The first of these passages uses verbal repetition to underline the connection between past and present: the members of Magdalen *still* speak of Addison, his favourite walk under the elms is *still* pointed out.[22] The second passage uses 'still' to establish links over an even greater period of time – indeed, beyond the dimension of history into that of myth. Addison's experience is linked with that of Virgil's hero, but the physical realities of river and shore make the connection concrete and therefore somehow literally as well as imaginatively valid.[23] In the third passage Addison is at a point in time when the connection between the distant past and the present is temporarily obscured; even so, certain permanent features – Vesuvius, the bay of Naples – remain, bringing together all three moments into a single continuity. The three passages, with their use of particularized detail, their movement from the known to the unknown, are extremely characteristic of Macaulay, and they embody his conception of the relevance of past to present, the continuity of history and yet its temporal variety, far more powerfully than any theoretical discussion of historical perspective could have done.

The reader's sense of the connection between now and then derives in large measure from Macaulay's mastery of the social history of the period, his ability to evoke in detailed and concrete terms not only the literary world of the early eighteenth century but also its connections with the world of politics. He knows intimately the factors unrelated to literary excellence which affected the success of a play or an occasional poem; he can make a description of a particular event into an emblem of an entire political and literary situation. The account of the production of *Cato*, for instance, includes the political circumstances influencing the decision to put it on – the hoped-for 'analogy between the followers of Caesar and the Tories, between Sempronius and the apostate Whigs, between Cato . . . and the band of patriots who still stood firm round Halifax and Wharton' (78:239) – but also a glimpse of the costumes which were used: Juba's waistcoat blazing with gold, Marcia's magnificent hoop, and Cato's fifty-guinea wig. The description of the composition of the audience manages to evoke the actual theatre on the first night, give the substance of the plot, and constitute at the same time an image of the contemporary political situation:[24]

> Steele undertook to pack a house. The boxes were in a blaze with the stars of the Peers in Opposition. The pit was crowded with attentive and friendly listeners from the Inns of Court and the literary coffee-houses. Sir Gilbert Heathcote, Governor of the Bank of England, was at the head of a powerful body of auxiliaries from the city; – warm men and true Whigs, but better known at Jonathan's and Garroway's than in the haunts of wits and critics.
>
> These precautions were quite superfluous. The Tories, as a body, regarded Addison with no unkind feelings. Nor was it for their interest – professing, as they did, profound reverence for law and prescription, and abhorrence both of popular insurrections and of standing armies – to appropriate to themselves reflections thrown on the great military chief and demagogue, who, with the support of the legions and of the common people, subverted all the ancient institutions of his country. Accordingly, every shout that was raised by the members of the Kit-Cat was re-echoed by the High Churchmen of the October; and the curtain at length fell amidst thunders of unanimous applause. (78:239–40)

Again, in telling the story of the origins of *The Campaign*, Macaulay conflates the sources available to him – in the works of Tickell and Budgell, and in the *Biographia Britannica* – into a persuasive and extremely vivid account which gives the reader a sense both of the political circumstances and of Addison's personal position: it is both emblem and biographical event. A brief conversation between Halifax and Godolphin about verse celebrations of the Battle of Blenheim conveys the relationship between the two men in a way that pages of analysis could not better:

> He [Godolphin] consulted Halifax; but Halifax affected to decline
> the office of adviser. He had, he said, done his best, when he had
> power, to encourage men whose abilities and acquirements might
> do honour to their country. Those times were over. Other
> maxims had prevailed. Merit was suffered to pine in obscurity;
> the public money was squandered on the undeserving. 'I do
> know,' he added, 'a gentleman who would celebrate the battle
> in a manner worthy of the subject. But I will not name him.'
> Godolphin, who was expert at the soft answer which turneth
> away wrath, and who was under the necessity of paying court to
> the Whigs, gently replied, that there was too much ground for
> Halifax's complaints, but that what was amiss should in time be
> rectified; and that in the mean time the services of a man such as
> Halifax had described should be liberally rewarded. (78:215)

Charles Montagu, Lord Halifax, is presented much more fully in the
History, but one aspect of his personality is captured here with great
economy. The handling of reported speech for dramatic effect, high-
lighted by the single sentence of direct quotation, is informed throughout by a clear sense of the manner in which one statesman gets his way
with another. The confrontation of the two men, with its interplay of
indirection, is thrown into relief by the specific details of how the
request was put to Addison:

> Addison then occupied a garret up three pair of stairs, over a
> small shop in the Haymarket. In this humble lodging he was
> surprised, on the morning which followed the conversation
> between Godolphin and Halifax, by a visit from no less a person
> than the Right Honourable Henry Boyle, then Chancellor of the
> Exchequer, and afterwards Lord Carleton. This highborn minister
> had been sent by the Lord-Treasurer as ambassador to the needy
> poet. Addison readily undertook the proposed task, a task which,
> to so good a Whig, was probably a pleasure. (78:215–16)

As in the account of the first night of *Cato* the physical details both
convey the actual scene and crystallize the larger situation; the inter-
connection of the literary and political life of the early eighteenth
century is captured in visual as well as in narrative terms.[25]

The Addison essay offers occasional encounters with the great public
men of the seventeenth and eighteenth centuries, the state officials and
leaders of parties who will figure largely in the *History*. Their outlines

are sketched in here, but we see in clear focus only certain limited aspects of their careers. Of Charles Montagu we are told that he is 'distinguished financier, debater, courtier, and party leader' (78:203), but although we are given – in that conversation with Godolphin – a momentary impression of his political abilities, the conversation itself relates, as does almost everything concerning Montagu in this essay, to his interest in literature. We watch Montagu from one angle only, in contrast to the varied perspectives of the History, for it is Addison who stands at this moment at centre stage. A number of the final essays, most notably those on Madame D'Arblay and Addison, are concerned with the evocation of minor aspects of eighteenth-century life, treating as foreground what would only be background in the History. That Macaulay viewed his 'Frederic the Great' essay in just this light is clear from his letter to Napier of 1 December 1841:[26]

> there are many characters and events which will occupy little or no space in my history, yet with which, in the course of my historical researches I shall necessarily become familiar. There cannot be a better instance than Frederic the Great. His personal character, manners, studies, literary associates, – his quarrel with Voltaire, his friendship for Maupertuis, his own unhappy métromanie, and so forth will be very slightly, if at all alluded to in a history of England. Yet in order to write the history of England it will be necessary to turn over all the memoirs and all the writings of Frederic, connected as he was with us as an ally in a most important war.

The authority of the presentation of context and background in the History depends precisely upon the fact that Macaulay has seen it from other angles, knows it intimately, has gone all round it in his mind before selecting which elements to make predominant and which to subordinate. But if the essays enable us to see something of that part of the iceberg which lies beneath the History's surface,[27] their 'Life and Times' formula also made its own special contribution to the whole organization of the larger work, and especially to the handling of the central role of William III. Macaulay had always insisted on the times as much as on the man – this was an essential element in his anti-Carlylean conception of the hero – and on the larger canvas of the History he at last had a chance to work out the proportions to his own satisfaction, to correct the perspective both for the human figures and for the historical landscape they inhabited.

7

Theory and Practice

Volumes One and Two of the *History of England*

When Sir Robert Peel's government finally fell in June 1846, immediately following the repeal of the Corn Laws, Lord John Russell was asked to form a Whig administration. That he succeeded in doing so despite the fact that his party was actually in a slight minority was a measure of the division and disarray into which the Tories had been thrown as a result of Peel's conversion to free trade. Macaulay accepted what he regarded as the relatively undemanding post of Paymaster-General to the Army and, as was then the custom, his entry into office required him to seek re-election. This time he was opposed, but although the contest was sharp his eventual victory was never seriously in doubt. 'I had become somewhat effeminate in literary repose and leisure', he wrote to Hannah from Edinburgh while the struggle was in progress. 'You would not know me again, now that my blood is up. I am such as when, twelve years ago, I fought the battle with Sadler at Leeds.'[1] Within a year, on the occasion of the July 1847 general election, Macaulay found himself once again on the Edinburgh hustings. The opposition now had a new candidate and better organization, and they succeeded in arousing deep Protestant resentment over Macaulay's Maynooth vote and what was regarded as his support for Irish Catholicism. There was also some dissatisfaction – particularly among the dealers in spirits who had vainly sought his support for changes in the excise laws – with the way in which Macaulay's elevated conception of parliamentary responsibility made him somewhat unresponsive to pressures from local interests.

On 30 July the poll was held, and Macaulay was beaten – a result brought about, according to the correspondent of *The Times*, 'by a heterogeneous combination of parties, including the bulk of the old Dissenters and Free Churchmen, the Radicals, the Tories, and the Excise Traders, whose bond of union was not so much superior admiration of any other candidate as a determination to get rid of Mr. Macaulay by whatever means.'[2] That night Macaulay wrote cheerfully to Hannah and to Ellis, but he also wrote, then or shortly afterwards, a poem which expressed his determination to remain faithful to his work and his ideals even at moments[3]

> when friends turn pale, when traitors fly,
> When, hard beset, thy spirit, justly proud,
> For truth, peace, freedom, mercy, dares defy
> A sullen priesthood and a raving crowd.

Five years later the electors of Edinburgh were to choose Macaulay as their representative without prior undertakings on his part, without his even visiting the city to campaign or accept nomination. For the moment, however, he withdrew in silence from political life, refused to consider an alternative seat (though one could readily have been found for him), and devoted his enforced leisure to the completion of volumes I and II of the *History of England*. The immense and immediate success of these volumes, first published in December 1848, scarcely needs to be documented. What will receive discussion in this and the two following chapters are the sources of that success, the nature of the ideas about history and about men in relation to history which inform this supreme achievement of Macaulay's career, and the particular strengths and weaknesses it displays as a work of literary art.

In 1843, when he was already embarked on the writing of the *History*, Macaulay deliberately omitted the 1828 *Edinburgh* essay on history from the collection of his essays which he agreed to republish in volume form. It seemed no doubt a dangerous document, one from which an antagonistic reviewer might select a whole armoury of brash assertions by the young essayist with which to belabour the shoulders of the mature historian.[4] Even if no such use were to be made of the article, there is little doubt that Macaulay was by this time embarrassed by the assemblage of assertions and judgments which he had once expounded so confidently and illustrated so exuberantly. It was not so much that he had changed his mind about the separate statements – many of them repeated in essays he did republish – as that by 1843 he was aware of his own limitations as a theoretician, whether in matters of criticism, history, or government. This recognition is marked implicitly by the decline in theoretical content between his early and late essays, and explicitly by his remarks in letters. Writing to Napier in June 1838 to decline a request for an article on Scott, Macaulay acknowledged his lack of real critical insight:[5]

> I have a strong and acute enjoyment of great works of the imagination; but I have never habituated myself to dissect them. Perhaps I enjoy them the more keenly for that very reason. Such books as Lessing's Laocoon, – such passages as the criticism on Hamlet in Wilhelm Meister fill me with wonder and despair.

In another letter, of February 1839, he expressed his confidence that he could 'dispose completely of Gladstone's theory' of the relation of Church and State, but then added: 'I wish that I could see my way clearly to a good counter theory. But I catch only glimpses here and there of what I take to be truth.'[6]

Macaulay perhaps exaggerated his own incapacity for sustained abstract speculation. He had, indeed, no coherent philosophy of history, and it would be pointless to attempt to construct one for him, but his early theoretical statements are not without interest or importance. The essayist had been the mature historian in embryo, and the continuity between early statement and late practice is usually obvious enough, particularly in matters relating to the actual business of writing history – arrangement, selection, style, and all the tools of the narrative historian's trade. Since, indeed, it never occurred even to the young Macaulay to concern himself with metaphysical questions about the nature of man's understanding of the past, most of the early pronouncements were in fact directed to the problem of conveying historical information effectively to others. And it is as specific formulations of literary-historical method rather than of historical theory that Macaulay's youthful statements retain their significance.

Much of the History essay is taken up with Macaulay's attempt to characterize the perfect historian. At the beginning he roundly declares:

> A perfect historian must possess an imagination sufficiently powerful to make his narrative affective and picturesque. Yet he must control it so absolutely as to content himself with the materials which he finds, and to refrain from supplying deficiencies by additions of his own. He must be a profound and ingenious reasoner. Yet he must possess sufficient self-command to abstain from casting his facts in the mould of his hypothesis. (47:331)

By the end of the essay the terms of the definition have become even more positive and specific:[7]

The perfect historian is he in whose work the character and spirit of an age is exhibited in miniature. He relates no fact, he attributes no expression to his characters, which is not authenticated by sufficient testimony. But by judicious selection, rejection, and arrangement, he gives to truth those attractions which have been usurped by fiction. (47:364)

Macaulay seems to have felt an almost missionary zeal not merely for conveying the felt life of the past but for making such historical narrative attractive. This zeal may have arisen from the struggle within himself between, on the one hand, an unacknowledged conviction – the product perhaps of his Evangelical boyhood – that fact was better than fiction and, on the other, his own insatiable appetite for novels good and bad. That some such confusion underlay his intentions seems a possible explanation for the crude and self-damaging statements he sometimes made about his historical ambitions.

Macaulay told Napier in a letter of 5 November 1841:[8]

I have at last begun my historical labours, I can hardly say with how much interest and delight. I really do not think that there is in our literature so great a void as that which I am trying to supply. English history from 1688 to the French revolution is even to educated people almost a *terra incognita*. I will venture to say that it is quite an even chance whether even such a man as Empson or Senior can repeat accurately the names of the prime ministers of that time in order. The materials for an amusing narrative are immense. I shall not be satisfied unless I produce something which shall for a few days supersede the last fashionable novel on the tables of young ladies.

The ability to repeat, no matter how accurately, the names of prime ministers can hardly be considered a sophisticated test of historical knowledge, and the desire to supersede the latest novel in the favour of young ladies is not a very elevated ambition for a serious historian, except in so far as he might have intentions of a specifically polemical kind. Yet this latter criterion of success was not simply the thought of the moment, dashed down in a personal letter. In 1835 he had praised Mackintosh's incomplete history for displaying 'the diligence, the accuracy, and the judgment of Hallam, united to the vivacity and the colouring of Southey', adding: 'A history of England, written through-out in this manner, would be the most fascinating book in the language.

It would be more in request at the circulating libraries than the last novel' (61:271). And in the History essay he had supported his contention that histories might be popular without violating truth by pointing to the success of many biographies:

> Whenever any tolerable book of the same description [i.e., a biography] makes its appearance, the circulating libraries are mobbed; the book societies are in commotion; the new novel lies uncut; the magazines and newspapers fill their columns with extracts. In the meantime histories of great empires, written by men of eminent ability, lie unread on the shelves of ostentatious libraries. (47:361)

It is in pursuit of a precedent for livelier forms of historical writing that Macaulay turns at the end of the History essay away from the historians themselves to the great historical novelist, Sir Walter Scott. Although he seems not to have approved of Scott as a man, some kind of general indebtedness to Scott's writings has always been recognized in Macaulay's work, indicated at the most obvious level by the frequent references to the titles, characters, and incidents of the Waverley novels throughout the essays and the *History of England*. Sir Piercy Shafton of *The Monastery* (1820) is mentioned in the Croker essay (54:37), for example, and the Nabobs who send up the price of eggs in the second chapter of *St. Ronan's Well* (1824) are perhaps also at work in the Clive essay (70:351); more substantially, there are (as we shall see) obvious similarities between the account of Charles II's court in chapter IV of the *History* and the description of the Restoration court in *Peveril of the Peak* (1822),[9] while an echo of *The Abbot* (1820) during the evocation of William III's thoughts before the Battle of the Boyne suggests that Scott's portrayal of a troubled Scotland may often have been in Macaulay's mind as he worked on the Irish section of the *History* or dealt with contemporary Ireland in his speeches.[10] But the real importance of the relationship between historian and novelist is far more than a matter of allusion and echo, involving as it does the whole question of the presentation of that 'domestic history of nations' which Macaulay saw as having been neglected by the historians proper and allowed to suffer annexation into the territory of fiction. Sir Walter Scott, writes Macaulay in the History essay,

> has used those fragments of truth which historians have scornfully thrown behind them, in a manner which may well excite their

envy. He has constructed out of their gleanings works which, even considered as histories, are scarcely less valuable than theirs. But a truly great historian would reclaim those materials which the novelist has appropriated. The history of the government, and the history of the people, would be exhibited in that mode in which alone they can be exhibited justly, in inseparable conjunction and intermixture. We should not then have to look for the wars and votes of the Puritans in Clarendon, and for their phraseology in Old Mortality; for one half of King James in Hume, and for the other half in the Fortunes of Nigel. (47:365)

This early essay, more of a battle cry than a plan of campaign, makes no attempt to define the ways in which the historian's use of the previously discarded 'fragments of truth' would differ from that of the novelist. Indeed, the long paragraph offered as a foretaste of the manner in which an ideal historian would narrate the early history of England reads like little more than an assiduous culling of the most colourful details from Scott. Yet the declaration that it would be possible to produce a portrait of Elizabeth 'at least as striking as that in the novel of Kenilworth, without employing a single trait not authenticated by ample testimony' (47:366), shows that even while embracing Scott's romantic conception of social history the young would-be historian still kept his most essential bearings. The important points here for Macaulay's own later practice are the emphases on the conjunction of the domestic and the political – the weight of popular life on political event which makes itself felt both in Scott and in chapter III of the *History of England* – and on the authentication of the materials used in characterization. The essayist's extravagance of colour – that crowd of 'Palmers, minstrels, crusaders' and their companions 'the privileged burgher' and 'the degraded villain' (47: 365) – should not be allowed to distract attention from these essentials. Macaulay was always to have a liberal hand with such details, but what marks his own practice as distinctively that of the historian is his incorporation of them in the presentation of major events and his insistence that, when so used, they must be specifically verifiable.

Macaulay aspired to vivacity of presentation, but he was not willing to dispense with accuracy of record. Popularity, indeed, was not for him an end in itself, no matter how brashly his own statements might suggest the contrary, but rather the index of a complex achievement –

the uniting of truth with art in the production of an image of the character and spirit of past ages such as would speak directly to the emotions and imagination of the reader. George Levine, in his recent important study of Carlyle, Macaulay, and Newman, goes to the heart of the matter when he comments:[11]

> The great Victorian Sages necessarily employed the techniques of fiction to dramatize their views and convince their audiences; and those techniques were not merely rhetorical tricks in a great argument but essential elements in the expression of a personal vision. The aesthetics of sympathy, which filtered through the period from several directions, made it appear to many writers that only by engaging the audience could the artist really tell the truth.

Macaulay had himself perceived from the beginning of his career an alternation between imagination and reason in historical writing, a crucial dichotomy between two kinds of narrative about the past – the one vivid, romantic, and particular, the other prosaic, factual, and generalized – and in the 1827 essay on Machiavelli he had allowed himself to wonder whether 'the best histories are not those in which a little of the exaggeration of fictitious narrative is judiciously employed. Something is lost in accuracy; but much is gained in effect' (45:294). By the following year, however, he seems already to have decided that he could not allow himself the luxury of continued flirtation with any fictitious element in history, and Herodotus, chosen earlier as an exemplar of the more romantic tradition, is finally placed outside the bounds of the debate on the direction history should take: 'He has written something perhaps better than the best history; but he has not written a good history; he is, from the first to the last chapter, an inventor' (47:332). Characterizing history as a 'debatable land' – a phrase which perhaps owes something of its metaphorical force to Scott's frequent invocation of it in *The Abbot* to designate the disputed border country lying between England and Scotland – Macaulay declared that it lay

> on the confines of two distinct territories. It is under the jurisdiction of two hostile powers; and, like other districts similarly situated, it is ill-defined, ill cultivated, and ill regulated. Instead of being equally shared between its two rulers, the Reason and the Imagination, it falls alternately under the sole and absolute

dominion of each. It is sometimes fiction. It is sometimes theory.
(47:331)

The vices resulting from the excessive sway of reason are seen as no less dangerous – though a good deal less attractive – than those produced by the dominance of imagination: the modern alternatives to Herodotus had tended to be either arid factual compilations or biased presentations in which facts were made subservient to the propagation of political theories.

This view of the nature and development of historical writing has, of course, a good deal in common with the theories of poetry expounded in the Milton and Dryden essays, for Macaulay sees history as essentially a branch of literature.[12] And, as in the early essays on poetry, Macaulay's clarity of expression and amplitude of illustration go a long way towards making the theory advanced seem coherent and persuasive. But that the result is at best an extreme over-simplification scarcely needs to be argued: what is interesting is Macaulay's reason for positing a pattern of this kind. It allows him to suggest a middle way which will escape the apparently inevitable decline into dullness and argument which he sees as resulting from the increasing dominance of reason in historical writing. History must not retreat back into fiction; it must, however, learn from the masters of fiction how to achieve truth of effect – not through exaggeration or invention but through selection, structural organization, and the management of perspective. By a shift of focus in both the selection of facts and the method of their narration history can regain some of its lost vitality and colour.

Selection, arrangement, proportion, transition – these are the topics which recur again and again in Macaulay's published and unpublished statements on history and on particular historians and biographers, whether he is criticizing Nares for his lack of any notion of 'the rules of historical perspective' and his utter inability to 'arrange the materials which he has collected' (55:272), or Courtenay for not studying the 'arts of selection and compression' (68:114), or the wretched Gleig for his 'three big bad volumes, full of undigested correspondence and undiscerning panegyric' (74:160). Even when Macaulay discusses Orme, whose 'style and power of painting' he much admired, he finds him, at times, 'minute even to tediousness' (70:296). His two favourites, Herodotus and Thucydides, do not escape unscathed. Returning to the Greek historians in 1848, on the completion of his own first two volumes, he found much to admire, much that he recognized as beyond his own range, but he nevertheless noted in his *Journal* on 20 November: '[Herodotus] is an admirable artist in many respects; but undoubtedly his arrangement is faulty.'[13] And on 4 December 1848 he wrote: 'On the whole Thucydides is the first of historians. What is good in him is better than anything that can be found elsewhere. But his dry parts are dreadfully dry; and his arrangement is bad. Mere chronological order is not the order for a complicated narrative.'[14]

Macaulay was undoubtedly concerned lest his own dry parts, particularly in the second pair of volumes, might also seem too dry; on 27 January 1849 he recorded his worries in his *Journal*: 'I feel extremely anxious about the second part. Can it possibly come up to the first? Does the subject admit of such vivid description & such exciting narrative?'[15] But during the actual process of composition he continually gave his attention to the arts of arrangement as much as to the problem of vividness. On 10 April 1850 he commented in his *Journal* on the account of the Jacobite conspiracy of 1690 on which he was then engaged:[16]

> This is a tough chapter. To make the narrative flow along as it
> ought, every part naturally springing from that which precedes,
> – to carry the reader backward & forward across St George's
> Channel without distracting his attention, is not easy. Yet it may
> be done. I believe that this art of transition is as important or
> nearly so to history as the art of painting.

In attempting to assess how far Macaulay succeeded in embodying such perceptions about the writing of history in the *History of England* itself, one must inevitably confront the fact that the five volumes represent merely a fragment of a larger intended whole. Judgments on the presentation of social detail, the handling of major and minor characters, the depiction of dramatic episodes in relation to the larger narrative, must all be hedged about with reservations as to how these matters might finally have appeared within the total context had Macaulay reached that moment within living memory he originally saw as the endpoint of his *History*. The problem is particularly acute in relation to questions of arrangement and proportion, and it is perhaps fairest to Macaulay to look closely at a section of the work which does have an independent unity of its own.

The publication of the first two volumes before Macaulay began work on the second pair gives authorial sanction to the consideration of them as a separate unit. Ending as they do with the climax supplied by the proclamation of William and Mary, their narrative shape has a satisfying completeness lacking in the next two volumes, even though the second pair has its own minor climax in the treaty of Ryswick. There seems little doubt that Macaulay saw quite plainly where he was going in the first two volumes; and although the treatment of events during the latter part of James's reign may have become slightly more extended than originally intended, he apparently did not deviate very far from the planned structure which he had set out in a letter to Macvey Napier of 20 July 1838:[17]

> As soon as I return [from the visit to Italy] I shall seriously com-
> mence my history. The first part which, I think, will take up
> five octavo volumes will extend from the Revolution to the
> commencement of Sir Robert Walpole's long Administration, –
> a period of three or four and thirty very eventful years. From the
> commencement of Walpole's Administration to the
> commencement of the American war, events may be dispatched
> more concisely. From the commencement of the American war
> it will again become necessary to be copious. These at least are
> my present notions. How far I shall bring the narrative down I
> have not determined. The death of George the Fourth would be
> the best halting place. The history would then be an entire view
> of all the transactions which took place between the revolution,
> which brought the crown into harmony with the parliament,
> and the revolution which brought the parliament into harmony
> with the nation. But there are great and obvious objections to
> contemporary history. To be sure, – if I live to be seventy, the
> events of George the Fourth's reign will be to me then what the
> American war and the Coalition are to me now.

As the second two volumes progressed, Macaulay must clearly have recognized that the aim of reaching 1722 or 1723 within five volumes was not attainable. For although he never loses control of proportion and pace, the narrative in these volumes persistently expands to include greater and still greater detail, so that the work which had begun by promising – comprehensively enough – to be a history of England from the accession of James II, with a backward glance at the previous history of the nation, turns progressively into a history of the reign of William III, with just the possibility of reaching forward to the reign of Anne, or at the utmost, George I. No matter how concisely certain portions of the eighteenth century might be dispatched, the eve of the Reform Bill became an infinitely receding prospect, and one hardly needs the comments in the *Journal* about ill-health and the increasing likelihood of an early death to indicate that Macaulay himself recognized the impossibility of completing the design he had outlined so confidently in 1838.

William Madden has recently argued for the existence of a deep psychological need on Macaulay's part *not* to finish the History, *not* to approach the present moment too closely:[18]

> To have realized that plan, to have brought the history of
> England down to the real and threatening present, would have
> meant leaving that 'past and unreal' world in which he
> essentially lived in his later years and in which his preconceptions
> were secure, his emotional life unthreatened, and his histrionic
> temperament free to exercise itself without restraint.

It is certainly true that Macaulay had declined much earlier in his career to involve himself with personalities and events still fresh in men's minds. But his argument then had been in terms of the impossibility of painting a sufficiently life-like picture of men he had known only slightly or not at all. Those who had known Scott, Romilly, even Lord Holland intimately were unlikely to be satisfied by any picture he could paint. He put the matter most forcibly in a letter to Napier of 20 July 1842:[19]

> A stranger who writes a description of a person whom
> hundreds still living knew intimately is almost certain to make
> mistakes; and even if he makes no absolute mistake, his portrait
> is not likely to be thought a striking resemblance by those who
> knew the original. It is like making a bust from description. The
> best sculptor must disappoint those who remember the real face.
> I felt this even about Lord Holland, and nothing but Lady
> Holland's request would have overcome my unwillingness to say
> anything about his parliamentary speaking which I had never
> heard. I had however known him familiarly in private. But
> Romilly I never saw except in the House of Commons.

But whatever the reasons, conscious or otherwise, which may have affected Macaulay's early indecision about where to end the *History*, and his later expansion of its narrative proportions, there is little doubt that by the time volumes III and IV appeared he already knew that the work could never be more than a fragment. Tristram Merton, like his predecessor Tristram Shandy, had set himself an impossible narrative task.

But Macaulay did not succumb to Shandyism in its most familiar form. The 'pre-natal' narrative is remarkable for its brevity, clarity, and controlled proportion, and it is the handling of the early history of England, with the gradually intensifying detail of treatment as the accession of James II is approached, which gives to the first two volumes a great deal of their attractiveness for the reader, and makes them interesting to the critic as examples of Macaulay's ideas on historical writing put into actual practice. When the first two volumes came out at the end of 1848 Macaulay had no reason to regard his task as impossible of attainment; he had, on the contrary, every reason to feel satisfied with the proportion and structure of the first unit of his work.

The opening paragraphs of the *History* have been often discussed, most recently and most incisively by George Levine, who sees them as announcing the essential aim of the *History* – 'to yield all the pleasures of fiction and all the satisfaction of knowing that one reads not fiction but fact' – and as illustrating the 'double vision' on which the work is built, a vision which allows a vivid and sympathetic evocation of the past to be combined with praise of 'the present which grew out of the past by the natural "tendency towards perfection" which time brings with it'.[20] While it seems unnecessary to analyse these paragraphs again in detail, it may at least be useful to recall those touches which establish the structural patterns and narrative aims of the volumes they introduce.

The book begins with one of Macaulay's favourite constructions, the resolved contrast – what William Madden has called that 'antithetical mode of thought and style' which was 'instinctive' with Macaulay.[21] First there is the paragraph whose motif is advance and success, second the paragraph outlining disasters and setbacks, third the paragraph in which the direction of this alternating movement – characterized in a favourite phrase as 'this chequered narrative'[22] – is shown as tending even so in the direction of progress and thus justifying an optimistic view of England's present situation. The pattern of the narrative which is to follow is here established as essentially dynamic and forward-moving, its goal announced in the very first sentence of all: 'I purpose to write the history of England from the accession of

King James the Second down to a time which is within the memory of men still living' (I,[1]). When Macaulay makes in the fourth paragraph an apparent shift from the question of design to that of content – the relating of 'the history of the people as well as the history of the government' – he nevertheless brings the outline of his pattern to completion by asserting his desire to place 'before the English of the nineteenth century a true picture of the life of their ancestors' (1,3). As the story moves forward, and the true pictures mount up, a moment within living memory will eventually be reached when the pictures no longer need to be created by the historian but are already to be found in the mind of the reader; the design will then have been accomplished.

Throughout the *History* we are thus aware of a movement towards an established goal, a bringing of the story forward to a point where historian and reader are one in their shared knowledge of nineteenth-century men and events, and where the *History* itself may come to an absolutely natural conclusion. This point of unity is both narrative end and narrative means, since it controls the perspective from which events are recounted: author and reader both look at the past from the vantage point of the nineteenth century and use it as their standard for comparison, explanation, and evaluation. The initial pace of this movement towards the nineteenth century forms the subject of the fifth and final introductory paragraph, in which, after invoking the metaphor of the 1688 Revolution as the climactic act in a drama whose earlier scenes one must remember in order to comprehend it fully, Macaulay remarks: 'I shall therefore introduce my narrative by a slight sketch of the history of our country from the earliest times. I shall pass very rapidly over many centuries: but I shall dwell at some length on the vicissitudes of that contest which the administration of King James the Second brought to a decisive crisis' (1,3–4).

By describing content and form in this way in the opening paragraphs, and by firmly establishing the modern perspective, Macaulay is renouncing a certain kind of narrative suspense. Although in the letter to Napier of 5 November 1841 he had stressed the ignorance of otherwise learned men about this period, Macaulay sought none of the enhancement of narrative interest that simple factual ignorance could supply. Both in the large terms of the paragraphs initiating the whole work and at the beginning of the accounts of particular episodes, the outcome of events is sketched in or foreshadowed at the outset. This charting of the pattern before the story is told works with the reader's awareness of moving towards an end within living memory to remind him continually that what Macaulay is here seeking to provide is not simply narrative information but rather historical understanding. Any suspense which exists relates to the desire to see the pattern work out. If Macaulay is in any sense competing with the experience of fiction, in this respect at least it is not with the pleasures of fashionable novels, whose attractions consist very largely in satisfying curiosity about what will happen, but rather with the pleasure which comes from the re-reading of great novels or, indeed, great poetry and drama: that of experiencing and understanding events whose outcome is already familiar. The key word, repeated many times in the first paragraphs is not the 'Why' of causal explanation and theorizing, but 'How', the word for exposition and sequential explanation. And this expository effect is reinforced by the reiteration of 'it will be seen' in the second paragraph. Certain answers to the 'whys' of history may be recognized by the reader as implicit in Macaulay's narrative, but its ostensible function is to present events and make them comprehensible rather than to posit theories of historical explanation or to point morals.[23]

At the opening of the first volume it is not therefore of fashionable novels but rather of epics and dramas that we are reminded. As George Levine comments:[24]

> No muse or holy spirit is directly invoked, but in other respects – in its proposal of a great subject relating to the fate of an entire nation, in elevation of tone, in rhythmic concentration, in sustained dignity of diction – the paragraphs might very well be out of a traditional epic invocation.

Macaulay himself speaks of the events he proposes to relate as forming 'only a single act of a great and eventful drama extending through ages' (1,3). And on 4 December 1848, just as the first two volumes were going on sale, he noted in his *Journal*:[25]

> At all events, I have aimed high; I have tried to do something that may be remembered; I have had the year 2000 & even the year 3000 often in my mind; I have sacificed nothing to temporary fashions of thought or style; and, if I fail, my failure will be more honorable than nine-tenths of the successes that I have witnessed.

There is an ironic unawareness here of how peculiarly of its age the *History* would seem to later generations; the ambition so frankly expressed, however, is for something immeasurably beyond a few days' pre-eminence on the tables of young ladies.

As we read the *History* our experience of Macaulay's handling of arrangement, proportion, transition, and other structural techniques, is essentially an experience of narrative pace, a question of how slowly or how quickly the story moves towards its goal, how closely the twin points of then and now move towards each other on the diagram of comparison. In the first two chapters he must, as he himself says, 'pass very rapidly over many centuries' (1,3). The pace of the narrative decreases gradually so that more time is given to later than to earlier events, but there are also deviations from this pattern of movement, as pauses are made for the exploration of matters crucial to the later action – in chapter 1, for example, the English constitution and the Church of England are allowed extended treatment. For Macaulay is not in fact merely sketching in 'the plot of the preceding acts' in these chapters, he is introducing some of his major subjects.

It is tempting to speak in terms of overtures and the introduction of themes, and such imagery is not entirely inappropriate. But it is perhaps unwise to emphasize the separateness of the first three chapters, for Macaulay himself was very firm about their being an integral part of the larger whole. He wrote to Longman in June 1848, when the first volume was printing:[26]

> If you wish to say, 'History of England from the Accession of James II,' I have no objection; but I cannot consent to put in anything about an Introductory Essay. There is no Introductory Essay, unless you call the first book of Davila, and the first three chapters of Gibbon, Introductory Essays.

The themes emphasized, the patterns invoked, even the groups and individuals introduced, all confirm the intimate connection of the first three chapters with the rest of the *History*. In chapter I the reader is given a paragraph which underlines by its syntax as much as by its content that pattern of temporal inter-connection which governs the whole work. The thirteenth century is compared, in a simile of epic grandeur if not of epic elaboration, to the 'wild and barren mountain tracts' in which the 'noblest rivers' have their source; Macaulay continues:

> Then it was that the great English people was formed, that the national character began to exhibit those peculiarities which it

has ever since retained, and that our fathers became emphatically islanders, islanders not merely in geographical position, but in their politics, their feelings, and their manners. Then first appeared with distinctness that constitution which has ever since, through all changes, preserved its identity; that constitution of which all the other free constitutions in the world are copies, and which, in spite of some defects, deserves to be regarded as the best under which any great society has ever yet existed during many ages. Then it was that the House of Commons . . . Then it was that the common law . . . Then it was that the courage of those sailors . . . Then it was that the most ancient colleges . . . Then was formed that language . . . Then too appeared the first faint dawn of that noble literature, the most splendid and the most durable of the many glories of England. (1,17–18)

The points on the graph are here at their farthest apart, but the whole paragraph is full of potential movement; as the parallel sentences pile one upon another the reader is carried in a series of great swoops forward from the thirteenth century to the nineteenth, and made dizzy by an almost physical sensation of England's progress.

In chapter II the narrative expands, and particular historical events and situations dominate the foreground much more completely, although the references to the late seventeenth and the nineteenth centuries are still very much in evidence. Charles II's reign is presented in some detail, and Macaulay begins both to depict the *dramatis personae* of the main action and to make use of some of the techniques he will employ in presenting that action. A whole series of character sketches, the semi-dramatized presentation of opposing viewpoints, the use of phrases of actual dialogue to heighten a concrete effect – all these and many other techniques are brought into play, while at the same time the colourful details of manners, dress, customs – readily and attractively available in Restoration literature – are exploited to the full. The build-up of such details prepares the way for the third chapter's famous survey of the condition of England in 1685, but in the meantime Macaulay never loses sight of the central issues of his narrative. The opening sentences of chapter II thus recapitulate the constitutional theme which had received expanded treatment in chapter I:

The history of England, during the seventeenth century, is the history of the transformation of a limited monarchy, constituted

after the fashion of the middle ages, into a limited monarchy
suited to that more advanced state of society in which the public
charges can no longer be borne by the estates of the crown, and
in which the public defence can no longer be intrusted to a
feudal militia. (1,151)

And it is with the constitutional conflict at crisis point that the chapter
ends: 'signs not to be mistaken indicated that the great conflict between
the prerogatives of the crown and the privileges of the parliament, was
about to be brought to a final issue' (I,278).

Following the overview of the third chapter, chapter IV resumes
the narrative pattern of chapters I and II, moving forward at a diminishing pace towards the double goal of the 1688 Revolution and the nineteenth-century standpoint from which events are being presented.
But there is an immediately apprehensible difference in the nature of
the pauses which occur in the narrative. Whereas in the first two
chapters the expansions tend to explore institutions, issues, or social
groups, the opening out of the narrative in the fourth and subsequent
chapters is often for the scenic development of some crucial moment.
The combination of pictorial depiction of individual men at a specific
place and time with the dramatization of their actions and words is
instituted on a full scale with the presentation of the death of Charles II.
Many other large and small scenes follow, so that the reader as he
moves through the first two volumes towards that known end announced in the opening sentence has the impression of passing by a
series of brilliantly illuminated tableaux. It is no accident that in the
opening paragraphs Macaulay invokes not only the epic and the drama
but speaks of supplying readers with 'a true picture of the life of their
ancestors'. If the tableaux, themselves so pictorial and permanent, do
not seem to detract from the impetus of the forward movement, that
is because each set piece is presented as an historically significant
moment, pregnant with implications for the subsequent course of
events.

The impulse to paint a vivid picture is, however, controlled – here
as elsewhere in the *History* – by Macaulay's awareness that, by a careful
selection of detail, by deftly inserted glosses upon characters and
customs, by the use of phrases indicative of recurrence and typicality,
he can make a scene realized with great particularity into a representative image for a whole period and an entire situation. Whitehall 'had
seldom presented a gayer or more scandalous appearance than on the

evening of Sunday the first of February, 1685' (I,429), nevertheless Whitehall was always gay and scandalous at this period; the richly dressed royal mistresses appear as they must have done on many occasions and the page sings amorous verses as often before; Hortensia Mancini's character and history are presented in some detail, with the implication that while she is no doubt an extreme example the careers of the other women may not be greatly dissimilar; Charles attempts to talk on the morning of 2 February, 'in his usual gay style' (I,431); Huddleston comes in by an entrance used on earlier occasions, though probably for 'visitors of a very different description' (I,437). Many other examples could be given of details which extend outwards to allow of the rendering of a whole way of life through the depiction of a particular moment.

The handling of detail in this scene brings out clearly the essential differences between the methods of the historian and those of the novelist. The similarities of outline and colouring with the description of Charles II's court in the fourth volume of Scott's novel, *Peveril of the Peak*, are too striking to be ignored, although the phrasing is everywhere different and close analysis reveals, in fact, nothing in Macaulay's version which can confidently be assigned to Scott rather than to the sources they shared. Macaulay knew the novel well – he had criticized its characterization of Buckingham in his 1831 essay on Moore's *Life of Byron* (53:566) – and while he was no doubt careful to avoid repeating Scott he was perhaps not unwilling in this first set piece of his main narrative to challenge comparison with the novelist. Where Scott's description refers to a fictional occasion and includes invented personages and dialogue, Macaulay's is everywhere specific: it is a particular evening, 1 February 1685, and although the account is intended to be representative as well as individual almost every concrete item is accompanied by a footnote indicating its source. Scott's singer of amorous ditties is simply 'a young syren',[27] but Macaulay's is identified – on the authority of Evelyn and Saint Evremond (I,430) – as Hortensia Mancini's page, and the distinction is important. Macaulay is here attempting not that portrait of a monarch he spoke of in the History essay but rather the portrait of an age; he tries to do it, none the less, 'without employing a single trait not authenticated by ample testimony' (47:366).

The entire episode is shaped by historical irony. The reader knows that Charles is about to die, having been reminded of this both at the end of chapter II and at the beginning of chapter IV, so that in place of any larger narrative suspense there is the invitation to concentrate attention on details and personages and on the question of the dying king's religion. Nor is the reader allowed to forget how much is here at stake. In particular, the fate of Rochester hangs in the balance:

> To that morning the contending factions in his council had, during some days, looked forward with anxiety. The struggle between Halifax and Rochester seemed to be approaching a decisive crisis. . . . But a great turn of fortune was at hand. (I,431)

But the reader knows that this great turn of fortune will affect not merely Rochester but his brother-in-law, the royal Duke who scurries so busily about his own affairs while his brother, the king, lies dying. It will also affect the king's eldest son, significantly absent from the deathbed. The dramatic crisis of this episode, involving as it does the king's adherence to Catholicism, forms a prologue to the series of crises over religion which will occupy the next three years: it is a poised moment in which much of the previous period is typified, much of the subsequent period foreshadowed. As at many other such moments in the *History*, the concreteness of detail seems to perform a kind of rhetorical function, emphasizing historical significance at the same time as it renders specific particularity.

Through the contrast between Charles and James, Macaulay is able to reflect essential elements both in past events and in events to come. He manages to maintain at this point in his presentation of Charles a delicate balance between nineteenth-century disapproval of the king's dissolute behaviour and the indication of those qualities of personality and manner – not necessarily good in themselves – which made Charles popular among his courtiers and among his subjects. Walking in the park and feeding the ducks does not make a good ruler; concern for the comfort of his courtiers, deathbed regret at having grieved the queen by his infidelities, the willingness to be reconciled to a religion at which he had scoffed in the days of his health – all this does not make a good man. But wit, charm, politeness, humour, and the ability to bear pain without too much complaint, are attractive qualities, and the reader recognizes during this scene and subsequently that they are qualities singularly absent from the make-up of the younger brother. Energy, the desire to make efficient preparations for all eventualities, a concern (even if somewhat belated) for his brother's soul – these qualities are intrinsically more worthwhile; but James's lack of intelligence, charm, and humour are ultimately to prove fatal.

Much of this is present dramatically in the account of Charles's death. Exposition and analysis of James follow in good measure in later chapters, but behind them lies the dramatized moment at the beginning of chapter IV when varieties of selfishness are contrasted and the culpable self-indulgence of Charles emerges as less dangerous than the single-minded pursuit of the unattainable on which James is about to embark. Due weight is given to the irony of James's behaviour: if at this moment he fails to recognize a dying brother's religious needs as he pursues his own political ends, he will later lose sight of political reality through dedication to religious aims.

The episode moves to its climax through the brilliantly economical use of a few sentences of direct speech, so selected and restricted as to take on an almost symbolic significance. James has his brief escape from self-absorption – 'if it costs me my life . . . I will fetch a priest' (I,436) – Charles his moment of personal concern at the end of a life of public carelessness – 'And do not . . . let poor Nelly starve' (I,438). These almost ritualistic phrases stay in our memories alongside certain actions and gestures: the Duchess of Portsmouth hanging over Charles's bed 'with the familiarity of a wife' (I,431) until driven away by the entrance of the queen; Charles attempting to kneel to receive the Host. We are also given a series of pictures which mass together to provide a background for these gestures and phrases: the beautiful women, the courtiers around the gambling table 'on which gold was heaped in mountains' (I,430), and Huddleston, 'A cloak . . . thrown over his sacred vestments, and his shaven crown . . . concealed by a flowing wig' (I,437).[28]

These pictures are essentially narrative in function; they belong with those Victorian paintings of seventeenth-century subjects which they no doubt helped to inspire rather than with the pictures which Lely painted of many of these same men and women. They are seen with an historian's eye, aware always of the significance of the scene and its characters in relation to earlier and, above all, to later events. Every picture indeed tells a story such as no contemporary portrait could attain. Real sitters pose for deliberate portraits at moments of leisure – almost, one might say, at moments outside of time – and although their dress and attitude may symbolize their station and their public or domestic role, they have little in common with Macaulay's historian's pictures. He depicts figures very much inside of time, at crucial moments on which great and small matters hinge, and throws upon them the light of historical irony and of subsequent precise knowledge

135

– knowledge such as no contemporary painter, whatever his skill in reading character and understanding society, can ever possess. This light no doubt distorts, heightening the historically significant details at the expense of throwing into shadow others equally present. But it is precisely to this kind of heightening and selecting for historical purposes that Macaulay aspired, and all his dramatized scenes and episodes are controlled by it.

Sir Charles Firth, in his illustrated edition of the *History*, was careful to represent the seventeenth-century personages only by contemporary portraits and caricatures. These were, as Firth notes in his Preface, the raw materials from which Macaulay derived his pictorial impressions: 'there are few authors who more constantly refer, either directly or indirectly, to engravings and pictures in order to elucidate their descriptions of persons and places.'[29] Nevertheless, the interspersion of Macaulay's text with these seventeenth-century images proves strangely disturbing, for instead of offering complementary illumination their effect is often contrastive. Static and isolated, the portraits lack the scenic and dramatic dimensions of Macaulay's verbal pictures, and without the special light of historical hindsight which he shafts on to his figures the features seem curiously flat. The impulse to imitate the vivid texture of past life is very strong in Macaulay, but the representation gains its power precisely from the fact that it is almost never indulged in for its own sake but directed to specifically historical ends.

Concrete details seen in all their historical significance are, of course, the stuff of the third chapter, devoted as it is to men, buildings, customs, manners, trades, entertainment, and diet. No abstract issues are explored, but the life of England in 1685 is placed before the reader as clearly, accurately, and vividly as the sources and the historian's eye will allow. The details are not allowed to degenerate into mere local colour; each one plays its part in creating a strictly historical impression. The third chapter was the most obviously innovatory feature of the first two volumes, for in it the muse of history turned – as Macaulay had continually advocated that she should – to matters which were normally beneath her gaze. But it is not so much the newness of the subject-matter as the extraordinary particularity with which it is presented which makes the chapter memorable. And its static, surveying form, coming at a moment when the narrative has been hastening forward and the reader is waiting to witness events after the death of Charles, helps to make it stand out still further.

To use the word 'static' is, however, to risk misrepresentation of the chapter's overall effect; for not only is it the chapter in which the doctrine of progress is most explicitly and firmly asserted, but all its descriptions, definitions, and assessments depend upon comparisons – most of them quite explicitly made – between 1685 and 1848. In a paradox which no doubt appealed to Macaulay, the longest pause in the *History* is the point at which one senses most powerfully the forward movement of English history:

> No ordinary misfortune, no ordinary misgovernment, will do so much to make a nation wretched, as the constant progress of physical knowledge and the constant effort of every man to better himself will do to make a nation prosperous. (I,279)

Every detail in the third chapter is selected and arranged to illustrate and amplify the Whig progressive view. In the edition Macaulay revised towards the end of his life even the historian's scholarly apparatus of footnotes became the vehicle of a further demonstration of the continuation of progress beyond the endpoint of the *History*'s original composition and thus, in terms of its narrative conventions, into the future. In a footnote dated 1857 Macaulay comments:[30]

> During the interval which has elapsed since this chapter was written, England has continued to advance rapidly in material prosperity. I have left my text nearly as it originally stood; but I have added a few notes which may enable the reader to form some notion of the progress which has been made during the last nine years; and, in general, I would desire him to remember that there is scarcely a district which is not more populous, or a source of wealth which is not more productive, at present than in 1848.

There are a number of other footnotes, dealing with such matters as the rising population of Leeds or the increased business of the Post Office, which supply further evidence of the progress here outlined.

It would, however, be a mistake to regard the emphasis on progress and the comparative structure in nearly every paragraph in this chapter as intended simply or even largely to celebrate the virtues of the nineteenth century. Difference and change are what is being emphasized – 'Everything has been changed, but the great features of

nature, and a few massive and durable works of human art' (I,281) –
and the continuation of this process on into the future is so emphasized
as to make nonsense of any interpretation of this chapter which sees it
merely as a hymn to Victorianism. Mario Praz, for example, seems to
miss this essential point – the *continuity* of progress – when, in writing
of Macaulay's 'preposterous optimism', he asserts that he 'saw the
epoch in which he was living as the culminating point and justification
of the whole preceding course of history; and the Revolution of 1688
appeared to him to have been accomplished on purpose to prepare the
advent of Queen Victoria.'[31] The nineteenth century marks, neither
more nor less than the seventeenth, simply a point on the diagram of
advance, but since it is for the author and the reader a shared, known
point it can be used to define and make comprehensible the past. The
purpose of the third chapter is made very clear at its outset: it is to
'correct some false notions which would render the subsequent
narrative unintelligible or uninstructive' (I,279). What is different in
the past must be identified and defined 'If we would study with profit
the history of our ancestors' (I,279). But while difference is emphasized,
continuity and points of contact are also indicated; after describing the
wild state of the Border country in the seventeenth century, Macaulay
draws upon Lockhart's biography of Scott in order to observe:[32]

> Within the memory of some who are still living, the sportsman
> who wandered in pursuit of game to the sources of the Tyne
> found the heaths round Keeldar Castle peopled by a race scarcely
> less savage than the Indians of California, and heard with surprise
> the half naked women chaunting a wild measure, while the men
> with brandished dirks danced a war dance. (I,286)

The reader is made to feel here almost in physical touch with the
strange wild men of the Borders at the same moment as the reference
to the Indians of California makes them seem even more alien.

Although Macaulay prefaced his description of the seventeenth-
century country gentry with a careful reminder of their difference
from 'their descendants, the county members and chairmen of quarter
sessions with whom we are familiar' (I,319), that did not prevent the
wrath of some of those descendants being loosed on his head, while
his portrait of the clergy was, if anything, even more strongly attacked.[33]
These attacks served to underline the very point Macaulay was
making: 'If we would study with profit the history of our ancestors,
... [we] must never forget that the country of which we read was a

very different country from that in which we live' (I,279). Macaulay may have erred in certain details, and he probably relied too much on literary sources; moreover, as he himself acknowledged, 'a description, composed from scanty and dispersed materials, must necessarily be very imperfect' (I,279). But the main problem was that many of his readers refused to read the *History* historically, despite all his warnings, and were only too ready to take up the cudgels on behalf of those with whom they identified by reason of descent, politics, or religion. It was perhaps naïve of Macaulay to think it could be otherwise: no matter how much he castigated those historians who used the past in the service of current political strife, he was far from objective himself, and he was certainly on shaky ground when he chose to interpret as evidence of his objectivity the fact that he had given offence to all sides of a particular question. On 7 February 1849 he responded to a report of Lord Shrewsbury's complaints about the treatment of Catholics in the *History* with the following *Journal* note: 'I am rather pleased on the whole with this clamour raised on every side. For it proves that I have been impartial.'[34]

The third chapter of the *History* is the outstanding example of Macaulay's putting into practice his ideas about the subject-matter of history and about the particular importance of social history: praising the wealth of information about furniture, fittings, and so on in some memoirs of Bath written by a certain Dr Pierce, he expresses the wish 'that historians of far higher pretensions had sometimes spared a few pages from military evolutions and political intrigues, for the purpose of letting us know how the parlours and bedchambers of our ancestors looked' (I,348). These ideas about the proper materials of history constitute the first of three often overlapping groups into which Macaulay's statements about the writing of history can conveniently be divided. The second group emphasizes the vivid portrayal of men and events so as to make the past come alive for the reader and (in combination with the social details) attract him with all the power of a fictional narrative by Scott – ambitions most immediately in evidence in the brilliant set-piece scenes, beginning with the death of Charles and followed by such episodes as the battle of Sedgemoor, the trial of the Seven Bishops, James and the Kentish fishermen, the flight of Jeffreys from the London mob. The third group comprises those ideas which are concerned with selection, arrangement, perspective, proportion, and transition: it is this group that in a technical sense controls the other two, manifesting itself particularly in terms of the amount and selection of social detail, the placing of dramatic episodes in relation to the narrative progression, and so on. If one looks closely at the later chapters of volume I and II it is easy to see how Macaulay is everywhere concerned with narrative technicalities, while his success is indicated by the fact that in an ordinary reading these structural arrangements are for the most part unobtrusive.

The spacing out of the big scenes is only the most obvious example of arrangement in these volumes; the alternation of different kinds of chapter is less noticeable but no less skilful. Chapters IV and V contain a series of highly dramatic episodes, many of them violent in their content and bloody in their results, so that James II and Jeffreys, master and man, are irrevocably associated in the reader's mind with all forms of cruelty and injustice. Chapter VI comes almost as a relief; it contains no really major scene and is almost entirely narrative and expository, presenting the first stages in James's thoroughgoing attempt to extend Catholic domination over England, Scotland, and Ireland. James thus holds centre stage for three chapters, but in chapter VII William and a series of men associated with him are introduced: this chapter, indeed, relies for its undoubted variety and interest not on dramatic scenes or social detail, but rather on the characterization of this new and assorted group of figures. For the rest of the first two volumes narrative interest is controlled by the paired patterns: first, that of the steady advance of William, particularly emphasized in chapter IX as he moves with ever-increasing support through the west country towards London, an implicit ironic contrast with Monmouth everywhere apparent; second, the oscillations and infinite variations of James as he thrashes about in search of some escape from a pattern of events that is made to seem almost inevitable – the echoes here are of his father's behaviour between 1639 and 1642, and of his own busy activity to secure his rights at the death of his brother. In these final chapters of volume II Macaulay manages the transitions from William to James and the echoing of previous events with great dexterity, and he so handles his techniques of presentation that characterization, scene, and narrative are kept in balanced proportion, providing his reader both with a sense of movement forward and a sense of pattern. The omnipresent nineteenth-century perspective casts over all the events an aura of inevitability, of advancing towards a known end, which helps to underline the steady fixed determination of William and, by contrast, the foolish inconsistencies of James.

The final pages in celebration of the preserving revolution of 1688 which secured England from a violent revolution in 1848 serve both to confirm the pattern of the first two volumes and to justify the increasing detail devoted to events subsequent to the introduction of William:[35]

> For the authority of law, for the security of property, for the peace of our streets, for the happiness of our homes, our gratitude is due, under Him who raises and pulls down nations at his pleasure, to the Long Parliament, to the Convention, and to William of Orange. (II,670)

Though divine authority is acknowledged, it is on the debt to William that the emphasis falls in the final words of the first two volumes. And if we consider the expansion of detail at the end of volume II – an expansion which becomes still more apparent in volumes III and IV – simply as a manifestation of Macaulay's desire to retreat from the present, we are perhaps in danger of allowing a psychological insight about the man to blind us to a deliberate decision on the part of the historian.

Jeffrey, in a letter to Empson of 20 March 1849, placed especial emphasis on the created order of the *History*, an order which is essentially a literary effect designed to convey what Macaulay saw as an historical truth:[36]

> The vivacity and colour of his style may have been the first attraction of many to his volumes; but I feel assured that it is the impression of the weight, and novelty, and clearness of the information conveyed – the doubts dispelled – the chaos reduced to order – the mastery over facts and views formerly so perplexing, and now so pleasingly imparted, that have given the book its great and universal charm, and settled it in the affections of all its worthy admirers.

Order, clarity, and the dispelling of doubt about the past are very effective preliminaries to the advocacy, implicit or explicit, of current lines of action. And Macaulay retained too acute and active a political sense not to recognize or indeed to seek the possibilities for influencing present action by the depiction of the past. It is arguable that it was precisely Macaulay's concern for the present and his belief in the crucial relevance of the events of William's reign to the nineteenth-century situation which led him to examine those events in such detail. If 1688 explains 1848, only through a full understanding of 1688 can nineteenth-century England select the right path for further peaceful advance in the future. Where nineteenth and seventeenth centuries are brought so frequently into juxtaposition, the examination of the earlier period cannot be wholly isolated and defined as a retreat from the later – particularly when the final sense of shapeliness in the work rests on an order both of content and of form.

8

The Method in Detail
The Chapter on Ireland

To see Macaulay's narrative techniques operating in terms of an actual coherent body of material it is worth considering an individual chapter of the *History* in some detail; and while it may seem invidious to choose one rather than another, the claims of chapter XII for special consideration are very strong. This chapter, which presents the story of the year 1689 in Ireland up to the relief of Londonderry and the Battle of Newton Butler, has a unity and shapeliness of structure, and an excitement of actual event, which make it among the most memorable in Macaulay's second pair of volumes. It also affords, in its dependence upon Macaulay's own visits to Ireland as well as upon written sources, an opportunity for watching him put together different kinds of material, while the record of his *Journal* allows us to follow the order of the writing, discover the points at which various structural changes were made, and catch occasional glimpses of what Macaulay saw as the problems calling for solution. But the overriding interest of the chapter consists in Macaulay's handling of the historical narrative for a nineteenth-century audience within the acknowledged context of the nineteenth-century political situation. Nowhere in the work is the relevance of the seventeenth century to the nineteenth more painfully apparent, and Macaulay's exploration of that relevance has both a tangible literary effect on the structure and content of the chapter itself and an intended political effect on the minds of its readers.

Ireland was the first subject to which Macaulay turned his attention when he began work in earnest on the second two volumes of the *History*. As early as February 1849, before the reviews of his first two volumes were in and while he was still revising the text for later printings, he was already working out for himself the way in which he would write volumes III and IV. The new plan of campaign involved three stages: first, the collection of material for the whole of William's reign, a process he envisaged as taking eighteen months or so; then the actual writing; finally, the 'polishing, retouching, & printing'.[1] On the very day on which he sketched out this scheme in his *Journal*, 8 February 1849, Macaulay went to work making copious extracts from Avaux's Irish dispatches, and during the ensuing months a good proportion of his reading was supplied by books and pamphlets relating to Ireland. But although Macaulay was no Von Ranke, the collection of material meant for him more than reading printed sources: he must examine archives in England and abroad, and he must see with his own eyes, whenever possible, the sites of the events he wished to describe. In August 1849 he set off for Ireland, to visit the Record Office in Dublin, and to see for himself Kerry, Limerick, Cork, Armagh, and Londonderry.

Once the Irish materials, documentary and visual, were in his head, Macaulay found it impossible to adhere to his plan and leave the actual composition until he was ready to write about the whole of William's reign. Having collected, as he noted in his *Journal*, 'a large store of images & thoughts',[2] he was no sooner at home than he was busily drawing on that store for the narrative of Irish events which now forms chapter XII of the *History*. The freshness and vividness of that narrative no doubt owes something to the change of plan. The writing began on 18 September 1849, and he commented in his *Journal* the next day that he would go on for a month or so before pausing for revision.[3] It is clear from the *Journal* that Macaulay intended to have three separate sections of Irish narrative which would combine with English and Scottish sections to form three mixed chapters with which to open his third volume. On 6 October he noted: 'finished the Irish part of my first Chapter. Tomorrow I shall proceed to the Irish part of my 2nd Chapter – then to the Irish part of my 3d – Then I think I shall take the Scotch part – but perhaps I ought to see Killie-crankie first.'[4] On 15 November he had still not gone on to Scottish events, and warned himself: 'I must begin on Scotland, I think. I shall be much vexed if I cannot finish one entire chapter before this year is out.'[5] But although the work on Scotland began, work on the Irish narrative continued alongside, and on 5 December he read that narrative to his sister, Hannah. That it already extended as far as the siege of Londonderry seems clear from the fact that, as Macaulay noted in his *Journal*, Hannah cried and he himself had difficulty controlling his voice as he read.[6]

The decision to keep as a single unit the account of Irish events in 1689 before the landing of Schomberg may perhaps have been taken in January 1851, when Macaulay seems to have felt that a reshaping of some or all of his new volume was needed. He commented in his *Journal* on 10 January 1851: 'Wrote – little out of heart – the events take new shapes. I find that what I have done must be done over again – Yet so much the better. This is the old story. How many times it was so with the first 2 vols, and how well it ended at last. I took heart again & worked.'[7] But he may not have settled on the final order until February 1854, when he recorded in his *Journal* that he had 'worked hard at altering the arrangement of the 1st 3 Chapters.'[8] It is clear that arrangement was much in Macaulay's mind at this time; on 5 January 1854 he commented: 'Arrangement and transition are arts which I value much, but which I do not flatter myself that I have attained.'[9] Whenever the decision was finally taken to put chapter XII in its present form, it is clear that the whole narrative was originally written under the pressure of a single impulse, when the documentary materials were fresh in Macaulay's mind, the settings clear in his memory, and the impetus accompanying the beginning of work on his new volumes at its greatest.

Macaulay had not given very much space to Ireland in his first two volumes, although certain leading figures such as Tyrconnel were established there. But in the final pages of chapter VI he had sketched in something of the post-Cromwellian state of affairs and demonstrated how James II's handling of Ireland served to exacerbate a situation he might have done much to remedy. The paragraph with which Macaulay introduces the Irish narrative in chapter VI is a prologue not merely to the pages which immediately follow it but to the presentation of Irish events as a whole:

When the historian of this troubled reign turns to Ireland, his task becomes peculiarly difficult and delicate. His steps, – to borrow the fine image used on a similar occasion by a Roman poet, – are on the thin crust of ashes, beneath which the lava is still glowing. The seventeenth century has, in that unhappy country, left to the nineteenth a fatal heritage of malignant passions. No amnesty for the mutual wrongs inflicted by the Saxon defenders of Londonderry, and by the Celtic defenders of Limerick, has ever been granted from the heart by either race. To this day a more than Spartan haughtiness alloys the many noble qualities which characterize the children of the victors, while a Helot feeling, compounded of awe and hatred, is but too often discernible in the children of the vanquished. Neither of the hostile castes can justly be absolved from blame; but the chief blame is due to that shortsighted and headstrong prince who, placed in a situation in which he might have reconciled them, employed all his power to inflame their animosity, and at length forced them to close in a grapple for life and death. (II,127)

It is the business of chapter XII to recount the initial stages of that grapple for life and death. The story is one of conflict, and it is organized in terms of the opposition implied here by the motif of Spartans and Helots. But chapter XII belongs in the end to the Spartans, for as disasters and mistakes accrue to the Jacobite side there can be seen emerging from the basically contrastive structure an increasing stress on the Protestant resistance, culminating in the climax of that resistance at the siege of Londonderry.

The story of the Protestant colonists is told by Macaulay in terms of three representative groups introduced early in the chapter – the people of Kenmare, of Enniskillen, and of Londonderry. As always in the *History*, Macaulay manages to make out of particularization a device tending paradoxically to economy rather than expansion, for through these three communities he is able to present in pictures which impress themselves on the reader's mind all the alternatives open to the colonists in 1689. The particularity which comprehends the exact number of inhabitants, houses, and fishing barks in Kenmare, the origins of iron-smelting in the area, the relative advantages and disadvantages of having seals on the coast, makes the little town into a precisely evoked image of industry and order on the edge of the wilderness. Macaulay's description of Kenmare and its neighbourhood although some of its details undoubtedly derive from his reading, dramatizes itself around something he had himself experienced – the perspective of the nineteenth-century traveller for whom this is 'the most beautiful tract in the British Isles' (III,135), where myrtle and arbutus flourish and 'The turf is of a livelier hue than elsewhere: the hills glow with a richer purple: the varnish of the holly and ivy is more glossy; and berries of a brighter red peep through foliage of a brighter green' (III,136).[10] Even the syntax is comparative and cumulative, and the effect is to emphasize not specific details but the general aesthetic superiority of the region, thus giving an added poignancy to the atmosphere of waste and lost opportunity with which Macaulay surrounds every part of his Irish narrative. Description here serves as powerfully as the discursive commentary in other parts of the chapter to remind the reader of the might-have-beens in the history of this Edenic island.

Also invoked are other lost opportunities of a more typically Macaulayan kind. The entrepreneurial activities of 'the benevolent and enlightened Sir William Petty' (III,136) are praised, so that Macaulay seems on the surface to be having it both ways: on the one hand he celebrates the beauties of Kerry, drawing for some of his details on an eighteenth-century volume, very much in the picturesque manner, which he praises warmly in a footnote;[11] yet a couple of pages later he seems to stand somewhat apart from the 'lovers of the picturesque' who 'still regret the woods of oak and arbutus which were cut down to feed [Petty's] furnaces' (III,137). Macaulay does not attempt to resolve the conflict, and it works to his rhetorical advantage, the unappreciated beauty and the unexploited economic opportunity remaining side by side as twin reminders of chances missed and delights unrecognized.[12] It is of course possible to argue that the presentation of the beauties of Kerry shortly before the account of Petty's activities is intended as an implicit comment on that colonist mentality which in its pursuit of material prosperity never counts the aesthetic cost. But this was certainly not Macaulay's intention – he was still the same man who over twenty years before had criticized Southey for making 'the picturesque the test of political good' (50:540) – and his arrangement is specifically designed to guard against such an a-historical interpretation, the transition from the beauties of Kerry to Sir William Petty and his enterprises being achieved through a description of Kerry as it appeared not to nineteenth- but to seventeenth-century eyes:

> If ever it was mentioned, it was mentioned as a horrible desert, a chaos of bogs, thickets, and precipices, where the she wolf still littered, and where some half naked savages, who could not speak a word of English, made themselves burrows in the mud, and lived on roots and sour milk. (III,136)

The account of Kenmare is, in fact, a perfect example of Macaulay leading his readers to those discriminations which free them from the error of identifying past attitudes and situations with those of the present.

The virtues of industry and order prove in the end insufficient to protect the men of Kenmare in their isolated situation, and they must flee to England. But the men of Enniskillen, presented as embodying both the virtues and the flaws of the Protestant military type, find themselves in a more numerous company in the north of Ireland, and are able to move from resistance to attack. Meanwhile it is the plight of Londonderry which becomes the major focus as the chapter moves to a climax:

> There, at length, on the verge of the ocean, hunted to the last asylum, and baited into a mood in which men may be destroyed, but will not easily be subjugated, the imperial race turned desperately to bay. (III,163)

The activities of the Enniskilliners are slightly underplayed, and the Battle of Newton Butler becomes an appendix to the greater symbolic triumph of the breaking of the boom and the relief of Londonderry – a pointer to the ultimate defeat of James rather than something to be insisted upon in its own right. Another and greater battle is, after all, in store when William himself comes to lead his troops at the Boyne.

Although Macaulay touches in various characteristics of the Protestant colonists so as to make comprehensible the events at Kenmare and Enniskillen, their main portrayal is reserved for that part of the chapter which deals with the siege of Londonderry. The introduction of a generalized characterization at this point supplies added weight to the account of the climactic struggle, while the actual details of that struggle itself serve to extend and illustrate the characterization. The long paragraph which depicts the defenders of the city is framed by opening and closing reminders of their plight: 'And now Londonderry was left destitute of all military and of all civil government. No man in the town had a right to command any other: the defences were weak: the provisions were scanty: an incensed tyrant and a great army were at the gates' (III,192). Thus the opening; the close is a variation of the same statements, so that while the intervening sentences take account of both virtues and vices it is on virtue in adversity that the stress naturally falls.

Macaulay was very much aware of the difficulty of balancing the good against the bad in his account of the men of Londonderry, confiding to his *Journal* on 10 October 1849 that 'the character of dominant castes' was 'a difficult & ticklish subject'.[13] When faced with the problem of definition or explanation Macaulay's instinct was to be illustrative and analogical rather than analytic, and on this occasion he moves outwards from the inhabitants of Londonderry to a wider characterization of colonists and aristocracies of race in general; the behaviour of the seventeenth-century Irish Protestants can thus be seen as exemplifying a general mode of human behaviour. From a reference to the arrogance of the Protestant colonists as having 'something of the Castilian haughtiness of manner' (III,193),[14] Macaulay shifts to a description of the customary virtues and vices of dominant castes in a manner reminiscent of his Clive essay, and especially of its presentation of Clive's deviation from the ruler's code in his treatment of Omichund: 'The member of a dominant race is, in his dealings with the subject race, seldom indeed fraudulent, – for fraud is the resource of the weak, – but imperious, insolent, and cruel' (III,193). Moving still further outwards, Macaulay proceeds to a more extensively developed analogy between the colonists and the Spartans – an analogy which on its brief introduction into the prefatory passage in chapter VI had looked like a piece of isolated ingenuity, but which here takes its place as part of an ordered sequence, a related set forming almost a grammar of imperialism. In such passages of Macaulay's each item in the series illuminates the others without coalescing with them; comparative placing stresses individuality even as it intensifies the sense of the qualities shared. The inhabitants of Londonderry are not Spartans, and no one sits 'calmly dressing his hair' (III,194); nevertheless something of the aura of Thermopylae surrounds the Irish city.

Through the alternation of good and evil in Spartan behaviour when viewed from different angles, Macaulay is able to remind his readers of the mixture of 'tyrant and hero' (III,194) in the Irish colonists; he can also glance forward to the manifestations of tyranny in 'the hateful laws which, within the memory of men still living, disgraced the Irish statute book', and to the continuation of tyranny into the present day, when it still 'sometimes breaks out in excesses pernicious to the commonwealth and dishonourable to the Protestant religion' (III,194). The nineteenth-century perspective which governs the whole paragraph is here made explicit in advance of a return to the specific situation of the inhabitants of Londonderry, governorless, isolated, besieged.

Macaulay dramatizes that situation for the reader in terms of items as precise and varied as the exact number of clergymen within the walls and the positioning of particular pieces of artillery. Even the nineteenth-century perspective is transformed into something concrete by the insistence on the survival not only of memories but of actual physical fragments:[15]

> Several boats full of stones were sunk. A row of stakes was driven into the bottom of the river. Large pieces of fir wood, strongly bound together, formed a boom which was more than a quarter of a mile in length, and which was firmly fastened to both shores, by cables a foot thick. A huge stone, to which the cable on the left bank was attached, was removed many years later, for the purpose of being polished and shaped into a column. But the intention was abandoned, and the rugged mass still lies, not many yards from its original site, amidst the shades which surround a pleasant country house named Boom Hall. Hard by is the well from which the besiegers drank. A little further off is the burial ground where they laid their slain, and where even in our own time the spade of the gardener has struck upon many sculls and thighbones at a short distance beneath the turf and flowers. (III,200–1)

One can argue for symbolic meaning in a passage such as this, for an intention to establish the turf and flowers beneath which skulls and thighbones lie as an image of nineteenth-century Ireland, a companion to that metaphor in chapter VI of the 'thin crust of ashes, beneath which the lava is still glowing' (II,127). But Macaulay's major intention was less metaphorical; he wanted, by the invocation of actual objects, to make of the past something immediately tangible to his readers. For Macaulay himself physical objects surviving from the past had a very powerful effect, and the daydreaming out loud in which he indulged for the entertainment of his sisters, and later of his nephews and nieces, often took the form of peopling the buildings and streets of London and the cathedral and university cities of England with the men and women who had walked there in earlier times.[16] Again and again Macaulay seeks in his descriptive passages not merely a visual effect designed to make his readers see, but this extra tactile quality as well. The events of the siege of Londonderry, which Macaulay had earlier connected with colonial situations at many times and places in the continuum of world history, are here quite specifically linked through surviving material objects with the actual moment of writing.

The employment of physical detail in this chapter is one of its most notable features. Such detail is not used exclusively to establish continuities and connections; some of it serves rather to emphasize the special and distinctive horror of these events, and in particular of life within the beleaguered city at a time when 'Dogs, fattened on the blood of the slain', were considered a precious source of food, so that 'The price of a whelp's paw was five shillings and sixpence' (III,233),[17] and when the black humour of desperate men spoke of 'First the horses and hides; and then the prisoners; and then each other' (III,234). The details are more than lurid colours for the portraiture of horror; they are emblems both of Protestant sufferings at that moment and of the emotions underlying subsequent Protestant oppression. They are, in fact, the emotional counters with which Macaulay evokes a moral response to Irish history before and after 1689, and even to events in the future – onward from 1855 – should nothing be done to change matters. Macaulay wants his readers to see the sufferings, feel the horrors, and hence to understand imaginatively; but he also wants them to understand morally, to judge, and then to act in the present by choosing wisely among contemporary political alternatives. The significance of Londonderry as symbolic memorial is pointed very clearly near the end of the chapter: 'the whole city is to this day a monument of the great deliverance' (III,239). But Macaulay insists that his readers look forward as well as back, that they 'respect the sentiment which indicates itself by these tokens', yet recognize that 'it is impossible for the moralist or the statesman to look with unmixed complacency on the solemnities with which Londonderry commemorates her deliverance' – for 'Unhappily the animosities of her brave champions have descended with their glory' (III,240–1). Moral responsibility for attempting to change matters had rested in the 1680s with James II; in the 1850s it rested with the English electorate and their chosen government.

The use of physical details with moral potentiality is perhaps even clearer in the accounts of the marauding rabble of Catholic peasants than it is in the description of the siege of Londonderry itself. It is on the contrast between the two kinds of horror that the narrative is balanced, and from the reader's experience of the contrast that understanding is intended to emerge. The descriptions of anarchy and destruction take their place in a context prepared by comments, earlier in this chapter and in chapter VI, designed to indicate the injustice of a situation in which almost all the power and property in

Ireland was in the hands of a tiny minority, while the majority were driven towards violence by neglect, injustice, persecution, incitement, ignorance, and, above all, by the failure of the government designated by James to actually govern. In 1688 'the two infuriated castes were alike convinced that it was necessary to oppress or to be oppressed, and that there could be no safety but in victory, vengeance, and dominion' (III,134).

To understand the behaviour of the Catholic majority is not, however, to excuse it. If Macaulay intends his readers to know the causes of the destruction, and its actual effect, he also intends them to feel disgust at wanton violence and the breakdown of civilized order. A long paragraph is given to the destruction of property by the Rapparees. Beginning with general comments from various sources, it moves through valuables like silver to 'the chief riches of Ireland' (III,158), her cattle and sheep:

> The freebooters who now overspread the country belonged to a class which was accustomed to live on potatoes and sour whey, and which had always regarded meat as a luxury reserved for the rich. These men at first revelled in beef and mutton, as the savage invaders, who of old poured down from the forests of the north on Italy, revelled in Massic and Falernian wines. The Protestants described with contemptuous disgust the strange gluttony of their newly liberated slaves. The carcasses, half raw and half burned to cinders, sometimes still bleeding, sometimes in a state of loathsome decay, were torn to pieces and swallowed without salt, bread, or herbs. (III,158–9)

Although this passage is clearly intended to evoke in its readers a moral revulsion based on physical disgust, the revulsion is not intended to be a blanket response of unthinking horror at the behaviour of the freebooters. Their conduct is partly explained by the comparison with that of the Goths and Vandals in Italy and is presented initially in terms of the latter's relatively harmless revelling in Massic and Falernian wines. The 'contemptuous disgust' of the Protestant onlookers at the actions of their 'newly liberated slaves' serves, when invoked at this point, to emphasize the responsibility of those Protestants for much of the disaster now overtaking them; racial scorn and the enslavement it produced and throve on must share the blame for the eventual revolution. But Macaulay does not pause here; he goes straight on to the nauseating description of slaughter and gluttony, and thus in some measure explains the scorn of the Protestants. Even so, the reader's disapproval is intended to be discriminated from theirs, and indeed to encompass masters as well as slaves. The paragraph continues with illustrations from a Grub Street play and with details of cows killed for the sake of a pair of brogues and sheep slaughtered for their fleeces while 'the bodies were left to poison the air' (III,159), and although the horror is framed, at the end of the paragraph as at the beginning, by material of a statistical and hence less emotional kind, the poison in the Irish air permeates the whole chapter. That spreading poison – whether emanating from the slaughtered sheep of Kerry or the rotting bodies inside the walls of Londonderry – has by no means been entirely dispelled by 1855.

The details thus exploited to evoke an emotional and moral response also serve to fill out the background of major events, and, as instances of the kind of material the muse of history had so often considered to be beneath her notice, they form an important element in what might be called the Third-Chapter strand running through the *History* as a whole. The same double function can be observed in other social details in the chapter. In the description of the natural scenery of Kerry, or of the streets and buildings of Cork, Macaulay is painting in the background of the action, but out of the contrasts between the seventeenth and nineteenth centuries, and the continuities linking those centuries, he forms a composite image which functions in temporal as well as spatial terms. *Then* things were so, *now* they are thus, but these particular things continue *still* the same. Thus Macaulay fixes the points on the graph of time, giving the reader not one picture but two, superimposed one upon the other; the superimposition makes it possible to experience the samenesses and the differences all the more sharply, and it is the result of the comparison rather than the pictorial details themselves which takes on a quasi-symbolic force.

It is of some interest in this connection to compare the description of Cork in the *History* (III,171–2) with the impressions which Macaulay set down in his *Journal* during his visit to the city in August 1849:[18]

> I now paced exactly the limits of the old walled town – the two channels N. & S. On the east the Grand Parade – on the West Duncan Street, once Grattan Street – Main Street runs through the middle & has a bridge at each end. It was the only street of the old city in wh two cars could cross – From it to

right & left branched off & still branch off a succession of lanes
miserable beyond the most miserable closes of London – noisome
to the scent, though mine has not of late been a very fine scent,
& to the eye of an Englishman insupportable. One of them is
called – & by comparison justly – Broad Lane – a viler place than
the vilest in Spitalfields – perhaps 10 feet wide – On the site of
some hideous labyrinths of burrows of this sort has now been
built Gt George's Street – a stately handsome street of red brick –
handsome shops – and a Court House really worthy to have
stood in the Forum of Rome or to be now a palace at Paris. I
have not seen a finer Corinthian Portico.

All the elements of this preliminary sketch, from the smells to the
Corinthian portico, are used in the final version. In the *History* the
nineteenth-century perspective and the contrasts between then and
now are insisted upon at the outset – 'We should greatly err if we
imagined that the road by which he [James] entered that city bore any
resemblance to the stately approach which strikes the traveller of the
nineteenth century with admiration' (III,171) – but the note of progress
thus sounded at the opening modulates by the close into a reminder of
the persistence in the noisome alleys of Cork of conditions worse than
anything to be found in nineteenth-century England.

A much simpler use of social detail can be seen, in this chapter, in
the presentation of certain minor figures: Sir William Temple in
retreat with his books, tulips and pineapples; Richard Hamilton, with
his family of Restoration wits and beauties, and his own past successes
at the Court of France, bringing briefly into the narrative of Irish
events the careless gaiety and immorality of the courts of Charles II
and Versailles. The contrast with the Irish agony is not stressed, but it
emerges powerfully none the less:

The long fair ringlets, the radiant bloom, and the languishing
blue eyes of the lovely Elizabeth still charm us on the canvass of
Lely. . . . One of her brothers, Anthony, became the chronicler
of that brilliant and dissolute society of which he had been one
of the most brilliant and most dissolute members. . . . Another
brother, named Richard, had, in foreign service, gained some
military experience. His wit and politeness had distinguished
him even in the splendid circle of Versailles. It was whispered that
he had dared to lift his eyes to an exalted lady, the natural
daughter of the Great King, the wife of a legitimate prince of the

House of Bourbon, and that she had not seemed to be displeased by the attentions of her presumptuous admirer. (III,151)

It is from the comforts and the artificiality of the Court of France that James and Avaux have come to Ireland. Not for them the starvation of Londonderry or the bleeding steaks of the freebooters, but certainly a discomfort made acute by contrast with the life to which they are accustomed:

> At Charlemont a bag of oatmeal was with great difficulty, and as a matter of favour, procured for the French legation. There was no wheaten bread except at the table of the King, who had brought a little flour from Dublin, and to whom Avaux had lent a servant who knew how to bake. Those who were honoured with an invitation to the royal table had their bread and wine measured out to them. Every body else, however high in rank, ate horsecorn, and drank water or detestable beer, made with oats instead of barley, and flavoured with some nameless herb as a substitute for hops. (III,184)

This is not the hardship of Londonderry – and the comparison, though implicit throughout, is never stated – but it is poor fare for a king. It is, moreover, the best that an Ireland ravaged by her own population can offer.

The details are striking, but they are not – considering Macaulay's memory and his reputation as an innovator and practitioner of social history – especially numerous. Nor, clearly, are they provided simply to fill out the background, enliven the story, or enrich the social texture. It is tempting, in fact, to regard them as symbolic; and if that term overstates the case it seems at least to point in the right direction. Sir William Temple grew many things besides pineapples and tulips, but it would be hard to better those products as emblems of a certain kind of Epicureanism, very English in its modesty and very seventeenth-century in the specific objects of its delight. James's followers had greater hardships to suffer than the doling out of bread and wine at his table, but the particular indignity serves to image, and in a deliberately unspectacular manner, the predicament to which a great monarch had reduced himself by his own folly. As a young essayist, Macaulay had a wonderful eye for the telling detail. If the details in the volumes of 1855 tend to be less flashy than those of earlier years, the eye has lost none of its sharpness: its perceptions, moreover, are now reinforced by a much greater awareness of the didactic potential such details may possess. Macaulay came to regard the mass of social data neglected by earlier historians as a source, not of colourful material to be lavishly applied whenever it would diversify the narrative, but rather of particular discriminated touches which would enforce and extend his account of events and, at the same time, serve as a kind of notation for moral judgment and emotional response. His success in selecting and applying such touches throughout the chapter on Ireland is one of many justifications for the feeling Macaulay recorded in his *Journal* after reading the first draft to his sister, Hannah: 'if I ever wrote well, I have done so here.'[19]

The peculiar intensity with which Macaulay thought and wrote about Irish affairs can be directly related to the frequency with which the condition of Ireland was debated in the House of Commons throughout the nineteenth century and to the recurrent onsets of misery and strife by which those debates were prompted. Macaulay himself spoke frequently on Irish subjects. During his political apprenticeship in the early 1830s he found himself somewhat uncomfortably attempting to reconcile Whig principles of individual liberty and the sacredness of constitutional rights with the Whig government's recourse to the same kind of repressive measures as successive governments of all parties had adopted to deal with Irish disorders.[20] By the 1840s Macaulay's knowledge of Irish history had deepened, his awareness of the problem inherent in the dominance of one race over another had been sharpened by the experience of India, and, after August 1841, he enjoyed for a few years the freedom of the opposite benches, from which pleas for historical perspective and for long-term solutions could be more easily voiced. Although as committed as ever to the maintenance of the Union, Macaulay now expressed strong support for other measures designed to remove some of the grievances of the Catholic majority in Ireland. He supported the bill to increase government financial aid to the Catholic college at Maynooth, and looked forward to the disestablishment of the Irish Church, assuring parliament in April 1845: 'of all the institutions now existing in the civilised world, the Established Church of Ireland seems to me the most absurd.'[21] Macaulay had a peculiar horror of the violent bigotry which too often characterized the demands of the Ulster Protestants and their supporters in parliament, and his most famous speech on Ireland contained a powerful denunciation of Peel for pandering, when out of office, to the prejudices he found it necessary to control once he was in power:[22]

All those fierce spirits, whom you hallooed on to harass us, now
turn round and begin to worry you. The Orangeman raises his
war-whoop: Exeter Hall sets up its bray: Mr. MacNeile shudders
to see more costly cheer than ever provided for the priests of
Baal at the table of the Queen; and the Protestant Operatives of
Dublin call for impeachments in exceedingly bad English. But
what did you expect? Did you think, when, to serve your turn,
you called the Devil up, that it was as easy to lay him as to raise
him? Did you think, when you went on, session after session,
thwarting and reviling those whom you knew to be in the right,
and flattering all the worst passions of those whom you knew to
be in the wrong, that the day of reckoning would never come?
It has come. There you sit, doing penance for the disingenuousness
of years. If it be not so, stand up manfully, and clear your fame
before the House and the country.

Macaulay himself refused to make concessions to bigotry for political
advantage; his speeches on Ireland, when in and when out of office,
gave little pleasure to the Edinburgh electorate, and, as we have seen,
they undoubtedly contributed to his 1847 defeat. He was, indeed, no
more prepared to appease anti-Catholic prejudice among his Scottish
constituents than among his London neighbours, meting out much the
same kind of high-handed treatment to those who urged him to
belabour the Catholics in parliament as to those who wanted him to
make a Guy Fawkes address in the streets near the Albany. This latter
visitation Macaulay recorded in his *Journal* for 22 November 1850
and reported in a letter to Ellis of the same date: 'I have just had a
deputation of my parish here begging me to go and make a Guy Faux
harangue tonight. I sent them away wiser than they came, which is
not saying much. However they will, I believe, abstain from demanding of the Queen a repeal of the Emancipation Act and a general
persecution of Papists.'[23]
His personal religious indifference no doubt made it easier for
Macaulay to give support to Catholic rights; his position was, however, firmly based on intellectual conviction, on moral principle, and
on common sense. His belief in individual freedom of conscience and
in the non-interference of the state in matters of religion had found
public expression as early as the Southey essay,[24] and he recognized the
folly of seeking to govern peaceably a people whose religious suscepti-
bilities you were constantly offending. Yet it is clear that behind these

intellectually controlled attitudes there lay an emotional distaste for Catholicism itself. Catholicism, while occasionally delighting Macaulay's sensibility by its richness, offended his rationalism by its element of mystery and by what he considered to be its demand for blind faith in its dogmas, and although he could justify his distaste to himself as a libertarian dislike of absolutism, or as an historian's judgment that the Catholic church had proved an anti-progressive force in countries where it retained religious dominance, the tone of nearly all his comments on the subject betrays a revulsion of a fundamental, instinctive kind. Thus his *Journal* contains, during the period of his travels in France and Italy in 1839–40, numerous adverse comments on Catholic liturgy and customs and on the political administration of Catholic countries, especially as it manifested itself in the behaviour of petty officials.

Macaulay's Evangelical upbringing no doubt accounted in large measure for such reactions, just as habits of mind derived from the whole Evangelical, anti-slavery tradition influenced his thinking on other aspects of the Irish situation. When he applies the terms Helot and slave to the Irish peasantry, for example, the imagery is far from accidental. He had, after all, been brought up by a father who thought of little else but slaves and subject peoples, and his own earliest public successes had been achieved in the Anti-Slavery cause. The tradition had its limitations. Zachary Macaulay had brought little boys from Sierra Leone to be educated in England, but they died one by one in the Clapham cold;[25] Macaulay himself had seen no alternative for Indian education other than to become entirely English in content and in form. These were not necessarily wrong or inhumane decisions at the time they were taken, but they illustrate the tendency to identify liberation from enslavement or racial disadvantage with the transformation of the liberated into the likeness of the liberator. It is to Macaulay's credit that while it came quite naturally to him to see Irish Catholics as slaves, and while he could not rid himself of a distaste for Catholicism and a disapproval of those aspects of the Irish character which seemed to militate against industry and progress in favour of lethargy and disorder, he nevertheless recognized that in this instance the way of transformation and conversion had never been seriously attempted, and would not, if invoked at this late stage, have the slightest chance of success. Cromwell had tried extirpation, James II might have tried reconciliation, but for the nineteenth century there remained the sole option of attempting to work through the only instrument available for enlightenment and civilization, the Roman Catholic Church. Macaulay believed that by a generous attitude towards that Church it might be made, at least in Ireland, a force for progress.

Macaulay's more liberal readers were no doubt grieved, as he was, by the current situation in Ireland, by the horrors of the potato famine and the apparent ineffectiveness of charity in a country where hunger and confusion, though temporarily assuageable, seemed inevitably to recur in aggravated form.[26] Such readers were disturbed and angry at the failure to achieve lasting peace or progress, and it was to them that Macaulay addressed himself both in his parliamentary speeches and in the *History*. His writings are essentially all of a piece. Phrases and images first used in the House of Commons in 1844 or 1845 reappear in various guises in the *History*,[27] illustrating an habitual tendency to cling to an analogy once made or a phrase once selected – so that statement and image are welded into a single counter which comes readily to hand whenever an argument is reviewed or an incident recounted – and underlining the extent to which Macaulay saw in his speeches and historical writings alike the possibility of advancing rational and moral attitudes through the process of illumination and explanation. Behind the historian's desire to make his readers see and understand lies always the passion of the orator to persuade and the zeal of the missionary to convert. Convinced himself of the connection between past and present, a connection which in the case of Ireland could not be charted in terms of the patterns of progress he saw as applicable to the rest of British history, Macaulay sought to work out for himself and his readers a comprehensible design, to make possible a just assessment of responsibility, and to create, through the informed understanding produced by the historian, the climate of opinion required for effective legislation.

The instinctive distaste for Catholicism none the less remains, as does its obverse, an irrepressible admiration for certain aspects of the colonists' behaviour, and there is a sense in which the unmistakable presence of these emotional responses serves to keep the *History* honest as a work of literature. The presentation of Irish history in chapter XII grows out of a confrontation between principle and instinct which is not disguised. Macaulay did not admit in the actual pages of the *History* as he did in the pages of his *Journal* that he wrote of the men of Enniskillen and Londonderry 'con amore',[28] but the warmth of commitment to these men – going beyond respect for them as representatives of order and progress and admiration for their discipline and courage – can readily be perceived. Macaulay loved the defenders of Londonderry because they were brave – brave like the Spartans at Thermopylae, brave like Horatius on the bridge. In a very straightforward and, to the twentieth-century reader, almost culpably naïve way, Macaulay loved physical courage displayed in the face of great danger. He could recognize the imaginative and moral limitations which were often the concomitants of such courage, but he still joined with Horatius in asking:[29]

> And how can man die better
> Than facing fearful odds,
> For the ashes of his fathers
> And the temples of his Gods . . .

9
Characterization in the *History*
The Case of William the Third

Macaulay praised Addison, in his essay of 1843, as 'an observer of life, of manners', and sought to capture in his own pages something of his predecessor's vivid impression of social reality. But he also praised Addison for his observation 'of all the shades of human character' (78:229), and for his capacity to embody his perceptions in specific characterizations:

> And what he observed he had the art of communicating in two widely different ways. He could describe virtues, vices, habits, whims, as well as Clarendon. But he could do something better. He could call human beings into existence and make them exhibit themselves. (78:229)

Macaulay is here making a distinction between the methods of the Clarendonian 'characterists' – whose epitomizations compose the individual traits of their subjects into static portraits – and the ways in which novelists create individualized men and women who reveal themselves progressively in their actions, words, and feelings.[1] The *Spectator* essays thus represent for Macaulay a landmark in literary history, a bridge between two kinds of narrative – between seventeenth-century historical writing and the eighteenth-century novel – and fascinate him as a practising historian by the possibility they suggest of annexing to history proper methods of characterization developed in the borderland between factual reporting and fictional invention.

The difficulty with Macaulay's attempts to invoke the methods of fiction for the purposes of characterization is that he seems almost instinctively to restrict himself to the kind of portraiture which presents men whole rather than as they gradually develop. In the depiction of social groups and types his method does sometimes recall certain kinds of Restoration play or eighteenth-century novel, or even the *Spectator* essays themselves. Yet despite the play of colour and detail around the basic outlines of such portraits, the final impression is of a clarity and fixity not so very different in structural and narrative effect from Macaulay's more orthodox historical Characters:[2] his nameless squires and clerics are still very much counters in the pattern of historical explanation, and they remain lively compilations rather than living beings. Here is Macaulay's description of the life of a young chaplain:

> A young Levite – such was the phrase then in use – might be had for his board, a small garret, and ten pounds a year, and might not only perform his own professional functions, might not only be the most patient of butts and of listeners, might not only be always ready in fine weather for bowls, and in rainy weather for shovelboard, but might also save the expense of a gardener, or of a groom. Sometimes the reverend man nailed up apricots, and sometimes he curried the coach horses. He cast up the farrier's bills. He walked ten miles with a message or a parcel. If he was permitted to dine with the family, he was expected to content himself with the plainest fare. He might fill himself with the corned beef and the carrots: but, as soon as the tarts and cheesecakes made their appearance, he quitted his seat, and stood aloof till he was summoned to return thanks for the repast, from a great part of which he had been excluded. (I,327–8)

As the picture of the squirearchy which precedes this clerical portrait has perhaps suggested, we are not very far here from the neighbourhood of Squire Western, and upon encountering a couple of pages later, among the references to Fletcher, Vanburgh, Shadwell, and Swift, one to *Tom Jones* itself, the reader has a sense of being carried, if not absolutely into the territory of fiction, then well into that debatable border land of which Macaulay had written in his History essay of 1828.

The issue is not so much that reliance on literary sources for which Macaulay was criticized as soon as his first two volumes appeared – though his debt to such material is undoubtedly heavy – but rather the historian's use of fictional modes of presentation.[3] Macaulay himself clearly believed not only that the light literature of the seventeenth and eighteenth centuries was the richest source of information, but that it could also supply appropriate models for the creation of typical portraits of whose truth the final test was essential rather than particular. Macaulay moves with great ease from statistical and factual evidence, through particular examples, to individualized portraits of an irresistible vitality; but the technique is in the end illegitimate, for in calling into being a young Levite with so specific and concrete a daily round Macaulay pushes out of his *History* the many other clergymen with different functions and habits. A single simplified image usurps the place that might have been supplied by a more comprehensive survey, and Macaulayan particularity – with its corned beef and carrots – achieves here not simply vividness and economy, but serious distortion. When general characterization merges into allegory the historian has wandered too far into the land of fiction.

Macaulay had written of Addison that he 'could call human beings into existence and make them exhibit themselves'. And he was certainly aware that this power of dynamic self-revelation had taken various and subtle forms in the works of fiction which succeeded Addison's pioneering achievements. In the Madame D'Arblay essay of 1843 he gives a eulogy of Jane Austen which speaks of her portrayal of clergymen very different from his own young Levite:

> She has given us a multitude of characters, all, in a certain
> sense, common-place, all such as we meet every day. Yet they
> are all as perfectly discriminated from each other as if they were
> the most eccentric of human beings. There are, for example,
> four clergymen, none of whom we should be surprised to find
> in any parsonage in the kingdom, Mr Edward Ferrars, Mr Henry
> Tilney, Mr Edmund Bertram, and Mr Elton. They are all
> specimens of the upper part of the middle class. They have all
> been liberally educated. They all lie under the restraints of the
> same sacred profession. They are all young. They are all in love.
> Not one of them has any hobbyhorse, to use the phrase of Sterne.
> Not one has a ruling passion, such as we read of in Pope. Who
> would not have expected them to be insipid likenesses of each
> other? No such thing. Harpagon is not more unlike to Jourdain,
> Joseph Surface is not more unlike to Sir Lucius O'Trigger, than
> every one of Miss Austen's young divines to all his reverend
> brethren. And almost all this is done by touches so delicate,
> that they elude analysis, that they defy the powers of description,
> and that we know them to exist only by the general effect to
> which they have contributed. (76:561–2)

In the same essay Macaulay denied the highest rank to writers like Ben Jonson and Mme D'Arblay who depicted characters in terms of humours; the greatest praise must be 'reserved for the few who have excelled in the difficult art of portraying characters in which no single feature is extravagantly overcharged' (76:562).

Clearly Macaulay did not aspire to the company of Jane Austen, but was prepared to settle, in his own practice, for something closer to the 'humours' tradition, no doubt feeling that for the purposes of an historical narrative an individual like Judge Jeffreys or a composite figure like the Tory squire of the third chapter almost demanded to have single features 'extravagantly overcharged'. In choosing to rely, on the one hand, on the methods of the historical Character and, on the other, on those of the literary caricature Macaulay was settling for the one supreme advantage which both these forms possessed – clarity. The advantages for exposition and argument of sharp and colourful emblems seemed to him to be indispensable, and since his conception of history was essentially unheroic, a matter not so much of particular men as of patterns of events and forces, he no doubt regarded the loss of complexity in human presentation as a small price to pay for the clear delineation of the course of events. Macaulay's purpose was not, after all, to discriminate a Henry Tilney from an Edmund Bertram, but to impress upon his readers the social and economic disadvantages experienced by seventeenth-century minor clerics; not to dramatize the hero of a novel in all his individual complexity and developing life, but to present with clarity the role of a William the Third in the pattern of history.

It is hardly surprising that a man who knew his Clarendon and Burnet as well as Macaulay should have been influenced by the tradition of the seventeenth-century English Character. As David Nichol Smith has pointed out, that tradition was essentially the creation of seventeenth-century historians and memoirists, and although undoubtedly influenced by classical and French models, and probably by the example of the English drama, it remained essentially true to its historical origins. Although characterizing yielded place to the biographical impulse in the course of the eighteenth century ('When the facts of a man's life, his works, and his opinions claimed detailed treatment, the fashion of the short character had passed'[4]), the compact and finite Character form retained considerable attractions for the historian with many protagonists to portray.[5]

For the Character-writer the life of his subject is perceived as a whole rather than as something developing in time; qualities and actions are treated of in essence rather than in sequence; works and opinions are invoked as illustrations in the service of a static judgment and not as the motive power by which a dramatic presentation is moved forward. The Character-writer views his subject either as outside of time or from some point after the subject is assumed to have fully displayed himself – often, indeed, when the subject is dead. The aim is to present what a man adds up to in the end rather than to portray the actual process of addition; change thus tends to be seen as a two-dimensional pattern of variation, and if development be depicted at all it is generally in terms of demonstrated fulfilment or of the completion of some already perceived design.

The great attraction of the Character method for Macaulay was that it lent itself perfectly to his instinct for seeing patterns and wholes in the most diverse materials; it also allowed him to achieve superlative clarity and precision of presentation, as in the brilliant Character of Halifax in chapter II of the *History*. The method's limitations become apparent as the reader encounters in later chapters a Halifax who seems never to change or grow; the experience is one of continual reinforcement rather than of renewed freshness of perception, and the expository advantage of clarity has now to be seen as off-set by the narrative disadvantage – especially if the *History* is to be compared with certain kinds of drama and novel – of lack of development and surprise. The influence of the seventeenth-century Character is, however, discernible in the *History* in almost every kind of portrait, from the briefest to the most extended, and it is discernible above all, compact with all its strengths and weaknesses, in the full-scale treatment of William the Third, Macaulay's central figure.

William the Third had provided the subject of the Cambridge Prize Essay of 1822, with which Macaulay achieved his first public success as an essayist; one of the last episodes of the *History* on which Macaulay worked just before his own death in 1859 described the death of William. It seems symbolically appropriate that Macaulay's career should be thus framed, for no character is more central to his conception of English history or to the validity of the *History of England* as a work of literature. The survival of the Prize Essay allows us to compare an early presentation of William with that in the first two volumes of the *History*, and what immediately emerges from such a comparison is the extent to which the essentials of Macaulay's mature conception of William are already present in the Prize Essay, and in remarkably complete form. As G. O. Trevelyan acutely remarks, the essay seems 'just such as will very likely be produced in the course of next Easter term by some young man of judgment and spirit, who knows his Macaulay by heart, and will paraphrase him without scruple.'[6] Trevelyan's comment might perhaps be emended to read 'parody him without scruple', for the carefully balanced sentences with their frequent antitheses verging all too often on the paradoxical, represent an earlier and cruder version of that style with which Macaulay was to astonish both the editor and the audience of the *Edinburgh Review*. The antitheses are employed not only to exhibit the contradictory elements in William's make-up – the contrast, for example, between his insignificant appearance and his courage and energy on the battlefield – but to oppose him at every point to Louis XIV, whose portrait occupies the first position in the essay's gallery. It is with an attempt to epitomize the distinction between the two kings that the Character of William ends:[7]

> On a general comparison of the qualities of the two great
> antagonists, we may pronounce that the character of William
> was suited to the domestic hearth, that of Lewis to the courtly
> circle; – that William appeared to most advantage on the field
> of battle, and Lewis in the chariot of triumph.

The desire to 'pronounce' betrays Macaulay into too neat an antithesis, for although William's tenderness for his wife has been mentioned in the portrait, the insistence on the 'domestic hearth' conflicts with an earlier emphasis on hunting and warfare. The encouragement which the Character as a genre gave to such pronouncing was undoubtedly one of its attractions for Macaulay, but in the course of his career he learned both to select with more care the details out of which he contrived his epigrammatic effects, and to balance the advantages of climax and finality against the desirability of smoother and more cohesive transitions.

Surprisingly enough, William remains almost unmentioned in Macaulay's writings between the Prize Essay of 1822 and the *History* of 1848. He makes his reappearance in chapter II of the *History*, where his future role is insisted upon from the first:

> a few days after William's [William II of Holland's] death, his
> widow Mary, daughter of Charles the First, King of Great Britain,
> gave birth to a son, destined to raise the glory and authority of

the House of Nassau to the highest point, to save the United
Provinces from slavery, to curb the power of France, and to
establish the English constitution on a lasting foundation. (I,217)

This is followed, not by a full-scale Character of William, but by a
narrative of Dutch sufferings during the conflict with France, thus
reversing the order Macaulay had adopted in 1822, when the Character
of William preceded the account of these same events. In the *History*
the full depiction of William must wait until chapter VII, but we are
given in the meantime sufficient details of his actions as a young man
to illustrate his potential for fulfilling the destiny marked out for him:
'Young as he was, his ardent and unconquerable spirit, though disguised by a cold and sullen manner, soon roused the courage of his
dismayed countrymen' (I,218). The resistance of William and the
Dutch is thrown into particularly sharp relief, coming as it does just
after the description of Charles II's subservience to Louis and its
culmination in the secret clauses of the Treaty of Dover, and as if to
drive the point about William's military determination home, the
paragraph ends with a description of Louis' withdrawal from the
scene of battle 'to enjoy the adulation of poets and the smiles of ladies
in the newly planted alleys of Versailles' (I,219). Yet it is perhaps
inaccurate to speak of passages about Charles and Louis setting
off the presentation of William: at this early stage in Macaulay's
narrative these men are balanced one against the other in a mutually
defining pattern, and if any figure is dominant it is that of Louis.
For all the insistence on William's destiny, Macaulay does not
allow his figure early prominence, reserving the major emphasis
for the moment when his actions become crucial to the history of
England.

Macaulay's arrangement sustains an appearance of following
William's development: the young Stadtholder is presented in chapter
II, and, in chapter VII, William at thirty-six poised for some intervention in the affairs of England. The formal Character in chapter
VII is distinct from the overview of the Prize Essay in that it is
associated with a particular moment in time, the year 1687. Yet, despite
this very specific placing, the picture is painted with all the insight that
nineteenth-century knowledge and the historian's assessment of the
significant can supply. It begins, appropriately enough, with visual
details, as William's various portraits are invoked as a way of linking
the nineteenth and seventeenth centuries:[8]

His external appearance is almost as well known to us as to his
own captains and councillors. Sculptors, painters, and medallists
exerted their utmost skill in the work of transmitting his
features to posterity; and his features were such as no artist could
fail to seize, and such as, once seen, could never be forgotten.
His name at once calls up before us a slender and feeble frame, a
lofty and ample forehead, a nose curved like the beak of an
eagle, an eye rivalling that of an eagle in brightness and
keenness, a thoughtful and somewhat sullen brow, a firm and
somewhat peevish mouth, a cheek pale, thin, and deeply
furrowed by sickness and by care. That pensive, severe, and solemn
aspect could scarcely have belonged to a happy or a good-
humoured man. But it indicates in a manner not to be mistaken
capacity equal to the most arduous enterprises, and fortitude not
to be shaken by reverses or dangers. (II,162–3)

William is, in fact, seen here from a combination of three different
perspectives: the contemporary one of his captains and counsellors,
that of men of later generations who view his portraits, and that of
the historian who interprets the features in terms of demonstrated
capacity for action in historical situations. Throughout the presentation which follows Macaulay manipulates these viewpoints, giving
the reader something of the detail through which William can be
known as a living being; but the dominant impression is still determined by that pattern of significances, as opposed to particulars, which
comprises the historian's essential portrait.

After the visual opening, William's early life is surveyed in order
to illustrate both his inherent characteristics and the effects of his
education and experience. Although the emphases – on his ability to
keep his own counsel, his military courage even in defeat, and his
aversion to religious persecution – have a special relevance for his
subsequent as well as his earlier career, the appearance of restricting
the portrait to what could be known of William at thirty-six is firmly
maintained, even though the limits are stretched to include material
for which only later events could be said to supply the full evidence.
Macaulay no doubt has William's behaviour at the death of Mary in
mind when he comments: 'When death separated him from what he
loved, the few who witnessed his agonies trembled for his reason and
his life' (II,170). But the specific occasion is not, in fact, mentioned
here, and it is only in the richly detailed survey of the material provided

by the Bentinck correspondence that the 1687 dateline is absolutely crossed; even then, Macaulay's footnotes alone reveal that the specific instances of what were no doubt recurrent feelings and attitudes are sometimes drawn from letters written later in William's life.

It is through the account of William's friendship with Bentinck that his private as well as public self is brought into the picture – the other side of the medallist's impression given in the opening portrait. It is by the same means that the description of William is gently extended beyond the finite, generalized form of the Character so as to include considerable biographical detail. This movement outwards from the static portrait to link up with the narrative thread of the *History* is continued in the accounts of William's feelings for his mistress, Elizabeth Villiers, his relationship with Mary, and Bishop Burnet's intervention between husband and wife in order that the course both of marriage and of history might run smooth. Transition and arrangement here are handled with great skill, Macaulay effecting an easy shift from portrait to narrative and on again to another portrait, very different in kind from William's, that of Bishop Burnet. Since William's role is to assume steadily greater importance in the events which follow, the more open-ended portrait has its own appropriateness, and by thus extending the Character Macaulay is able to make full use of what was fresh primary material, the details of the Bentinck friendship as revealed by William's personal correspondence.[9]

It is undoubtedly true, as Macaulay's critics were quick to point out,[10] that William is let off very lightly for his infidelities, and that Macaulay seems to accept too readily Burnet's account of the estrangement between William and Mary and of a subsequent reconciliation easily achieved through the dropping of a shrewd hint or two by the Bishop himself. The story is a delightful one and effects a splendidly concrete introduction to the Character of Burnet, but Macaulay's use of it does indeed seem somewhat uncritical, and the spirited defence of Burnet as an historian, in text and footnote, serves to heighten rather than diminish this impression. The simple explanation, as the critics saw it, was that, when it came to William and Mary, Macaulay was disingenuous or gullible, or both. In his 1837 essay on Bacon, Macaulay had criticized Basil Montagu for proceeding 'on the assumption that Bacon was an eminently virtuous man', commenting: 'This mode of defending Bacon seems to us by no means *Baconian*. To take a man's character for granted, and then from his character to infer the moral quality of all his actions, is surely a process the very reverse of that which is recommended in the *Novum Organum*' (65,ii:4–5). There are some grounds for charging Macaulay, in his presentation of William, with failing to live up to the standards and procedures he had himself earlier advocated.

But the matter can also be looked at in a way which at least throws a somewhat happier light on Macaulay's motivation, for he seems not to have sought to give a false impression, but to have wanted very much to give a clear impression. William's faults are admitted from the first – even in the brief sketch in chapter II there is an allusion to the stains attaching to his name following the death of De Witt and the Massacre of Glencoe – but they are deliberately underplayed by Macaulay in order that those qualities which enabled William to become the chief agent of the Glorious Revolution may be seen to predominate. For Macaulay, historical truth undoubtedly meant historical significance as well as historical fact – as in his summary dismissal, in the Milton essay, of those defenders of Charles I who invoked the king's private virtues to excuse his public conduct: 'A good father! A good husband! – Ample apologies indeed for fifteen years of persecution, tyranny, and falsehood!' (42:330). Because he did not see all facts as equal in importance, Macaulay did not hesitate to emphasize good qualities in William and evil ones in James: in keeping with his basically developmental concept of history, he believed that in relation to the larger course of events these were the qualities which counted. This is, of course, a dangerously relativistic view, but it is not the deliberate dishonesty of which Macaulay has been accused. The affair with Elizabeth Villiers, even the Massacre of Glencoe, seemed to Macaulay to be relatively unimportant in comparison with the courage and decisiveness which enabled William to seize his opportunities in 1687 and 1688 and to steer a steady course through all the difficulties of his ensuing reign.

For Macaulay, historical events were the products of a complex of forces – economic, geographic, social, religious, racial. He never sought to define the working of these forces in any coherent theory, but awareness of their operation affects his conceptions of individuals. Particular men, with their personal strengths and weaknesses, desires and fears, have a part to play in influencing the course of events, and are to be held morally accountable for that part; but they do not dominate. Evidence of this general view can be found in almost any of Macaulay's essays, although it is expressed more crudely and absolutely in the earlier works than in the later. Men are repeatedly presented as products of historical situations rather than as controllers of destiny: a particular conjunction of events may provoke a 'plain Buckinghamshire Esquire' like Hampden into obstructing 'the path of tyranny' (54:506); in 1678 or 1679, 'there would have been an outbreak, if [Oates and Bedloe] had never been born' (61:297).

This last quotation comes from the Mackintosh essay of 1835, the most extreme Whig document Macaulay ever composed, the article which lays the greatest stress on crucial events rather than crucial figures. It was in this essay that Macaulay wrote of those who wished to bring William of Orange over to England:

> Their first object was to seat William on the throne; and they were right. We say this without any reference to the eminent personal qualities of William, or to the follies and crimes of James. If the two princes had interchanged characters, our opinion would still have been the same. It was even more necessary to England at that time that her king should be a usurper than that he should be a hero. There could be no security for good government without a change of dynasty. (61:313)

This is the language of the polemicist, not of the judicious historian; all attempts at authorial detachment is surrendered and Macaulay identifies himself completely with one side of the question. Whatever reasons affected the emotional violence and lack of control of the article on Mackintosh, its very extravagance makes it in some ways the clearest, most unguarded statement of some of Macaulay's fundamental beliefs about men and history. Written shortly before he began seriously to contemplate his major work, the essay ends with paragraph after paragraph of insistence on what England owed to the Revolution, *not* what she owed to William – who is, indeed, barely mentioned.

Even when the more extreme assertions and tones of the Mackintosh essays are discounted and allowance is made for developments in Macaulay's thinking in the late 1830s and 1840s, there remains little doubt that when he embarked upon his *History* he believed that without William there would still have been a Revolution, although it would naturally have taken a different course. And he almost certainly saw that Revolution rather than William's part in it as his essential subject. Although the character of William was a vital element in the exposition Macaulay intended to offer his readers, it is clear from the choice of the Character genre as the basic means of portraiture that for the major as much as for the minor figures Macaulay felt individual psychology must give way to the analysis of that larger course of events in which any individual was only a contributory factor.

Yet by the end of the first two volumes of the *History* William's part in the Revolution has won for him pride of place: 'For the authority of law, for the security of property, for the peace of our streets, for the happiness of our homes, our gratitude is due, under Him who raises and pulls down nations at his pleasure, to the Long Parliament, to the Convention, and to William of Orange' (II,670). The contrast with the end of the Mackintosh essay, where the Revolution rather than William receives the tributes, is clear. In the course of writing his first two volumes not only has Macaulay's historical sense of the part played by William become heightened, but his imaginative commitment to his hero has grown accordingly. And the reader whose sense of William's personality and role has been created by the preceding narrative readily acquiesces in the prominence given to William in the final words of this first complete section of the *History*.

But William's story is not finished by the end of volume II. His reign in England remains to be narrated, and the question which faces the critic of the later volumes is whether there is any development in Macaulay's basic methods of characterization to correspond to his changed conception of the agency of William in events. While it would be a mistake to emphasize this latter change too strongly – Macaulay was always to see William as a man whose lines of action were severely restricted by historical circumstances – something more than the essentially static portraiture of volumes I and II was clearly required. There is certainly evidence in the *Journal* that Macaulay was anxious about the success of the second pair of volumes,[11] yet he seems to have been concerned chiefly because they could not match the first two in variety or vitality of incident or portrait rather than because they called for any radically different approach to questions of characterization or narration.

In chapter XI, the first of volume III, Macaulay gives considerable space to William's habits, manners, and mode of behaviour once he became king of England, and shows how coldness and abruptness of manner and simple foreignness – particularly when contrasted with the gaiety and sociability of Charles II – served to alienate the king from his subjects. Since William's lack of personal attractiveness formed part of the sketch in chapter II and of the fuller portrait in chapter VII, the details of chapter XI constitute a fleshing out of an already established outline, and only the emphasis on the effects of William's personality is new. Macaulay makes very clear the significance of these effects: the failure to win the hearts of others which to an ordinary man would be a personal misfortune can be to a king a political disaster. And every detail presented in this chapter is recorded on the political as well as the personal scale: an item may be trivial, but it is never insignificant. When William gobbles up the green peas without leaving any for his sister-in-law this registers not merely as domestic ill-manners but also as an insult to an English princess by a foreign king.

As volumes III and IV proceed, the reader feels more and more that whether he views William's social behaviour in chapter XI, his religious attitudes in chapter XIV, or his military conduct in chapter XVI, he is simply being supplied with further details in a pattern already laid down in the first two volumes. As with the presentation of Halifax, all is reinforcement; nothing is surprise. This is undoubtedly as Macaulay felt it should be with the characters of a history. He saw the historian's duty when handling character and event as a matter of extracting significance from the variety and complexity of the life of the past, rather than of seeking to give an impression of that life for its own sake. It seems likely, however, that Macaulay's inclusion of so many vivid episodes and so much social detail may have been prompted, at least in part, by some recognition of the life-denying effect of perpetual dedication to selection of the significant. The vitality of some of the more obvious glowing set pieces may be characterized as a compensatory effect, and the same is true of some of the lesser details as well: in the absence of a continuous attempt at lifelikeness we are given lively anecdotes of green peas.

For Macaulay the omniscience of the historian was very different from that of the novelist. It is not the knowledge which pertains to the creator of characters, but rather that long view of the 'philosophic historian' which he attributed to Halifax.[12] Such a view takes cognizance of all sides of a question and is deliberately detached from a contemporary perspective on events; indeed, when employed from the standpoint of the nineteenth century, it knows the outcome of all the events. But although motives are analysed and the validity of various arguments balanced against each other, the vision is limited to that of the shrewd interpreter of words and deeds; for the historian, unlike the novelist, cannot move freely inside the heads and hearts of his protagonists, nor can he place them in invented situations of a deliberately revelatory kind.

G. M. Trevelyan has argued that Macaulay's great failing was 'a disastrous habit of attributing motives', and he goes on to remark that Macaulay 'was never content to say that a man did this or that, and leave his motives to conjecture; he must always needs analyse all that had passed through the mind of his *dramatis personae* as if he were the God who had created them.'[13] While there is little doubt that Macaulay was too free in ascribing base motives to those he saw as villains – Penn, Marlborough, and James II, for example – Trevelyan's emphasis on creation seems slightly wide of the mark. Macaulay rarely analyses what passes through the minds of his characters; he does, however, attempt – and sometimes with considerable success – to give semi-dramatized form to the arguments which *might* have occurred to the figures concerned. This partial dramatization is intended to create an impression similar to that available to the novelist, the creator of character, and it is in a way a tribute to Macaulay that Trevelyan mistakes it for the same thing. But it remains in the end interpretation rather than creation, and the liveliness we perceive pertains to the manipulation of the arguments and positions rather than to any attempt at a realistic portrayal of the idiosyncratic movement of an individual mind operating through thought patterns as personal as a particular accent or tone of voice.

One of the most striking examples of Macaulay's use of a technique of semi-dramatization so as to give the impression of entering the mind of a character is the presentation in chapter XV of William's position when the Whigs prevent the amnesty he desires. 'The King watched these events with painful anxiety' (III,528), Macaulay tells us, and then, in a series of brief sentences, he lists the causes of this anxiety as they might well have occurred to William himself. But even here there is no attempt to catch the precise quality of William's mental processes, and when Macaulay goes on to sum up what must have been William's feelings – 'The King felt that he could not, while thus situated, render any service to that great cause to which his whole soul was devoted' (III,529) – the supportive details are only of a kind available to a shrewd observer. What Macaulay does do is heighten the already established rhythm of short sentences so that it builds up into a rhetoric of grievances and self-justification:

> As for the turbulent and ungrateful islanders, who detested him
> because he would not let them tear each other in pieces, Mary
> must try what she could do with them. She was born on their

soil. She spoke their language. She did not dislike some parts of
their Liturgy, which they fancied to be essential, and which to
him seemed at best harmless. If she had little knowledge of politics
and war, she had what might be more useful, feminine grace and
tact, a sweet temper, a smile and a kind word for every body. She
might be able to compose the disputes which distracted the State
and the Church. Holland, under his government, and England
under hers, might act cordially together against the common
enemy. (III,529–30)

These are the slightly peevish rhythms of injured merit as a state of
mind, rather than the idiolect of Dutch William meditating on the
ingratitude of seventeenth-century England. The realism pertains to
the emotion rather than to the personality.[14]

This faithfulness to the patterns and tones of mental and emotional
situations does much to give the appearance of life to the detailed
presentation of William in the later volumes of the *History*, even though
it finally contributes more to our understanding of his predicament
than to our sense of him as a man. And in certain of the more dramatic
episodes Macaulay can draw on William's actual words and gestures
to create something of the impression of a living, breathing man at the
centre of events. Thus Macaulay's powerful visualizing imagination is
applied to particularly good effect in the account of William's campaign in Ireland and the Battle of Boyne in chapter XVI. On the day of
the Boyne William was the cynosure of all eyes, and his success in the
battle ensured that his sayings and doings were treasured and subsequently recorded in such works as Story's *Impartial History of the
Wars of Ireland*. Macaulay combines such contemporary details with
information derived from nineteenth-century topographical works,
such as Wilde's account of the River Boyne, and from his own visit to
the scene of the battle, in order to achieve a concrete particularity of
effect capable of surviving the process of selection – as strongly active
here as elsewhere in the *History*.[15] We retain a sense of watching events
as they happen, and when Macaulay insists, as the campaign starts, that
'William was all himself again' (III,618), the reader feels for once that
he is watching the actual as well as the essential William.

Anecdote is once more invoked – this time to illustrate William's
sprightliness rather than his morose greed – but the gracious acceptance
of the cherries carries a lesser burden of implication than the gorging
of the peas, for many details of word, gesture, and action contribute

N

to the depiction of William's deportment at this time. Actual words are quoted sparingly, and the historian's discriminating hand has clearly chosen them for their significance; even so, they do serve to capture something of the texture of William's mood. We are given his dry comments as he views the enemy forces – 'I am glad to see you, gentlemen, . . . If you escape me now, the fault will be mine' (III,622); the deliberately calm understatement when he is wounded – 'There is no harm done, . . . but the bullet came quite near enough' (III,628); the brief indulgence in sarcasm at the expense of the traitor Richard Hamilton – 'Your honour! . . . your honour!' (III,634); and the growl of disapproval at the Reverend Mr Walker's pushing so far into the thick of battle as to get himself killed at the ford – 'What took him there?' (III,638). Each phrase combines typicality and authenticity and in this episode at least the balance is maintained.

A skilfully managed evocation of material which must have presented itself to the mind of William occurs in a passage which precedes the account of the battle itself. In the course of his description of Ireland at the time of William's arrival Macaulay shifts from a nineteenth-century perspective, comparing the Belfast of William's day with the Belfast of the present, through a seventeenth-century perspective – 'Not a human being was to be found near the road, except a few naked and meagre wretches who had no food but the husks of oats, and who were seen picking those husks, like chickens, from amidst dust and cinders' (III,620)[16] – to the viewpoint of William himself:

> Perhaps he [William] thought how different an aspect that
> unhappy region would have presented if it had been blessed
> with such a government and such a religion as had made his
> native Holland the wonder of the world; how endless a succession
> of pleasure houses, tulip gardens and dairy farms would have
> lined the road from Lisburn to Belfast; how many hundreds of
> barges would have been constantly passing up and down the
> Laggan; what a forest of masts would have bristled in the
> desolate port of Newry; and what vast warehouses and stately
> mansions would have covered the space occupied by the noisome
> alleys of Dundalk. 'The country,' he was heard to say, 'is worth
> fighting for.' (III,620)

This is, of course, another example of Macaulay's favourite device of definition by comparison, but the substance of the passage has a concreteness whose effect is amplified by the appropriateness of these thoughts to the particularized perspective of William. The contrast between Holland and Ireland is full of significance for the conduct of William and James, and for the different traditions of government they represent; it is not, however, to this significance alone that the reader responds, but to the way in which the depth of William's feeling about Holland is here powerfully dramatized, and to the representation of his mind in the actual process of making comparisons and discriminations.[17] An added poignancy attaches to the passage in that he who perhaps had these or similar thoughts is also the person who might have effected beneficial changes in Ireland; yet the nineteenth-century reader, aware of the larger perspectives earlier invoked, knew that although material improvements had occurred, sectarian bitterness persisted in Ireland with a fierceness and a potential for violence almost the equal of the seventeenth-century situation.

The actual words quoted at the end of the passage are both the historian's justification for what precedes them and the final concrete touch driving home the point of the meditation. It is for some similar fusion of the historical sense with the presentation of an individual mind in action at particular realized moments in time that the reader yearns at other points in the narrative of William's career in these final volumes.[18] All too often the lack of particularity combines with the very coherence of the presentation to transform the attitudes and actions which so neatly illustrate the original Character into the movements of a puppet on the historian's string. All too often we are told about William; all too rarely does he become the vehicle of perceptions. It is no doubt unreasonable to expect Macaulay to combine the impression of particularized life with the treatment of whole areas of William's thought and behaviour: not only was he unable to draw at all points on the kind of detailed material available for the narrative of the Battle of the Boyne, but he must have felt that an equally particular and personal presentation of every episode would be proper only to a biography of William, not to a history of England. Yet it is because the later volumes of the *History* – in their detail and in their concentration on William as the centre of all the threads of action – approximate so frequently to the patterns of biography that the reader wishes for further glimpses of William from a contemporary perspective, and more frequent opportunities to see with William's eyes. Macaulay would no doubt have considered too sustained a dramatization of the narrative from the point of view of William to be a betrayal of his demonstrative and explicatory function as an historian. The stress on historical significance none the less becomes increasingly artificial and oppressive, squeezing the life out of the actors who go so regularly through the authenticated motions.

There remains in the end a hollowness at the heart of the three later volumes of the *History* which makes them less satisfying than the original pair. It is not simply a matter of those salient qualities in the early volumes which are easily recognizable at a first reading – the series of highly-coloured episodes and dramatic personages, the rich and varied gallery of Characters, the wealth of social detail – for a closer examination reveals not only that some of these effects are relatively crude, but that the later volumes handle more detailed and complex material with considerable subtlety: monetary matters in William's reign are much less exciting than the Bloody Assizes, but Macaulay none the less manages to present clearly a mass of historical detail and to hold the reader's interest as he does so. Yet the hollowness remains, and can only be accounted for by the absence of the Prince of Denmark from the play. Although so much of the detail and the structure of the final volumes is brought to bear on the figure of William, such material can function only as further amplification of the static and finite Character of chapter VII. There is no movement in the central figure to correspond to the slow, detailed forward move-ment of events. In concentrating on what he saw as the vital elements in William, Macaulay denied him vitality as a personality. The death of William which Macaulay, himself a sick man, was so anxious to get down on paper, represents not the concluding moments in a career but the final touches in a portrait. We know already about the calm reli-gious faith, the love for Mary, the quietness and stoicism, which are here exhibited, and some readers may even feel a sense of relief that they will never be reminded of them again.

The Character, in the expanded form in which Macaulay learned to employ it, provides a most effective way for the historian to capture his personages. It controls them as temporal beings, taking their attributes out of the dimension of time so that their function in the pattern of events can be clearly seen at every point, not merely when the narration of their careers is complete. Details later revealed become illustrations controlled by the net of the initial Character rather than existential moments in their own right. For the presentation of a figure as continuously crucial to the narrative as William, however, the ten-sion between the static conception of the man and the dynamic process of events becomes in the end too great, so that the portrait designed for maximum coherence and clarity seems finally inadequate.

In the end the history of England defeats Macaulay, and it defeats him, ironically enough, in the person of William the Third. For not only did Macaulay allow the *History* to grow in length far beyond the proportions he originally envisaged, but he also came to see William's role as overreaching the bounds allotted to any individual in the conception of history with which he began. In crediting a single individual with a considerably greater influence on events than his own earlier ideas would seem to allow, and in depicting that influence in action in the detailed terms of the *History*, Macaulay was confronting himself – without fully recognizing the fact – with a new set of problems. The old solutions worked out in his essays for the handling of character, biography, and history were not adequate to the continuous presentation of the life and personality of a man who influenced not only contemporary events but the whole subsequent course of English history. In paying tribute to William at the end of volume II Macaulay was acknowledging that influence without having to come to terms with the difficulties of presenting it; in the later volumes those difficulties became steadily more obtrusive and more intractable.

Although Macaulay had always had a Whig conception of the crucial significance of the seventeenth-century revolution, he had never – even in the 1822 Prize Essay – attempted a narration of that revolution in combination with a presentation of the figure of William. The heroes in his major narrative and biographical essays are not shown in conjunction with events absolutely vital to the whole course of English history – for Macaulay, indeed, there were perhaps only two such moments, the 1640s and 1688 (with the possible addition of 1831-2). Clive, Hastings, even Pitt can all be assimilated to a view of the movement of history which lays emphasis on patterns of events and the general historical moment rather than on the mastery of individual men. But in dealing with William in the detailed, progressive narrative of the *History*, the old conceptions simply would not work.

It is not that room for William should have been found in that shadowy heroes' alcove Macaulay had half-granted to the figures of Julius Caesar, Cromwell, and Napoleon;[19] a complete shift to some kind of heroic view of history was never in question. What the later volumes of the *History* seem clearly to require is a more complex view of the interaction of men and events, the acknowledgment of a temporal dimension to human personality and of the capacity of men to affect events – and be affected by them – continuously and variously in the course of time. The retention of the static Character form in the presentation of William – for all the expansion of detail with which it is endowed – not only indicated Macaulay's failure to perceive the problem of character and history in a new way, but effectively prevented him from evolving a solution for it.

In this vital matter of characterization the *History* was the end of the line which began with the essays. And Macaulay's failure to complete the *History*, particularly when taken in conjunction with his paradoxical anxiety to get at least to the death of William, indicates an instinctive recognition of the impasse to which he had been brought by the articulation of his conception of seventeenth-century history through a combination of the static portraiture of men with an insistence on the dynamic of events. Walter Bagehot, one of the most perceptive critics ever to discuss Macaulay, had considerable praise for his powers of portraiture, commenting in a review article of 1855: 'No one describes so well what we may call the *spectacle* of a character.'[20] The spectacle of William of Orange is sharp and clear, but it increasingly impedes, by its fixity, the flow of Macaulay's narrative.

Macaulay was above all else an historian, and he became trapped within his historian's role. He needed always to be absolutely certain as to the point in time from which he was viewing his subject,[21] and this was at once a great strength and a great weakness. It enabled him to lead a contemporary audience back into the past without any danger of forgetting the nineteenth-century perspective and the wisdom of hindsight which later events provided. His position was always one of omniscience: not only did he know, or seem to know, everything about the men and events he described, he also knew so much about other times and places which could be brought relevantly to bear for purposes of definition or expansion. But because he could not in the end control his knowingness – any more than he could control that vast outpouring of allusion and opinion with which he astounded his acquaintances as a young man – he could not escape to a shifting vantage point from which to view his characters inside of time. He always saw them whole, and so he always saw them dead. This mattered very little within the limited, largely two-dimensional conventions of the essay. But when, by its detailed tracking of men and events through that small handful of years at the end of the seventeenth century, and by its assimilation of that colourful presentation of the social surface normally associated with the novel, the *History* reached towards some more essentially dynamic narrative form, Macaulay could not relinquish his omniscient stance. From an historian's point of view this may have been no bad thing, but when the *History* is considered as a work of literature, with structural and narrative needs of an organic kind progressively generated within itself, then the static quality associated both with the nineteenth-century perspective and with the presentation of the personages as Characters can only be seen as reducing to a spectacle a work which might have been so much more.

10

Conclusion

To Instruct by Pleasing

Macaulay's name had been familiar to the educated British public ever since the publication of the Milton essay in 1825; after the publication of the first two volumes of the *History of England* in December 1848 he was universally acknowledged, at home and abroad, as one of the greatest Englishmen of his day. Sales of the *History* surpassed all expectations and praise flowed in from all sides, qualified by only a few hostile articles, including one by Croker in the *Quarterly*, and a number of protests over the treatment of particular episodes and individuals – most notably, perhaps, the objections made by a delegation of Quakers to the representation of William Penn.[1] Though out of parliament, Macaulay continued to live in the Albany and to take some part in public life: the happy reconciliation with Sir Robert Peel just before the latter's death took place as a consequence of their encounters as Trustees of the British Museum. Macaulay attended the opening day of the Great Exhibition in May 1851 and found it 'a most gorgeous sight – beyond the dreams of the Arabian romancers. I cannot think that the Caesars ever exhibited a more splendid spectacle – I was quite dazzled. I felt as I did on entering St Peter's.'[2] In December of that same year he notes with regret the removal of Palmerston, whom he much admired, from the post of Foreign Secretary, and in January 1852 repeats in his *Journal* those reasons of 'health, temper, and tastes' which had induced him to decline an invitation from Lord John Russell to become a member of the Cabinet: 'I added that I would not sit for any nomination borough, & that my turn of mind disqualified me for canvassing great constituent bodies.'[3]

Remarkably enough, Macaulay was shortly to find himself the chosen candidate of a great constituent body without any kind of canvassing on his part. Approached by the contrite electors of Edinburgh before the general election of July 1852, he was prevented by a combination of principled aloofness and physical indisposition from taking any part in the election itself: G. O. Trevelyan speaks of his having been, on this occasion at least, 'probably the worst electioneer since Coriolanus'.[4] Shortly after learning of his success in the poll, Macaulay became quite seriously ill, apparently as the result of a heart attack, and was sent to Clifton, in Somerset, to recuperate. His condition gradually improved, but he never regained his old vigour. That winter he suffered from bronchitis, and in succeeding years he seems never to have been entirely free from attacks of asthma. In March 1853 he looked back to the previous July as 'a crisis in my life. I became twenty years older in a week. A mile is more to me now than ten miles a year ago.'[5] He managed in October 1852 to make the much-delayed trip to Edinburgh to thank the electors for the confidence in him which they had so signally displayed, and in November he resumed his seat in the House of Commons – commenting favourably on Disraeli's presentation of his budget on 3 December but adding that he himself could have done the job at least as well in two hours instead of Disraeli's five.[6]

The English party system at this time was still in confusion in the aftermath of Peel's about-face on the Corn Laws, and although the Conservatives under Lord Derby were in office their lack of Peelite support put them in a minority situation in the Commons. When, early in the session, the government was defeated on the question of Disraeli's budget, Macaulay was consulted about the formation of the new coalition ministry under Lord Aberdeen, but there was no question of his again taking office himself. In June 1853 he made an important speech on India and the introduction of competitive examinations for appointments to the civil service – a subject dear to his own heart and to that of his brother-in-law, now Sir Charles Trevelyan – and in July he spoke in the House of Commons for the last time. During the sessions of 1854 and 1855 his deteriorating health and the demands the *History* – of which the third and fourth volumes appeared in 1855 – made his parliamentary responsibilities seem increasingly burdensome, and he eventually resigned his seat in January 1856.

In the spring of 1856 Macaulay gave up his rooms in the Albany and moved to Holly Lodge, on Campden Hill, where he was to spend his few remaining years, taking great pleasure in the possession of an extensive garden and even embarking upon some modest horticultural efforts of his own. Writing to one of his nieces at this time, Macaulay chronicles his unending battles with the dandelions on the lawn: 'I thought that I was rid of the villains; but the day before yesterday, when I got up and looked out of my window, I could see five or six of their great, impudent, flaring, yellow faces turned up at me. "Only you wait, till I come down," I said. How I grubbed them up! How I enjoyed their destruction! Is it Christianlike to hate a dandelion so savagely? That is a curious question of casuistry.'[7] Apart from the occasional expeditions to the continent and to various parts of the British Isles in which he loved to indulge, usually in company with his friend, Ellis, Macaulay now spent his time almost exclusively at Holly Lodge, and G. O. Trevelyan paints, out of his own recollections, a happy picture of his uncle enjoying his increments of comfort, leisure, and wealth – Longman paid him a royalty cheque of £20,000 for sales of the *History* in 1856 alone – and taking special pleasure in entertaining visitors with lavish meals and brilliant conversation. He was indulgent to his servants and generous in his charity to those, known and unknown, who appealed to him for help.[8]

In August 1857 Macaulay was elevated to the peerage as Baron Macaulay of Rothley. He accepted the honour with unabashed pleasure, but his happiness was clouded by the almost simultaneous arrival of news of the Indian Mutiny. The *Journal* entry for 25 October 1857, his fifty-seventh birthday, reveals the complex state of his feelings at this period:[9]

> My birthday – Fifty-seven. I have had a not unpleasant year.
> My health is not good. But I suffer little: my head is clear: my
> heart is warm: my fortune is easy: I receive numerous marks of
> the good opinion of the public – a large public, including the
> educated men both of the old & of the new world. I have been
> made a peer with, I think, as general an approbation as I remember
> in the case of any man that in my time has been made a peer.
> ... What is much more important to my happiness than wealth,
> titles, & even fame, those whom I love are well & happy and very
> kind & affectionate to me. These are great things. I have some
> complaints however to make of the past year. The Indian troubles
> have affected my spirits more than any public events in the whole
> course of my life. To be sure the danger which threatened the
> country at the beginning of April 1848 came nearer to me. But
> that danger was soon over; and the Indian mutiny has now lasted
> several months, and may last months still. The emotions which it
> excites too are of a strong kind. I may say that till this year I

did not know what real vindictive hatred meant. With what horror I used to read in Livy how Fulvius put to death the whole Capuan Senate in the Second Punic War! And with what equanimity I could hear that the whole garrison of Delhi, all the Moulavies & Mussulman Doctors there, and all the accursed rabble of the bazaar had been treated in the same way – Is this wrong? Is not the severity which springs from a great sensibility to human suffering a better thing than the lenity wh. springs from indifference to human suffering? The question may be argued long on both sides.

By this time he had recognized that he would not live to complete his *History*, and that he might not even have the time or energy to finish the next volume. It was perhaps for that reason that he was willing, in his last years, to supply his old Edinburgh friend Adam Black with *Encyclopaedia Britannica* articles on some of those figures – among them Atterbury, Goldsmith, and William Pitt – whom his historical endeavours would never encompass. He may also have wanted to assure himself that his biographical gifts had not deserted him. It was certainly at this period that he took deliberate measures to ensure that his mental skills and faculties should not share in his physical decline: he refreshed his knowledge of German, engaged a tutor to converse with him in Italian, and read as widely as possible, annotating many of the volumes with a succinct and often pungent commentary. 'Of all the memorials of himself which he has left behind him,' writes G. O. Trevelyan, 'these dialogues with the dead are the most characteristic.'[10]

Early in 1859 Sir Charles Trevelyan accepted the Governorship of Madras and sailed once more for India, to be followed by his wife in a year's time. Once parted from Hannah, Macaulay could have no hope of ever seeing her again, and the news of the impending separation was a bitter blow to one who, only three years earlier, had found himself in tears after coming upon some old letters from his sister, Margaret: 'To think that she has been near 22 years dead; and I am crying for her as if it were yesterday.'[11] He tried to combat his depression by a strict regime of reading and writing specifically directed towards the completion of the next volume of the *History*. His *Journal* for 14 December 1859 reads: 'Finished at last the session of 1699–1700. There is a good deal in what I have written that is likely to interest readers. At any rate this employment is a good thing for myself & will be a better soon, when I shall have little else left.'[12] Two days later, however, the same *Journal* records a sharp recurrence of his illness – 'The depression, the weakness, the sinking of the heart, the incapacity to do anything that required steady muscular exertion were very distressing'[13] – and on 28 December he died quietly in his library chair. Beside him was the first number of the *Cornhill*, open at the first page of Thackeray's 'Lovel the Widower'. On 9 January 1860 he was buried in Westminster Abbey, at the foot of the statue of Addison.

In *The Public Life of Lord Macaulay*, published in 1862, the Rev. Frederick Arnold concludes a first-hand account of Macaulay's funeral with a fine rhetorical flourish: 'So fitly was he gathered to the Minster's kindred dust, among the nobles of the land to whose rank his own genius and labour had raised him, among our intellectual princes in whose noble company he bears no mean place, among eloquent and patriotic statesmen none of whom loved his country with a deeper, purer, and more enthusiastic love.'[14] This valedictory praise was not, however, unqualified: Arnold went on to acknowledge that Macaulay 'was not one of those who have stamped their character upon our national history or stirred the profoundest feelings of the soul or the subtlest reaches of the intellect'.[15] The limits of Macaulay's political career were obvious enough, and even before his death there had been those who accused him of intellectual superficiality, but in the phrase about 'the profoundest feelings of the soul' Arnold is presumably alluding to what must have seemed to him, as a clergyman, the extraordinary and damaging absence from Macaulay's public statements of any spiritual concern, any demonstration either of religious enthusiasm or of anxious doubt.

This lack of religious engagement certainly puzzled and disturbed a good many of Macaulay's contemporaries. Lord Shaftesbury, recording in his diary the news of Macaulay's death, remembered with gratitude his eventual support for the Ten Hour Bill, which restricted the hours which could be worked by young people in factories, and contrived to enrol him as a Christian on the somewhat negative grounds that his 'super-eminent and mighty talents, though never openly and directly employed for God's services, were, at least, never perverted to evil uses. Is there a sentence in any of his writings to offend decency, morality, the Christian faith? – not one.'[16] Shaftesbury later persuaded himself that G. O. Trevelyan must have omitted from the *Life and Letters* the evidence which would have provided a vital insight into Macaulay's 'real religious feelings and character'.[17] But despite those 'graceful, tender, touching, and delightful' letters to Hannah and

Margaret which Shaftesbury saw as outpourings of a 'loving and religious soul'[18] – despite, too, some conventional and prudential defences of the Protestant religion made on the Edinburgh hustings – there seems to be no evidence that this product of Clapham had any serious religious beliefs or emotions whatsoever.

Perhaps this is simply one aspect of that non-speculative and non-introspective cast of mind on which so many commentators have insisted. In any case, his chief concern with religious questions seems to have been that they should not be exploited for political ends. His hostility to all manifestations of a narrowly sectarian kind emerges clearly from an exchange which took place during the Leeds election of 1832. Challenged by a Methodist minister in the crowd to declare his religious faith, Macaulay demanded that the man stand up and identify himself and then plunged into an expression of his abhorrence of any mixing of politics and religion:[19]

> I must say that I have heard with the greatest shame and sorrow the question which has been proposed to me; and with peculiar pain and sorrow do I learn, that this question was proposed by a minister of religion. I do most deeply regret that any person should think it necessary to make a meeting like this an arena for theological discussion. I will not be a party to turning this assembly to such a purpose. My answer is short, and in one word – I regret that it should be necessary to utter it. Gentlemen, I am a Christian. (Cheers.) Gentlemen, this is no subject for hearty acclamation. I have done; I will say no more; no man shall have to say of me that I was the person who, when this disgraceful inquisition was entered into in an assembly of Englishmen, actually brought forward the most sacred subjects to be canvassed here – who brought forward these subjects to be a matter for hissing or for cheering.

The bluff common sense and forthrightness of this seem irresistible. One does not doubt the effectiveness of the tactic or the essential rightness of the sentiments. But there is nothing here to contradict Walter Bagehot's insistence, in his review of the third and fourth volumes of the *History*, that Macaulay had 'no passionate self-questionings, no indomitable fears, no asking perplexities',[20] and that he was therefore ill-equipped to understand men who were seized by power-ful feelings, whether spiritual or physical. Bagehot contrasts Macaulay's treatment of Cromwell with Carlyle's as a way of demonstrating the former's incapacity to grasp the depths of religious feeling and commitment which sustained the English Puritans.

Though Macaulay was less free from emotional complexities than these comments suggest – like Matthew Arnold, Bagehot took the smooth tenor of the work as a direct reflection of the author's own personality – he certainly had only limited insight into the nature of religious movements and the characters of passionate men. It was, however, a weakness which he seems to have taken either consciously or unconsciously into account, choosing to write for the most part about figures less than heroic and periods whose crises were chiefly constitutional. Some sense of his weaknesses as a psychologist may also have contributed to his decision not to resume those early experiments in fiction he had published in the pages of *Knight's Quarterly*. But if J. Cotter Morison, in his English Men of Letters volume of 1882, had grounds for declaring that Macaulay had 'no ear for the finer harmonies of the inner life',[21] he perhaps exaggerated Macaulay's avoidance of moral issues, his lack of what Morison calls ethical depth. Quoting the *Journal* reflection of 25 October 1857 on the Indian Mutiny, Morison responds to Macaulay's self-questioning 'Is this wrong?' with a resounding condemnation: 'Clearly it was wrong in a man of Macaulay's culture and experience. He might have remembered with what just severity he had branded cruelty in his *History* and *Essays*, with what loathing he had spoken of the Duke of York's delight in witnessing the infliction of torture.'[22] One can agree with this, and yet feel that Morison is himself lacking in historical perspective. Deeply disturbed as he was by events in India, and by the versions of those events which had reached England, Macaulay could not remain untouched by the national mood of shock, outrage, and desire for revenge. Given the savagery and universality of that mood, he must at least be given credit for the honesty with which he records and attempts to confront the upsurge of feelings to which he had previously been a stranger.

Try as he might to view all events, past and present, in a long perspective, Macaulay remained very much a man of his time and place, just as the *Lays*, the *Essays*, and the *History* itself can now be seen as distinctive documents of early Victorianism – optimistic, patriotic, liberal in principle, conservative in feeling. Leslie Stephen argues in *Hours in a Library* that Macaulay's power to speak so directly to contemporary readers stemmed from his fundamental identification with 'some of the most deeply-seated tendencies of the national character. . . . If he flatters his countrymen, it is the unconscious and spontaneous effect of his participation in their weaknesses.'[23] Although Stephen sees this identification as the source of 'some annoying peculiarities', including 'a certain brutal insularity' and touches of commonness and even vulgarity of style, he also recognizes that it gives Macaulay a kind of strength: 'His patriotism may be narrow, but it implies faith in the really good qualities, the manliness, the spirit of justice, and the strong moral sense of his countrymen.'[24] Whether or not these qualities are indeed recognizable as national characteristics of the British, they can reasonably be attributed to Macaulay himself. At the same time, any image of him as a public figure of somewhat John Bullish dogmatism, chauvinism and, in his last years, conservatism needs to be set against the impression irresistibly created by the *Life and Letters* and the reminiscences of those who knew him well – the impression of a private character warm, affectionate, charming, considerate, generous, and tolerant. According to Dean Milman's Royal Society obituary, even that overpowering conversational manner Macaulay often adopted on social occasions – largely, as Milman suggests, for the benefit for those who had come especially to hear him – was entirely abandoned in more intimate circumstances: 'But in the quiet intercourse with the single friend, no great talker was more free, easy and genial, than Macaulay. There was the most equable interchange of thought; he listened with as much courtesy, as he spoke with gentle and pleasant persuasiveness.'[25] The obvious comparison with Dr Johnson was happily made by Thackeray in the *Cornhill* immediately following Macaulay's death: 'The critic who says Macaulay had no heart, might say that Johnson had none: and two men more generous, and more loving, and more hating, and more partial, and more noble, do not live in our history.'[26]

The crucial dichotomy in Macaulay's life, however, is not that mild discrepancy between his public and his private face, but rather the persistent struggle between literature and politics for the domination of his career. Cotter Morison's view is that Macaulay had extraordinary gifts both as a politician and as a writer but was prevented by circumstances from realizing either side of his genius to the full: his lack of independent means handicapped his political career; his involvement in politics hampered him as a writer in so far as it encouraged his instinctive aversion from introspection and speculative thought. 'Macaulay's mode of life', Morison argues, 'was adverse to inwardness, reflection, meditation; and he had no such innate tendency in that direction that he could dispense with help from any quarter. Outward circumstances alone prevented him from taking a first rank in politics; circumstances and inward disposition combined to deprive him of the very highest rank in literature.'[27] The theory, though attractive, seems over-stated. If Macaulay had been independently wealthy, his career might indeed have been different, but he would then have been a different man. As things were, it is difficult to conceive of Macaulay behaving as anything other than what he so patently was – a man with an immense appetite for the world of great affairs, past and present, and with an unusual capacity for administration, whether of a government department or of a great literary project such as the *History of England*, but ultimately lacking in such indispensable qualities of the great political leader as driving ambition, flexibility, and acute insight into the characters and motives of others. It seems fair to say, indeed, that the qualities which made Macaulay stand out among his political contemporaries were precisely those which disqualified him from positions of leadership. If he was a great orator, he was a poor debater, and his influence in the House of Commons was the product not of a charismatic personality nor of a majestic voice but of a reputation for absolute probity and of a capacity to marshal facts and instances into a semblance of irrefutable logic. He was justly respected as a man of principle, but his principles were such as no political leader could have afforded. Despite his admiration for Halifax the great Trimmer and and the stance of 'the philosophic historian' (I, 243), he was in practice reluctant to abandon any position once deliberately arrived at – clinging even to the very phrases in which that position was originally formulated. Bagehot makes the point very effectively in his *Economist* obituary of Macaulay:[28]

> He was admirable in his treatment of a well-understood crisis, involving old, clear, and well-discussed principles, on which conflict ran high. But he had not that quick and ready appreciation of transient symptoms, – that half-instinctive, half-empirical tact, which is needed in the constitution of a party leader or a great statesman.

From our present perspective it is perhaps more to the point to acknowledge how remarkable it was that the author of the *Essays* and the *History of England* should also have figured so largely in the political life of his day and, more briefly but scarcely less significantly, in the history of the Indian sub-continent. And while involvement in

politics absorbed much of Macaulay's time and energy, it also contributed a great deal to his success as a writer. Conceivably, as Cotter
Morison would argue, it prevented him from becoming another kind
of writer, but Macaulay is so absolutely and almost unchangeably
himself from the very beginning of his literary career to the very end –
from the Prize Essay on William III to that last, posthumous volume
of the *History* – that it is hard to see any traces whatsoever of an alternative direction that he might have taken. His experience in the House
of Commons, in ministerial office, and in India gave him an acquaint-
ance with politics, with politicians, and with great events which was
to make a major contribution to the presentation of character and event
in the *History* and in some of the essays. It also enhanced that sense of
the continuity of British history, and of the pressing need to reassert
that continuity, which provides one of the *History*'s chief motivating
forces. In a very practical way, too, Macaulay's political career helped
him to become the man who would write the *History*: it gave him the
assurance that his views would be listened to with more than ordinary
attention, and it was the source of that wealth which eventually
permitted him the necessary leisure for the long processes of research
and composition. Thackeray, indeed, in his *Cornhill* obituary, speaks
of Macaulay's having gone to India to secure an independence not for
the sake of a political career but that he might devote himself more
exclusively to literature.

If Thackeray exaggerates here, it is because he always saw Macaulay
as first and foremost a man of letters. Reviewing the first collected
edition of the *Essays* in the *Pictorial Times*, he had spoken of the new
distinction which Macaulay had given to the profession of letters
itself:[29]

> He is the first literary man in this country who has made himself
> honourably and worthily the equal of the noblest and wealthiest
> in it; this may be no cause for respect with the reader, perhaps,
> but with every *writer* it should be, who is glad to see in another
> his own profession advanced, and success and honour bestowed at
> last upon one of a body of men who were but a few score years
> since begging guineas from my lord for a dedication; the bye-
> word for poverty, the theme for sneering wits.

One can set alongside this Frederick Arnold's acknowledgment of
Macaulay's interment in Westminster Abbey 'among the nobles of
the land to whose rank his own genius and labour had raised him' and

Lord Shaftesbury's diary entry on learning of Macaulay's elevation to the peerage: 'Macaulay is to be made a Peer. This is wise, politic, useful, conservative. . . . It will be taken as a compliment by literary men – small and great.'[30]

Macaulay has, then, his place in the history of the literary profession, as he certainly does in the history of both England and India. Nor can there be any doubt of his immense significance as a cultural phenomenon in the second half of the nineteenth century when the *History*, the *Lays*, and, above all, the *Essays* continued to command an enormous readership. It was this kind of popularity which led Matthew Arnold to characterize Macaulay as 'the great apostle of the Philistines'[31] and as one 'pre-eminently fitted to give pleasure to all who are beginning to feel enjoyment in the things of the mind.'[32] Several years earlier Bagehot had referred to the '*intellectual entertainment*' offered by the *History* and the *Essays* alike: 'To read Macaulay for a day, would be to pass a day of easy thought, of pleasant placid emotion.'[33] While Bagehot did not by any means think this the highest kind of writing, he could speak of it, without condescension, as both useful and attractive and suggest that Macaulay's great appeal lay in his capacity to make dull things interesting: 'He has something that suits the readers of Mr. Hallam; he has something which will please the readers of Mr. Thackeray. The first wonder to find themselves reading such a style; the last are astonished at reading on such topics – at finding themselves studying by casualty.'[34]

It seems safe to assume that Macaulay would not have repudiated the role of popular educator. He strove for clarity and immediate comprehensibility in all his writings, approaching each of them as if it were a particular kind of oratorical performance; he wanted his essays to reach a wide audience and took satisfaction in the large sales of the collected editions; his early ambition for the *History* was that it should retrieve for historical writing some of the popularity which had been engrossed by fiction. And whatever else may be said of his influence upon Victorian England, he certainly did much to sustain a national sense of historical and cultural continuity by reviving interest in the almost forgotten constitutional crises of the late seventeenth century, by keeping before the nineteenth-century imagination some of the major literary and political figures of the eighteenth century, and by giving eloquent expression to the principles underlying the preserving revolution of 1832.

Macaulay, clearly, is a writer not of exploration but of statement.

His thinking was unoriginal and his sensibility limited, but he had an unequalled capacity for organization and clarity. His role, as he himself fully recognized, was not critical or innovatory but didactic and expository, and his success in his own day was based upon an acute sense of audience. He has that capacity to instruct by pleasing on which Dr Johnson laid such stress, and his very weaknesses of dogmatism, hearty patriotism, and occasional vulgarity are inseparable from that superb assurance of manner and comprehensiveness of view which gives such impetus and verve not only to the oratory of the speeches and the balladry of the *Lays* but to the prose narrative of the *History* and the best of the essays. As Thackeray observed in reviewing the 1843 *Essays*:[35]

> It requires no more science than may be had from a circulating
> library or a Scott's [sic] novel to be delighted with narratives
> not less exciting than the best fictions of the novelist; while the
> reader who seeks for profit and study more than amusement, will
> better see the extraordinary powers of this brilliant intellect and
> the amazing variety and extent of learning which must have gone
> to the preparation of essays which all may so easily read.

Notes

Chapter 1   Beginnings

1 Frederick Arnold, *The Public Life of Lord Macaulay* (London, 1862), p. 363.
2 David Newsome, *The Parting of Friends: A Study of the Wilberforces and Henry Manning* (London, 1966), p. 21.
3 See Noel Annan, 'The Intellectual Aristocracy', in J. H. Plumb, ed., *Studies in Social History: A Tribute to G. M. Trevelyan* (London, 1955), pp. 243–87.
4 James Stephen, 'The Clapham Sect', *Edinburgh Review*, 80 (1844): 261.
5 Sydney Smith, *Works* (London, 1839–40), III, 329.
6 *Edinburgh*, 80:271.
7 Quoted in George W. E. Russell, *The Household of Faith: Portraits and Essays* (London, 1902), p. 225.
8 *Edinburgh*, 80:270–1.
9 Macaulay's manuscript *Journal*, now in the Library of Trinity College, Cambridge: Trinity MS 0–15–5, entry for 21 August 1852; George Otto Trevelyan, *The Life and Letters of Lord Macaulay* (London, 1908), p. 571. This work was originally published in two volumes in 1876, but all references are to the enlarged one-volume edition of 1908, subsequently referred to as *LL*.
10 E. M. Forster, *Marianne Thornton, 1797–1887: A Domestic Biography* (London, 1956), p. 46.
11 Ibid.
12 Ibid., p. 47.
13 *LL*, p. 20.
14 Trinity MS 0–15–5, 14 September 1852; *LL*, p. 573.
15 *LL*, p. 25.
16 Viscountess Knutsford, *Life and Letters of Zachary Macaulay* (London, 1900), p. 232.
17 Ibid., p. 234.
18 Ibid., p. 463.
19 *Edinburgh*, 80:270. Macaulay approved of Stephen's portrait of his father, and wrote to his sister Fanny on 10 July 1844: 'My influence over the ER

is so well known that a mere fulsome eulogy of my father appearing in that work would only call forth derision. I therefore am really glad that Stephen has introduced into his sketch some little characteristic touches which, in themselves, were not beauties' (Trinity MS o-15-71; *LL*, p. 50).

20 Memoir written by Macaulay's sister, Hannah Trevelyan, for her son, G. O. Trevelyan, to use in his biography of his uncle: Trinity MS o-15-12E; *LL*, p. 49.

21 Knutsford, op. cit., p. 233.

22 Ibid.

23 Ibid., p. 3.

24 Trinity MS o-15-12A; compare the later letter on the same subject, *LL*, pp. 34–35.

25 Trinity MS o-15-12E; partly quoted *LL*, p. 48.

26 Forster, op. cit., p. 79.

27 Knutsford, op. cit., p. 463.

28 Ibid., p. 271.

29 Ibid., p. 3.

30 Ibid., p. 5.

31 Trinity MS o-15-12E; *LL*, p. 44.

32 Knutsford, op. cit., p. 460.

33 Ibid., p. 343.

34 See *LL*, pp. 63–4.

35 Ibid., p. 82. See also the account of the meeting, apparently by Macaulay's younger brother, Charles, quoted in Knutsford, p. 420, and the description by Marianne Thornton in a letter to Hannah More, *LL*, p. 722 (the letter is partly quoted and the author identified in Forster, pp. 128–9).

36 For a full discussion of the identification of this first *Edinburgh* contribution see my article, 'Father and Son: Macaulay's *Edinburgh* Debut', *Review of English Studies*, 21 (1970):159–67.

37 Trinity MS o-15-73.

38 *LL*, p. 83.

39 Trinity MS o-15-12E.

40 See Knight's self-exculpatory 'Advertisement' to the last volume, *Knight's Quarterly Magazine*, 3 (1824):vii–viii.

41 All Macaulay's prose contributions to *Knight's Quarterly*, with the exception of the essay 'On West Indian Slavery' which formed the basis of his first *Edinburgh* article, were reprinted in the two posthumous volumes of *Miscellaneous Writings* (London, 1860), edited by his friend, Thomas Flower Ellis; a number of poems from the magazine were also included.

42 The two love poems were 'Oh Rosamund!' and 'By thy love, fair girl of France' (*Knight's Quarterly* 1 [1823]:219–20); the historical poems were the two Songs of the Huguenots (2 [1824]:33–5), and the two Songs of the Civil War (2:321–5).

43 *Knight's Quarterly*, 1:38.

Notes

44 Ibid., 3 (1824):121.
45 Ibid., 3:302.
46 Ibid.
47 *Edinburgh Review*, 42 (1825):306. Subsequent quotations from Macaulay's contributions to the *Edinburgh* are identified by volume and page numbers incorporated within parentheses in the text.
48 *Blackwood's*, 30 (1831):411.
49 Trinity MS O–15–12A.

Chapter 2 Apprenticeship in Polemics

1 Trinity MS O–15–12A; *LL*, p. 78.
2 Trinity MS O–15–12E; *LL*, p. 92.
3 Trinity MS O–15–12E.
4 'Mill's *Essay on Government*. Utilitarian Logic and Politics', 49 (1829): 159–89; 'Bentham's Defence of Mill. Utilitarian System of Philosophy', 49:273–99; 'Utilitarian Theory of Government, and the "Greatest Happiness Principle"', 50 (1829): 99–125; 'Sadler's *Law of Population, and Disproof of Human Superfecundity*', 51 (1830):297–321; 'Sadler's *Refutation* Refuted', 52 (1831):504–29.
5 *Critical and Historical Essays, Contributed to the Edinburgh Review* (London, 1843), I, viii.
6 *Blackwood's*, 22 (1827):403.
7 Ibid., 29 (1831):404, 405.
8 Ibid., 29:404.
9 Ibid., 27 (1830):679.
10 Trinity MS O–15–12E; *LL*, p. 101.
11 *Rural Rides*, ed. G. D. H. and Margaret Cole (London, 1930), II, 406.
12 There appears to be no basis for the often-repeated claim that Macaulay was seeking to avenge himself for parliamentary defeats suffered at Croker's hands during the debates on the Reform Bill: see E. S. de Beer, 'Macaulay and Croker: The Review of Croker's Boswell', *Review of English Studies*, 10 (1959):388–97. The editor of the *Croker Papers* claimed that 'The attack defeated itself by its very violence, and therefore it did the book no harm whatever. Between forty and fifty thousand copies have been sold, although Macaulay boasted with great glee that he had "smashed" it' (Louis J. Jennings, ed., *The Croker Papers*, London, 1884, II, 47). But the original five-volume edition of 1831 was apparently withdrawn: see G. Birkbeck Hill's edition (revised by L. F. Powell) of the *Life of Johnson* (Oxford, 1934–50), I, xli. What sold so well were the later editions – prepared by John Wright (1835, reissued 1836) and by Croker himself (1848) – which

removed from Boswell's text much of the interpolated matter to which Macaulay had objected.

13 Although Carlyle attacked Macaulay's paradoxes about Boswell in his *Fraser's* review of 1832, he was in total agreement on the question of the integrity of Boswell's text: the edition's 'grand fundamental failing' was that Croker 'instead of working on the margin with his Pen, to elucidate as best might be, strikes boldly into the body of the page with his Scissors, and there snips at discretion! ... But, in fine, what ideas Mr. Croker entertains of a literary *whole* and the thing called *Book*, and how the very Printer's Devils did not rise in mutiny against such a conglomeration as this, and refuse to print it, – may remain a problem' ('Boswell's Life of Johnson', *Fraser's*, 5 [1832]:381–2). For a discussion of the views of Macaulay and Carlyle and of other early nineteenth-century commentators as a reflection of Romantic conceptions of biography, see the fine article by Francis R. Hart, 'Boswell and the Romantics: A Chapter in the History of Biographical Theory', *ELH*, 27 (1960):44–65.

14 BM Add. MS 34,614; Macvey Napier, Jr, ed., *Selections from the Correspondence of the Late Macvey Napier, Esq.* (London, 1879), p. 77. This latter work will subsequently be referred to as Napier.

15 See, for example, Macaulay's letters of 29 April and 25 December 1830, and 11 January 1831, Napier, pp. 80, 99–100.

16 When, a quarter of a century later, Macaulay wrote a biographical article on Johnson for the *Encyclopaedia Britannica*, he considerably tempered his earlier views on Johnson himself. But Boswell fared no better than in the *Edinburgh*: his vanity and folly, his inability to reason, his garrulousness are once more detailed, and the paradoxical greatness of the *Life of Johnson* remains a puzzle – for, despite all the faults of Boswell the man, 'his writings are read beyond the Mississippi, and under the Southern Cross, and are likely to be read as long as the English exists, either as a living or as a dead language' (*Encyclopaedia Britannica*, 8th edn, Edinburgh, 1856, XII, 800).

Chapter 3 Reform, Revolution and Party

1 *Blackwood's*, 30 (1831):410.

2 G. H. Francis, *Orators of the Age* (London, 1847), p. 79.

3 Paul M. Zall, 'Selina Macaulay's Diary', *Bulletin of the New York Public Library*, 66 (1962):442.

4 Francis, op. cit., pp. 97–8.

5 Trinity MS 0–15–12; *LL*, p. 146.

6 Trinity MS 0–15–12A; *LL*, p. 166.

7 Trinity MS 0–15–12A; *LL*, p. 178.

8 *LL*, p. 90.

9 Trinity MS 0–15–6, 22 January 1853; *LL*, p. 613 (misdated).

10 There was talk of his writing articles on Burke in 1840 and again in 1844; see Napier, pp. 322, 466.

11 BM Add. MS 34,619; Napier, p. 265.

12 *Speeches of the Right Honorable T. B. Macaulay, M.P. Corrected by Himself* (London, 1854), p. 81.

13 In 1844, in his second essay on Chatham, Macaulay gave an eloquent summary of the position of Burke and the Rockingham Whigs: see *Edinburgh* 80:572.

14 *Speeches*, p. 163.

15 Ibid., pp. 26–7.

16 *The Works of the Right Honourable Edmund Burke* (London, 1854–7), II, 516.

17 Sir James Mackintosh, *History of the Revolution in England in 1688* (London, 1834), p. 302.

18 *Speeches*, pp. 18–19.

19 Burke, II, 516.

20 Ibid., II, 517.

21 *Speeches*, p. 3.

22 Ibid., p. 87. The phrase quoted does not occur in the Hansard report of the speech (Third Series, 10:926–34), but the general tenor of Macaulay's remarks is similar to the *Speeches* version of 1854.

23 See Burke, I, 447.

24 Ibid., I, 308.

25 For a full discussion of Burke's views on party see Harvey C. Mansfield, Jr, *Statesmanship and Party Government: A Study of Burke and Bolingbroke* (Chicago, 1965).

26 Burke, I, 375.

Chapter 4   The Indian Years

1 Quoted in A. S. Turberville and Frank Beckwith, 'Leeds and Parliamentary Reform, 1820–1832', *Publications of the Thoresby Society*, 41 (1943):67–8.

2 Frederick Arnold, *The Public Life of Lord Macaulay* (London, 1862), p. 143.

3 Trinity MS O–15–12A; *LL*, p. 209.

4 Arnold, op. cit., p. 144.

5 Trinity MS O–15–12B; *LL*, p. 228.

6 Trinity MS O–15–12B; *LL*, p. 234.

7 Trinity MS O–15–12D; *LL*, p. 263.

8 Gerald and Natalie Robinson Sirkin, 'The Battle of Indian Education: Macaulay's Opening Salvo Newly Discovered', *Victorian Studies*, 14 (1971): 409–10.

9 H. Woodrow, ed., *Macaulay's Minutes on Education in India* (Calcutta, 1862), p. 108.

10 Sirkin, op. cit., 411.
11 Woodrow, op. cit., p. 115.
12 *Miscellaneous Writings*, II, 438.
13 See *LL*, p. 225.
14 *Speeches*, p. 160.
15 C. D. Dharker, ed., *Lord Macaulay's Legislative Minutes* (Madras, 1946), p. 252.
16 In the Preface to her edition of *The Works of Lord Macaulay* (London, 1866), I, v, Lady Trevelyan writes: 'These papers were entirely written by Lord Macaulay, but the substance of them was the result of the joint deliberations of the Indian Law Commission, of which he was President.'
17 *A Penal Code Prepared by the Indian Law Commissioners, and Published by Command of the Governor General of India in Council* (Calcutta, 1837), 'Notes', p. 37.
18 Eric Stokes, *The English Utilitarians and India* (Oxford, 1959).
19 Trinity MS 0–15–12B; *LL*, pp. 234–5.
20 *LL*, pp. 249–50.
21 Trinity MS 0–15–12A; *LL*, pp. 165–6.
22 See, for example, Macaulay's comments to Napier of 20 July 1838 on Brougham's 'squandering the remains of his public character in an attempt to ruin the party of which he was a member then [in 1833] and of which I am a member still'. Earlier in the same letter he had warned Napier against allowing Brougham to use the *Edinburgh* in his campaign against his old colleagues:

> His wish, I imagine, is to establish . . . such an ascendancy as may enable him to drag the Review along with him to any party to which his furious passions may lead him, – to the Radicals, to the Tories, to any set of men by whose help he may be able to revenge himself on old friends whose only crime is that they could not help finding him a habitual and incurable traitor (BM Add. MS 34,619; Napier, pp. 262–3).

23 Trinity MS 0–15–12B, letter of 23 December 1833.
24 Trinity MS 0–15–12E.
25 A copy of this letter is in the possession of Mrs Humphry Trevelyan; partly quoted *LL*, p. 280.
26 Trinity MS 0–15–12; *LL*, p. 311.
27 Ibid.
28 BM Add. MS 34,623; Napier, p. 395. Macaulay was referring to B. G. Niebuhr, *The History of Rome*, trans. Hare and Thirlwall, 2 vols (Cambridge, 1828–32).
29 See *LL*, pp. 316–17.
30 This collection of ballads is now in the Library of Trinity College, Cambridge (MS 0–15–67). The printed text of the Leicester ballad bears Macaulay's holograph annotations identifying the protagonists; its authorship

is confirmed from a collection of Macaulay's poems copied out by his sister, Selina, Trinity MS 0–15–68.

31 BM Add. MS 34,623; Napier, p. 411.
32 *Lays of Ancient Rome* (London, 1842), p. 175.
33 Ibid., p. 36.
34 Ibid., pp. 43–4.
35 See *LL*, p. 422.
36 *Lays*, p. 9.
37 *LL*, p. 426.
38 *Lays*, p. 10.
39 *LL*, pp. 281.

Chapter 5   Time of Decision

1 Nowell C. Smith, ed., *The Letters of Sydney Smith* (Oxford, 1953), p. 675.
2 Ibid., p. 686.
3 BM Add. MS 34, 619; Napier, p. 258.
4 BM Add. MS 34, 619; Napier, p. 265.
5 Trinity MS 0–15–12; *LL*, 319–20.
6 See *LL*, pp. 364–5.
7 See, for example, the entry for 8 December 1838, Trinity MS 0–15–1.
8 See, for example, entries for 9 March and 22 April 1839, Trinity MS 0–15–1.
9 *LL*, p. 364.
10 BM Add. MS 34,618; Napier, pp. 192–3. The work Macaulay chose to review was Thomas Peregrine Courtenay, *Memoirs of the Life, Works, and Correspondence of Sir William Temple, Bart.* (London, 1836).
11 Trinity MS 0–15–72 (copy made by Macaulay's sister, Fanny).
12 BM Add. MS 34,618; Napier, p. 193.
13 See, for example, Macaulay's examination of Temple's proposal for the formation of the Council of Thirty in relation to the general issue of Cabinet government, 68:154–63.
14 For a full discussion of the Phalaris section of the essay see my article, 'Macaulay at Work: An Example of his Use of Sources', *Transactions of the Cambridge Bibliographical Society*, 5 (1970), 90–8.
15 The last name is a misprint for 'De Pauw'; the error was corrected in the 1843 collected edition of the *Essays*.
16 The book on Clive under review was Sir John Malcolm, *The Life of Robert Lord Clive* (London, 1836).
17 See, for example, the comments on Macaulay's treatment of Sir Elijah Impey in E. B. Impey's *Memoirs of Sir Elijah Impey* (London, 1846), Sir J. F. Stephen's *The Story of Nuncomar* (London, 1885), and [H. D. Traill], 'Macaulay and Sir Elijah Impey', *Macmillan's Magazine*, 52 (1885):422–34.
18 Macaulay also took the opportunity of showing the proofs to various

experts on India, and he asked for a revise as well as a proof of the essay – a clear indication of the care he took with it. See Napier, pp. 294, 313.

19 BM Add. MS 34,620; Napier, p. 291.
20 *LL*, pp. 263–4.
21 After his return from India Bentinck became M.P. for Glasgow and, as the proponent of somewhat radical ideas, a controversial figure: see *LL*, pp. 393–4. Napier was apparently reluctant to print the tribute, but Macaulay stood firm: see Napier, p. 314.
22 The history of the conquests of Mexico and Peru would, in fact, have been reasonably familiar to educated readers in the mid-nineteenth century, especially from Books V and VI of William Robertson's *History of America* (1777, and many times reprinted) or from the translation of Diaz del Castillo's *The True History of the Conquest of Mexico* (1800, 1811) – a work which Macaulay mentions in his *Lays*, in the preface to 'The Battle of Lake Regillus'. In June 1850 he read Prescott's *Conquest of Mexico* and *Conquest of Peru*, of which the first English editions had just appeared. As he commented in his *Journal*, the impression of Aztec civilization given by Prescott was different from that which he had himself formed, and which he had invoked in the Clive essay: 'Read Prescott's Mexico & liked it much – very much – But I imagine [?] that he overrates the civilization of the Aztecs – If not, how cd they, numerous & brave as they were, be conquered by 4 or 500 men?' (Trinity MS 0–15–3, 20 June 1850).
23 For an opposing view of Macaulay's 'schoolboys' see Sir Walter Raleigh *On Writing and Writers*, ed. George Gordon (London, 1926), pp. 176–7.
24 A couple of pages later Macaulay refers to Hastings's 'long public life, so singularly chequered with good and evil, with glory and obloquy' (74:163). Similar phrasing occurs in Macaulay's comments on his great contemporary, Peel, in the preface to the authorized edition of the *Speeches*: 'on a calm review of his long and chequered public life, I acknowledge, with sincere pleasure, that his faults were much more than redeemed by great virtues, great sacrifices, and great services' (*Speeches*, p. vii).

Chapter 6 Biography, History, Criticism

1 Trinity MS 0–15–1; *LL*, p. 393.
2 BM Add. MS 34,622; Napier, pp. 352–3.
3 *Speeches*, p. 261.
4 BM Add. MS 34,625; Napier, p. 500.
5 See the excerpts from Macaulay's *Journal* during his Italian travels in *LL*, pp. 352–4, 356–61, 362–70, especially the account of the visit to Naples, pp. 367–9.
6 *Essays* (1843), I, viii.
7 BM Add. MS 34,621; Napier, p. 343.

8 Trinity MS 0–15–4. The paragraphs persisted in the 1852 reissue of the 1850 one-volume edition of the *Essays*, but subsequently disappeared altogether.

9 *LL*, p. 431.

10 In two letters written at the time of the Madame D'Arblay essay (3 and 10 January 1843; not included in Napier, presumably because of their comments on Croker and Lord Hertford) Macaulay deals at some length with Croker's 'ferocious insults to women' (BM Add. MS 34,623).

11 BM Add. MS 34,623; Napier, p. 429.

12 BM Add. MS 34,623; Napier, pp. 427–8.

13 Trinity MS 0–15–1; *LL*, pp. 523–4.

14 Trinity MS 0–15–1, entry for 22 April 1849; *LL*, p. 526, incorrectly dated.

15 *Essays* (1843), I, viii–ix.

16 BM Add. MS 34,622; Napier, pp. 393–4.

17 Martin J. Svaglic, in his recent essay, 'Classical Rhetoric and Victorian Prose' (in George Levine and William Madden, eds, *The Art of Victorian Prose*, New York, 1968, pp. 268–88), argues persuasively for seeing Macaulay's Milton essay as written largely in reaction to Johnson's 'Life of Milton'.

18 BM Add. MS 34,622; Napier, p. 367.

19 See, for example, the references to *Dissertation upon the Epistles of Phalaris* (78:199), Congreve (200), Dryden (200), Frederic the Great's French poetry (206), Temple (229), Jeremy Collier and the drama (231–2).

20 This information was later incorporated into the *Essays* text of the essay. For references to research for various late essays see letters in Napier: 4 December 1840 (Comic Dramatists), p. 338; 30 April 1841 (Warren Hastings), p. 347; 20 September 1841 (Warren Hastings), p. 364; 23 February 1842 (Frederic the Great), p. 381.

21 Samuel Johnson, *Prefaces Biographical and Critical to the Works of the English Poets* (London, 1779–81), V, 155.

22 This passage is much revised in the manuscript: the second 'still' is an afterthought, and Macaulay first wrote 'strangers who visit it' and then cancelled the last three words, achieving the sequence: 'His college is still … His portrait still hangs … strangers are still told …' (BM Add. MS 34,629, f. 262).

23 This passage is also much revised in the manuscript, but it is not possible to reconstruct with confidence either the original version or the stages of revision. Clearly, however, the word 'still' was twice written and crossed out before Macaulay finally arrived at the phrase 'still overhung with dark verdure' (BM Add. MS 34,629, f. 281).

24 Compare the account of the first night of *Cato* in the 1835 essay on Mackintosh, where Macaulay comments: 'The history of that night was, in miniature, the history of two generations' (61:322).

25 Robert D. Horn's 'Addison's *Campaign* and Macaulay' (*PMLA*, 63 [1948]: 896), points out quite correctly that one of the telling details with which

Macaulay fleshes out his account of the bad Blenheim tributes involves a serious misquotation and the compression of a great many lines of verse into three. This was one time when Macaulay's famous memory seems to have let him down badly. However, in calling these misquoted lines Macaulay's 'most original contribution to the correction of Miss Aikin's errors in Addison scholarship', Mr Horn is being neither fair nor accurate, as he would himself quickly have discovered had he checked the first edition of Macaulay's essay in the *Edinburgh*, with its numerous footnotes correcting Miss Aikin – footnotes omitted from F. C. Montague's 1903 edition to which Mr Horn consistently refers.

26 BM Add. MS 34,622; Napier, p. 369. Many works on Frederic in English, French, and German are recorded in the shelf-list Macaulay had made of his books in 1852. This list is now in the library at Wallington, Northumberland, the former Trevelyan family home, now owned by the National Trust.

27 Thackeray commented admiringly on this aspect of Macaulay's writing in his obituary tribute, 'Nil Nisi Bonum', *Cornhill*, 1 (1860):133.

Chapter 7   Theory and Practice

1 Trinity MS 0–15–1; *LL*, p. 464.
2 Quoted Frederick Arnold, *The Public Life of Lord Macaulay* (London, 1862), p. 315.
3 *Miscellaneous Writings*, II, 433.
4 The History essay was in fact quoted by Bagehot in an extremely perceptive article on the *History of England* written on the appearance of the second two volumes ('Mr. Macaulay', *National Review*, 2 [1856]: 357–87). Despite Macaulay's decision not to reprint it, the essay was fairly widely available, not only in the pages of the *Edinburgh* but also in the pirated American editions of the essays which had entered England in considerable numbers before the appearance of the authorized edition of 1843.
5 BM Add. MS 34,619; Napier, p. 257.
6 BM Add. MS 34,620; Napier, p. 288.
7 G. Kitson Clark has recently demonstrated that in the *History of England* Macaulay did not always live up to the standards he outlined here as a young man. His discussion of Macaulay's presentation of the trial of Dame Alice Lisle shows convincingly not only that Macaulay attributed to his characters expressions 'not authenticated by sufficient testimony' but also that the process of 'selection, rejection, and arrangement' could have important consequences for historical accuracy as well as for literary effect. Macaulay no doubt believed that his presentation of Judge Jeffreys at the trial of Dame Alice offered an essentially true picture of his character, but Dr Kitson Clark is able to point to considerable discrepancies between

Macaulay's version and the account in the *State Trials* which had served as his source (G. Kitson Clark, *The Critical Historian*, London, 1967, pp. 99–107). George Levine, in *The Boundaries of Fiction: Carlyle, Macaulay, Newman* (Princeton, 1968), pp. 155–6, has an interesting discussion of the literary effect of the Dame Alice episode but does not consider Macaulay's use of his source.

8 BM Add. MS 34,622; Napier, p. 367.

9 See p. 133.

10 See chapter 9, n. 17.

11 Levine, op. cit., p. 116.

12 Ronald Weber, in 'Singer and Seer: Macaulay on the Historian as Poet' (*Papers on Language and Literature*, 3 [1967]:210–19), has argued persuasively that Macaulay envisaged 'a unique role' for the historian, 'one akin to and even replacing that traditionally held by the imaginative writer, and especially the poet' (210). While I cannot accept the analysis in its entirety, it offers important insights into the intimate connection between the theories of poetry and of history in Macaulay's early essays.

13 Trinity MS 0–15–1; *LL*, p. 515.

14 Trinity MS 0–15–1; *LL*, p. 516.

15 Trinity MS 0–15–1; *LL*, p. 519.

16 Trinity MS 0–15–2; Trevelyan gives a version of this passage (*LL*, p. 539) but incorrectly ascribes it to 15 April 1850.

17 BM Add. MS 34,619; Napier, pp. 264–5.

18 William A. Madden, 'Macaulay's Style', in Levine and Madden, eds, *The Art of Victorian Prose*, p. 149.

19 BM Add. MS 34,623; Napier, p. 397.

20 Levine, op. cit., p. 126.

21 Madden, op. cit., p. 133.

22 *The History of England from the Accession of James II*, 5 vols (London, 1849–61), I, 3. All subsequent references to the *History* are, unless otherwise stated, to the first editions of the various volumes and are incorporated within parentheses in the text. Volumes I and II bear the date 1849, although they appeared late in 1848; volumes III and IV came out in 1855 and volume V, posthumously, in 1861.

23 For a vigorous contemporary defence of Macaulay's historical method see Francis Jeffrey's letter to William Empson of 20 March 1849 in Lord Cockburn, *Life of Lord Jeffrey with a Selection from his Correspondence* (Edinburgh, 1852), II, 457–9.

24 Levine, op. cit., p. 122.

25 Trinity MS 0–15–1; *LL*, p. 517.

26 *LL*, p. 506.

27 *Peveril of the Peak* (Edinburgh, 1822), IV, 215.

28 Huddleston enters through the secret door presided over by Chiffinch, a door which provided access for an extremely varied range of visitors and

which takes on almost the function of a leitmotif in the narrative of Charles's and James's reigns: see, for example, II, 70, 553.

29 Sir Charles Firth, ed., *The History of England from the Accession of James the Second*, by Lord Macaulay (London, 1913–15), I, v.

30 *The History of England from the Accession of James the Second*, 7 vols (London, 1858), I, 292–3. The text for this small octavo edition was carefully prepared by Macaulay and was also used later in 1858 for a large octavo edition in four volumes.

31 Praz, *The Hero in Eclipse in Victorian Fiction* (London, 1956), p. 107.

32 See also the footnote about General Oglethorpe (I, 357), which has the same effect of emphasizing contact with the past.

33 See chapter 9, n. 3.

34 Trinity MS 0–15–1.

35 The note in 1848 is that of confidence, in 1822 it had been that of hope. The Prize Essay concludes: 'By such means was the constitution of England established. May similar moderation guide, and similar success reward the efforts of all who, in this and in every age, shall defend the great cause of human liberty and happiness!' (A. N. L. Munby, ed., 'Germ of a History: Twenty-three Quarto Pages of a Macaulay Cambridge Prize Essay', *The Times Literary Supplement*, 1 May 1969, p. 469).

36 Cockburn, op. cit., II, 459–60.

Chapter 8   The Method in Detail

1 Trinity MS 0–15–1; *LL*, p. 497.

2 Trinity MS 0–15–3, 28 August 1849.

3 Trinity MS 0–15–2, 19 September 1849.

4 Trinity MS 0–15–2, 6 October 1849.

5 Trinity MS 0–15–2, 15 November 1849.

6 See *LL*, p. 533. Macaulay had mentioned writing of the men of Enniskillen and Londonderry as early as 16 October 1849: *Journal*, Trinity MS 0–15–2.

7 Trinity MS 0–15–3; *LL*, p. 548.

8 Trinity MS 0–15–8; *LL*, p. 613.

9 Trinity MS 0–15–6, 5 January 1854; Trevelyan (*LL*, p. 613) incorrectly ascribes this *Journal* entry to 1 January.

10 Macaulay described the scenery of Killarney in his *Journal* on 23 August 1849: 'I never saw such turf, such moss, such a varnish on ivy, such a gorgeous scarlet on berries' (Trinity MS 0–15–3). See also the passage quoted from a letter to Ellis about Killarney, *LL*, p. 531.

11 Charles Smith, *The Ancient and Present State of the County of Kerry* (Dublin, 1756). Smith's descriptions of the Kerry scenery underlie Macaulay's account. Compare, for example, this passage by Smith about the Kerry mountains:

The grandeur, and magnificence of these mountains not only entertain and surprize the spectator, but he must be also agreeably amused, in contemplating the infinite variety of beautiful colouring they afford. For in one part may be seen the gayest verdure, blended with scarlet fruit, and snowy blossoms, well known properties of the *Arbutus*; and in other places, the most elegant variety of brown and yellow tints, caused by other kinds of trees and shrubs, appears: all these are intermixed with rock-work, and to soften the whole, a deep, smooth and noble bason of water extends it self beneath this scenary: but to give the reader an adequate idea of this place, would require the pencil of some excellent painter, rather than the pen of any prose writer (p. 123).

12 It is perhaps worth noting that Sir William Petty was an ancestor of Lord Lansdowne, for whose borough of Calne Macaulay first entered parliament in 1830, and for whom he felt a lifelong respect and affection.

13 Trinity MS 0–15–2, 10 October 1849.

14 The same pattern of associations, including the analogy with Mexico, occurs in the speech which Macaulay made on the state of Ireland on 19 February 1844, more than eleven years before the publication of chapter XII of the *History* in 1855. Macaulay had revised his speeches for volume publication in the summer of 1853, and it is possible that the passage dealing with 'dominant castes' in chapter XII was substantially revised after that date; in all probability, however, it was in much its present form as early as the autumn of 1849, and what we have here is an example of the way Macaulay's memory retained not only facts and judgments but the images and analogies in which they were first embodied in his thinking. For the speech see Hansard's *Parliamentary Debates*, Third Series, 72:1169–74, and *Speeches*, pp. 291–321.

15 Compare the account of his visit to Boom Hall which Macaulay wrote in his *Journal*, 31 August 1849; *LL*, pp. 498–9.

16 See *LL*, pp. 95 and 493.

17 Macaulay derived much of his information about the siege from the account by the Rev. George Walker, which includes a detailed price-list of food in the city. See George Walker, *A True Account of the Siege of London-derry*, in Bernard Nicholas, *The Whole Proceedings of the Siege of Drogheda; to Which is Added, A True Account of the Siege of London-derry* (Dublin, 1736), p. 148. This was the edition owned by Macaulay; it appears in lot 273 of the Sotheby sale of Macaulay's books in 1863. The catalogue of the sale is reprinted in A. N. L. Munby, ed., *Sale Catalogues of Eminent Persons*, vol. I (London, 1971), 251–333.

18 Trinity MS 0–15–3, 26 August 1849.

19 *LL*, p. 533.

20 See the report of Macaulay's 28 February 1833 speech on the disturbances in Ireland: *Hansard*, Third Series, 15:1326–37.

21 *Speeches*, p. 380.
22 *Speeches*, p. 377. This was the speech on the Maynooth College grant; on 27 September 1853, while he was correcting this passage for volume publication, Macaulay recorded in his *Journal*: 'After breakfast wrote a little – Maynooth – then walked – Home & wrote more – the famous peroration. How white poor Peel looked while I was speaking. I remember the effect of the words "There you sit" – ' (Trinity MS O-15-6; partly quoted *LL*, p. 453). The Hansard report (Third Series, 79:657) does not in fact contain the crucial phrase, and the wording suggests slightly less of a personal attack on Peel. But no doubt Peel knew for whom it was intended, and it is possible that Macaulay's memory of the 'There you sit' is more accurate than the shorthand-based report, since his rapid delivery made him notoriously difficult to take down. The differences between the two versions are matters not of substance but of phrasing, the volume text showing as usual superior polish and some improvement of the illustrations.
23 Trinity MS O-15-12.
24 See also the comments in his essay, 'Church and State', in particular *Edinburgh*, 49 (1839):276-80.
25 The account of the fate of the boys, originally twenty-five in number, in Viscountess Knutsford's *Life* of her grandfather is, to say the least, laconic:

> The superintendence of the young Africans whom he [Zachary Macaulay] had brought to England had hitherto occupied a considerable portion of his time. They were at last satisfactorily settled at Clapham under the eye of the excellent rector, John Venn, who had in conjunction with Thornton made a happy selection of a schoolmaster under whose charge they were placed. This man, Mr. William Greaves, who came from Yorkshire, did his duty thoroughly by his pupils; but the climate proved fatal to the constitutions of the greater number, and by the end of 1805 only six of the poor children remained alive. The disappointment was, however, made up to Mr. Greaves by many of the residents at Clapham Common sending their sons daily to profit by his tuition, a confidence of which he was well worthy, as his scholarship was good, and his kindly disposition and good temper won the attachment of the boys (Knutsford, p. 237).

It is perhaps only fair to add that Zachary Macaulay's own letters printed elsewhere in the biography show great concern for both the spiritual and physical welfare of his 'children', as he called them.
26 In March 1847 Macaulay was in correspondence with Ellis about the best place to send money to alleviate distress in Ireland. In the end he sent Ellis's contribution, on the recommendation of Charles Trevelyan, to a fund for the Highlands of Scotland, since it was likely to be used more effectively there than in Ireland (letters to Ellis of 3 and 15 March 1847, Trinity MS

0–15–12). See also the quotations from a letter of Macaulay's written from Ireland in August 1849, *LL*, p. 531, n. 2.

27 Many phrases of the 19 February 1844 speech recur in the *History*: for example, the statement that in his own country the Irish Catholic was 'a mere Gibeonite, a hewer of wood and a drawer of water' (*Speeches*, p. 296) is echoed in chapter VI of the *History* (II, 138). See also n. 14 above.

28 Trinity MS 0–15–2, 16 October 1849.

29 *Lays*, p. 58.

Chapter 9   Characterization in the *History*

1 The affinity between some of the *Tatler* and *Spectator* essays and seventeenth-century 'Characters' had been recognized by other critics before Macaulay: Johnson commented, for example, that the *Tatler* and *Spectator* 'like La Bruyere, exhibited the *Characters and Manners of the Age*' (*Prefaces . . . to the Works of the English Poets*, V, 31). In the manuscript of the Addison essay Macaulay followed Johnson in invoking La Bruyère when discussing Addison's characterization, but then deleted La Bruyère and substituted Clarendon (BM Add. MS 34,629, f. 303). That he did not do this merely to be different from Johnson or to remove a reference to a French author is suggested by the retention of La Bruyère's name later in the essay (78:237). The insertion of the name of the great English historian seems to have been integral to a deliberate revision of this whole passage: Macaulay had originally written 'create real men' but substituted 'call human beings into existence', presumably to bring into closer conjunction the methods and achievements of the historian and of the writer of fiction.

2 Throughout this chapter I have used 'Character' with an initial capital to distinguish the literary genre.

3 Macaulay's presentation of the clergy was challenged in the strongest terms by Churchill Babington, *Macaulay's Character of the Clergy in the Seventeenth Century Considered* (Cambridge, 1849). Babington is highly critical of Macaulay's use of literary sources, and is especially incensed by the account of clerical marriages, devoting a whole section of his critique to a defence of the honour and social status of the wives of seventeenth-century clergy. Bishop Phillpotts of Exeter engaged in a length epistolary controversy with Macaulay early in 1849 (it was published by the Bishop after Macaulay's death as *Correspondence Between the Bishop of Exeter and the Right Hon. T. B. Macaulay*, London, 1860), but his concern was with Macaulay's presentation of the theological beliefs of the post-Reformation clergy rather than with their social position. Gladstone also criticized Macaulay's treatment of the clergy in his review of Trevelyan's biography, *Quarterly Review*, 142 (1876):35. A specific comment on Macaulay's use of literary sources for the portraits of gentry and clergy is made by Sir Charles Firth:

The general lines of his pictures are correct enough, but individual features are over-coloured and over-emphasized till the result of the process is a caricature, not a portrait. The judgment which should be passed on his description of the clergy and the country gentlemen is not that he employs a kind of evidence which should not be used in such an account, but that he does not recognise that its value is limited, and that it should be employed with more caution (*A Commentary on Macaulay's History of England*, London, 1938, p. 97).

4 David Nichol Smith, *Characters from the Histories and Memoirs of the Seventeenth Century* (Oxford, 1918), p. ix.

5 The handling of character by Macaulay's predecessor, Hume, is discussed by Leo Braudy in his valuable study *Narrative Form in History and Fiction: Hume, Fielding and Gibbon* (Princeton, 1970). Mr Braudy sees Hume as turning 'away from the character sketch as a literary method and a historical truth because he feels the importance in history of the accumulations of time, the force of "mere chronology"' (p. 49).

6 *LL*, pp. 61–2.

7 *TLS*, 1 May 1969, p. 468.

8 It is interesting to compare with this the description of William with which Burnet opens his final Character of the king, following the account of William's reign and death: 'Thus lived and died *William* the Third, King of *Great-Britain*, and Prince of *Orange*; He had a thin and weak Body, was brown haired, and of a clear and delicate Constitution: He had a *Roman* Eagle Nose, bright and sparkling Eyes, a large front, and a Countenance composed to gravity and authority: All his Senses were critical and exquisite' (Gilbert Burnet, *History of His Own Time*, London, 1724–34, II, 304).

9 The Duke of Portland had allowed Mackintosh to make copies of the William-Bentinck correspondence; see Macaulay's footnote, II, 63.

10 The Bishop of Exeter, for example, was highly critical of the leniency with which Macaulay treated 'The deep strain of vice in his [William's] private morals' (*Correspondence*, p. 3).

11 See, for example, the *Journal* entries for 27 January 1849 (quoted above, p. 124) and 28 and 29 November 1855 (quoted *LL*, p. 618).

12 In chapter II of the *History* Macaulay defined that habit of mind of the great Trimmer which he saw as accounting for both the value of Halifax's writings and his failure to achieve quite the success in public life his great talents merited: 'he always saw passing events, not in the point of view in which they commonly appear to one who bears a part in them, but in the point of view which, after the lapse of many years, they appear to the philosophic historian' (I, 243).

13 G. M. Trevelyan, *Clio: A Muse, and Other Essays Literary and Pedestrian* (London, 1913), pp. 45–6.

14 For a full discussion of the historical accuracy of this episode, see Firth, *Commentary*, pp. 351–9.

15 See George Story, *An Impartial History of the Wars of Ireland, with a Continuation Thereof* (London, 1693) and William R. Wilde, *The Beauties of the Boyne, and its Tributary, the Blackwater* (Dublin, 1849). Macaulay's own visit to the Boyne took place on 21 August 1849 and is recorded in his *Journal*, Trinity MS 0–15–3.

16 Macaulay acknowledged in a footnote that he derived this detail from Story and it seems worth quoting part of Story's account for purposes of comparison: 'There was none of the *Irish* to be seen but a few poor starved Creatures who had scraped up some of the Husks of Oats nigh a Mill, to eat instead of better Food. It's a wonder to see how some of those Creatures live; I my self have seen them scratching like Hens amongst the Cindars for Victuals' (p. 72).

17 Although Macaulay could no doubt have cited historical chapter and verse for the feelings ascribed to William – the words actually quoted come almost directly from Story (p. 72) – the 'Perhaps' with which he opens the paragraph is the historian's acknowledgment of a speculative element in his narrative here. Since this is one of the points at which Macaulay comes nearest to claiming a novelist's freedom, it seems worth noting that the hint which transformed a traveller's comparison into an image both of character and of historical situation may well have been derived from a passage in Scott's *The Abbot* in which Sir Halbert Glendinning, just returned from the Low Countries, looks round at his own Scottish border lands and speaks to his wife of the contrast with the richly developed country he has just visited (*The Abbot*, Edinburgh, 1820, I, 61).

18 Macaulay earlier achieves a similar effect in the presentation in chapter V of the countryside which Monmouth sees from the top of Bridgwater steeple; for a discussion of that passage, see Levine, pp. 132–4.

19 These three were singled out in the 1828 essay on Hallam as having achieved glory of 'the most seductive and dazzling kind' (48:141) in founding monarchies on the ruins of republican institutions. The long and brilliant paragraphs in which the young Macaulay celebrates this glory are a mixture of disapproval and fascination, but the emphasis is on the rare power these men exhibited in changing the whole course of a nation's history.

20 *National Review*, 2 (1856):383; Bagehot is specifically contrasting Macaulay's pictorial methods of characterization with more dramatic techniques in which character is 'exhibited in its actions'.

21 See the discussion of the *Lays of Ancient Rome*, pp. 72–3.

Chapter 10   Conclusion

1 See *Journal* entry for 5 February 1849, *LL*, p. 521; see also chapter 9, n. 3, above.

2 Trinity MS 0–15–4; *LL*, p. 551.

3 Trinity MS 0–15–4; *LL*, p. 556.
4 *LL*, p. 566.
5 Ibid., p. 575.
6 See ibid., p. 579.
7 Ibid., p. 629.
8 G. O. Trevelyan records some of Macaulay's many acts of quiet generosity, *LL*, pp. 639–42.
9 Trinity MS 0–15–11; a number of excisions have been made from the original *Journal* page at this point and the resulting lacunae ('in my time . . . peer', 'what real', 'meant. With . . . hear that') are supplied from *LL*, p. 657.
10 *LL*, p. 677.
11 Trinity MS 0–15–9; *LL*, p. 643.
12 Trinity MS 0–15–11; *LL*, p. 683.
13 Trinity MS 0–15–11; *LL*, p. 684.
14 Frederick Arnold, *The Public Life of Lord Macaulay* (London, 1862), p. 362.
15 Ibid., p. 363.
16 Edwin Hodder, *The Life and Work of the Seventh Earl of Shaftesbury* (London, 1886), III, 73.
17 Ibid., III, 452.
18 Ibid.
19 Arnold, op. cit., p. 111.
20 *National Review*, 2 (1856):370.
21 J. Cotter Morison, *Macaulay* (London, 1882), p. 54.
22 Ibid., p. 179.
23 Leslie Stephen, *Hours in a Library* (new edn) (London, 1907), III, 270–1.
24 Ibid.
25 Reprinted as a foreword to Lady Trevelyan's edition of the final volume of Macaulay's *History of England* (1862), VIII, xxviii.
26 *Cornhill*, I (1860):134.
27 Morison, op. cit., p. 184.
28 *The Economist*, 17 (1859):1456.
29 Thackeray, *Stray Papers* (London, 1901), p. 203.
30 Hodder, op. cit., III, 72.
31 Matthew Arnold, *Essays in Criticism* (London, 1865), p. 251.
32 Matthew Arnold, *Mixed Essays* (London, 1879), p. 245.
33 *National Review*, 2:381.
34 *National Review*, 2:375.
35 Thackeray, *Stray Papers*, pp. 202–3.

Bibliography

Macaulay's contributions to the *Edinburgh Review* are listed in *The Wellesley Index to Victorian Periodicals, 1824 to 1900*, I (Toronto, 1966). For the fullest list of his speeches the reader must consult the indexes to Hansard. The useful bibliographies of primary and secondary materials in *The New Cambridge Bibliography of English Literature*, III (Cambridge, 1969) can be supplemented by those in Arthur Bryant, *Macaulay* (London, 1932), and in W. H. French and G. D. Sanders, eds, *The Reader's Macaulay* (New York, 1936); for a short and highly selective but absolutely sound listing, see John Clive and Thomas Pinney, eds, *Thomas Babington Macaulay: Selected Writings* (Chicago, 1972). A survey of Macaulay's unacknowledged and uncollected writings by Professor Pinney is forthcoming in the *Papers of the Bibliographical Society of America*.

A   Works by Macaulay

Collected editions

The Works of Lord Macaulay, ed. Lady Trevelyan, 8 vols, London, 1866. This edition, which is not absolutely complete, has been many times reprinted, most notably as the twelve-volume Albany edition of 1898.

Essays

'Germ of a History: Twenty-three Quarto Pages of a Macaulay Prize Essay', ed. A. N. L. Munby, *The Times Literary Supplement*, 1 May 1969, pp. 468–9. First publication of the essay on William III for which Macaulay won a Cambridge prize in 1822.

Critical and Historical Essays, Contributed to the Edinburgh Review, 3 vols, London, 1843. The first authorized collected edition of those essays from the *Edinburgh* which Macaulay himself wished to preserve. New issues and editions of this collection, the later ones containing additional post-1842 articles, appeared during Macaulay's lifetime in a variety of formats, and he exercised close personal supervision over the text of these editions at least as late as 1853.

Some, but not all, of the essays excluded by Macaulay appeared in the *Miscellaneous Writings* (below).

Biographies by Lord Macaulay Contributed to the Encyclopaedia Britannica, with Notes of his Connection with Edinburgh, and Extracts from his Letters and Speeches, Edinburgh, 1860. Collected edition of the five brief biographies contributed to the eighth edition of the *Encyclopaedia Britannica* between 1854 and 1859.

Miscellaneous Writings of Lord Macaulay, ed. T. F. E[llis], 2 vols, London, 1860. This collection, published immediately after Macaulay's death, reprinted all his prose contributions to *Knight's Quarterly Magazine* (1823–4), with the exception of the article 'On West Indian Slavery'. Also reprinted in these volumes were the poems on historical subjects from *Knight's Quarterly*, other occasional poems and ephemera, most of the articles from the *Edinburgh Review* not previously collected, and the *Encyclopaedia Britannica* biographies.

Poems

Pompeii, Cambridge, 1819; *Evening*, Cambridge, 1821. Macaulay's two undergraduate Prize Poems.

Lays of Ancient Rome, London, 1842. New edition with 'Ivry' and 'The Armada', London, 1848. Other uncollected and unpublished poems were included in the *Miscellaneous Writings*.

Speeches

Speeches of the Right Honorable T. B. Macaulay, M.P. Corrected by Himself, London, 1854. The authorized collection. Additional speeches can be found in Hansard and *The Mirror of Parliament*, and in the newspaper reports of his various political campaigns and of his activities in India.

Indian affairs

A Penal Code Prepared by the Indian Law Commissioners, and Published by Command of the Governor General of India in Council, Calcutta, 1837. Macaulay was largely responsible for the drafting of the code and himself wrote the Introduction and Notes.

Macaulay's Minutes on Education in India, ed. H. Woodrow, Calcutta, 1862.

Lord Macaulay's Legislative Minutes, ed. C. D. Dharker, Madras, 1946.

The Indian Civil Service, London, 1855. A parliamentary report prepared by Macaulay and others.

History of England

The History of England from the Accession of James II, vols I and II, London, 1848 (dated 1849); vols III and IV, 1855; vol. V, 1861. The last volume is incomplete and was prepared for the press after Macaulay's death by his sister, Lady Trevelyan. Macaulay made minor revisions and additions to the text for various issues and editions during his lifetime, the most careful revision – followed by a close supervision of the proofs – being made for the seven-volume edition of 1858.

Selections

Only the most significant of the numerous selected editions are listed below.

Selections from the Writings of Lord Macaulay, ed. G. O. Trevelyan, London, 1876.

The Reader's Macaulay, eds W. H. French and G. D. Sanders, New York, 1936.

Macaulay: Prose and Poetry, ed. G. M. Young, London, 1952.

Thomas Babington Macaulay: Selected Writings, eds John Clive and Thomas Pinney, Chicago, 1972.

B Biographies and Letters

Arnold, Frederick, *The Public Life of Lord Macaulay*, London, 1862. The first full-length study, it contains some material not found elsewhere.

Trevelyan, G. O., *The Life and Letters of Lord Macaulay*, 2 vols, London, 1876; one-volume enlarged and complete edition, 1908. The standard work written by Macaulay's nephew, and one of the best examples of the nineteenth-century Life and Letters genre. The portrait of Macaulay is full and fair, and the selections from his letters and journals, though treated with a certain amount of textual licence, are chosen with an unerring eye for the distinctive and illuminating passage. All later biographies derive from Trevelyan and only the brief study by Arthur Bryant (listed below) has real merit.

Stephen, Leslie, Life of Macaulay in the *Dictionary of National Biography*, vol. XXXIV, London, 1893.

Bryant, Arthur, *Macaulay*, London, 1932.

Beatty, Richmond Croom, *Lord Macaulay: Victorian Liberal*, Norman, Okla., 1938.

Napier, Macvey, Jr, ed., *The Correspondence of the Late Macvey Napier, Esq.*, London, 1879. Napier was editor of the *Edinburgh Review* during most of Macaulay's association with the journal and this volume includes the largest collection of published Macaulay letters apart from the Trevelyan *Life*.

Occasional letters by Macaulay appear in the biographies and memoirs of various nineteenth-century political and literary figures, and some of these are listed by Bryant and by French and Sanders. An accurate text of an important group of letters about the Reform Bill is printed in the volume of *Selections* edited by Clive and Pinney, and Professor Pinney is currently at work on the definitive edition of Macaulay's letters, the first volume of which should appear shortly.

C Works about Macaulay and his background

In the past one hundred and fifty years there have been innumerable books and articles which make brief or general comments on Macaulay; the following is a selected list of works which throw useful light on his literary achievement and the background to his career. For further titles see the bibliographies mentioned in the headnote. Works reviewed by Macaulay or used by him as sources are not included here, but references to them in the text are accompanied by a full citation in the notes.

Annan, Noel, 'The Intellectual Aristocracy', in *Studies in Social History: A Tribute to G. M. Trevelyan*, ed. J. H. Plumb, London, 1955, pp. 243–87.

Arnold, Matthew, 'A French Critic on Milton', in *Mixed Essays*, London, 1879, pp. 237–73.

Arnold, Matthew, 'Joubert', in *Essays in Criticism*, London, 1865, pp. 214–52.

Babington, Churchill, *Mr. Macaulay's Character of the Clergy in the Seventeenth Century Considered*, Cambridge, 1849.

Bagehot, Walter, Obituary of Macaulay, *The Economist*, 17 (1859), 1455–6.

Bagehot, Walter, 'Mr Macaulay', *National Review*, 2 (1856), 357–87.

Brown, Ford K., *Fathers of the Victorians: the Age of Wilberforce*, Cambridge, 1961.

Bush, Douglas, 'Early Victorian Minor Poets', in *Mythology and the Romantic Tradition in English Poetry*, Cambridge, Mass., 1937, pp. 265–96.

Butler, J. R. M., *The Passing of the Great Reform Bill*, London, 1914.

Clark, G. Kitson, *The Critical Historian*, London, 1967.

Clive, John, 'Macaulay, History and the Historians', *History Today*, 9 (1959), 830–6.

Clive, John, 'Macaulay's Historical Imagination', *Review of English Literature*, I, iv (1960), 20–8.

Clive, John and Pinney, Thomas, Introduction to *Thomas Babington Macaulay: Selected Writings*, Chicago, 1972.

Cockburn, Henry, Lord, *Life of Lord Jeffrey with a Selection from His Correspondence*, 2 vols, Edinburgh, 1852.

[Croker, John Wilson] 'Mr. Macaulay's *History of England*', *Quarterly Review*, 84 (1849), 549–630.

de Beer, E. S., 'Macaulay and Croker: The Review of Croker's Boswell', *Review of English Studies*, 10 (1959), 388–97.

Firth, Sir Charles, *A Commentary on Macaulay's History of England*, London, 1938.

Fisher, H. A. L., 'The Whig Historians', in *Pages from the Past*, Oxford, 1939, pp. 40–92.

Forster, E. M., *Marianne Thornton, 1797–1887: A Domestic Biography*, London, 1956.

Francis, G. H., *Orators of the Age. Comprising Portraits, Critical, Biographical, and Descriptive*, London, 1847, pp. 78–100.

Fraser, G. S., 'Macaulay's Style as an Essayist', *Review of English Literature*, 1, iv (1960), 9–19.

Gash, Norman, *Politics in the Age of Peel*, London, 1953.

Geyl, Pieter, 'Macaulay in his Essays', in *Debates with Historians*, London, 1955, pp. 19–34.

[Gladstone, W. E.] 'Lord Macaulay', *Quarterly Review*, 142 (1876), 1–50.

Hart, Francis R., 'Boswell and the Romantics: A Chapter in the History of Biographical Theory', *ELH*, 27 (1960), 44–65.

Hinton, R. W. K., 'History Yesterday: Five Points about Whig History', *History Today*, 9 (1959), 720–8.

Hodder, Edwin, *The Life and Work of the Seventh Earl of Shaftesbury*, 3 vols, London, 1886.

Holland, Saba, Lady, *A Memoir of the Reverend Sydney Smith*, 2 vols, London, 1855.

House, Humphry, 'The Mood of Doubt', in Harman Grisewood *et al.*, *Ideas and Beliefs of the Victorians: An Historic Revaluation of the Victorian Age*, London, 1949, pp. 71–7.

Howse, Ernest Marshall, *Saints in Politics: The 'Clapham Sect' and the Growth of Freedom*, Toronto, 1952.

Jones, M. G., *Hannah More*, Cambridge, 1952.

Knight, Charles, *Passages of a Working Life During Half a Century*, 3 vols, London, 1864–5.

Knowles, David, *Lord Macaulay, 1800–1859*, Cambridge, 1960 [A centenary lecture].

Knutsford, Viscountess, *Life and Letters of Zachary Macaulay*, London, 1900.

Levine, George, *The Boundaries of Fiction: Carlyle, Macaulay, Newman*, Princeton, 1968.

[Macaulay, Joseph Babington] ed. *Memoirs of the Clan Aulay*, privately printed, 1881.

Madden, William A., 'Macaulay's Style', in *The Art of Victorian Prose*, eds George Levine and William Madden, New York, 1968, pp. 127–53.

[Mill, J. S.] 'Macaulay's Lays of Ancient Rome', *Westminster Review*, 39 (1843), 105–13.

Millgate, Jane, 'Father and Son: Macaulay's *Edinburgh* Debut', *Review of English Studies*, 21 (1970), 159–67.

Millgate, Jane, 'Macaulay at Work: An Example of his Use of Sources', *Transactions of the Cambridge Bibliographical Society*, 5 (1970), 90–8.

[Milman, H. H.] Obituary notice of Lord Macaulay from the *Proceedings of the Royal Society*, reprinted in Lady Trevelyan's edition of Macaulay's *History of England*, London, 1862, VIII, i–xxx.

Morison, J. Cotter, *Macaulay*, London, 1882.

Munby, A. N. L., *Macaulay's Library*, Glasgow, 1966 [David Murray Foundation Lecture].

Munby, A. N. L., ed., *Sale Catalogues of Libraries of Eminent Persons*, vol. I. London, 1971. [The catalogue of the Sotheby sale of Macaulay's books appears on pp. 251–333.]

New, Chester W., *The Life of Henry Brougham to 1830*, Oxford, 1961.

Newsome, David, *The Parting of Friends: A Study of the Wilberforces and Henry Manning*, London, 1966.

Paget, John, *The New Examen*, Edinburgh, 1861.

Praz, Mario, 'Macaulay', in *The Hero in Eclipse in Victorian Fiction*, London, 1956, pp. 102–17.

Raleigh, Sir Walter Alexander, 'Thomas Babington Macaulay', in *On Writing and Writers*, London, 1926, pp. 17–86.

Roberts, S. C., 'Lord Macaulay, the Pre-eminent Victorian', in *An Eighteenth-Century Gentleman and Other Essays*, Cambridge, 1932, pp. 107–31.

Robson, Robert, ed., *Ideas and Institutions of Victorian Britain: Essays in Honour of George Kitson Clark*, London, 1967.

Russell, George W. E., *The Household of Faith: Portraits and Essays*, London, 1902.

Sirkin, Gerald and Sirkin, Natalie Robinson, 'The Battle of Indian Education: Macaulay's Opening Salvo Newly Discovered', *Victorian Studies*, 14 (1971), 407–28.

Smith, Nowell C., ed., *The Letters of Sydney Smith*, 2 vols, Oxford, 1953.

Southgate, Donald, *The Passing of the Whigs, 1832–1886*, London, 1962.

[Stephen, James] 'The Clapham Sect', *Edinburgh Review*, 80 (1844), 251–307.

Stephen, Leslie, 'Macaulay', in *Hours in a Library*, 4 vols, London, 1907, III, 227–71.

Stokes, Eric, *The English Utilitarians and India*, Oxford, 1959.

Stokes, Eric, 'Macaulay: The Indian Years, 1834–38', *Review of English Literature*, I, iv (1960), 41–50.

Svaglic, Martin J., 'Classical Rhetoric and Victorian Prose', in *The Art of Victorian Prose*, eds George Levine and William Madden, New York, 1968, pp. 268–88.

Taine, H. A., 'Criticism and History: Macaulay', in *History of English Literature*, trans. H. Van Laun, 2 vols, Edinburgh, 1871, II, 402–34.

[Thackeray, W. M.] 'A Few Words on Junius and Macaulay', *Cornhill*, I (1860), 257–63.

[Thackeray, W. M.] 'Nil nisi bonum', *Cornhill*, I (1860), 129–34.

Thackeray, W. M., 'Literature: Mr Macaulay's Essays', in *Stray Papers*, London, 1901, pp. 202–4.

Trevelyan, G. M., 'Macaulay', in *Clio: A Muse, and Other Essays Literary and Pedestrian*, London, 1913, pp. 1–55.

Trevor-Roper, Hugh, Introduction to *Macaulay's Essays*, London, 1965.

Trevor-Roper, Hugh, 'Macaulay and the Glorious Revolution', in *Men and Events*, New York, 1957, pp. 249–53.

Trevor-Roper, Hugh, 'Lord Macaulay', *Listener*, 74 (1965), 565–7.

Turberville, A. S. and Beckwith, Frank, 'Leeds and Parliamentary Reform, 1820–1832', *Publications of the Thoresby Society*, 41 (1943), 1–88.

Weber, Ronald, 'Singer and Seer: Macaulay on the Historian as Poet', *Papers on Language and Literature*, 3 (1967), 210–19.

Wedgwood, C. V., 'Macaulay's Lays', *Review of English Literature*, 1, iv (1960), 29–37.

[Wilson, John] 'Noctes Ambrosianae, XLVIII', *Blackwood's*, 27 (1830), 659–94.

[Wilson, John] 'Noctes Ambrosianae, LIX', *Blackwood's*, 30 (1831), 802–46.

[Wilson, John] 'Lays of Ancient Rome', *Blackwood's*, 52 (1842), 802–24.

Woodward, C. L., *Age of Reform, 1815–1870*, rev. edn, Oxford, 1962.

Young, G. M., 'Macaulay', in *Daylight and Champaign: Essays*, London, 1948, pp. 9–22.

Zall, Paul M., 'Selina Macaulay's Diary', *Bulletin of the New York Public Library*, 66 (1962), 440–3.

Index

Index